THE 7 HABITS OF JESUS

Praise for
The 7 Habits of Jesus

"The goal of the missional church is to make disciples not members. The book *The 7 Habits of Jesus* is an invaluable tool for congregations to teach what it means to be an apprentice of Jesus, by living out their baptism in daily life. I am pleased to recommend it to every pastor and lay leader who take discipleship seriously."

Rev. Dr. Rick Rouse
Co-author, A Field Guide to the Missional Congregation
Faculty, Lutheran Seminary Program of the Southwest

"In a rapidly changing religious landscape, the church of the 21st century will need to function more like the church of the 1st century. Jesus sent the church with the mandate to make disciples by baptizing and teaching. I am thrilled to recommend *The 7 Habits of Jesus* to every community that is passionate about shaping disciples for daily ministry in a 21st century world. Here we have a useful roadmap to equip the saints to participate in God's reconciling work in the world."

Rev. Robert G. Schaefer, *Bishop*
Florida-Bahamas Synod, ELCA

"Not only is *The 7 Habits of Jesus* a tremendous resource for today's church, it also addresses the need in our culture to get back to the basic habits of following Jesus. The way we relate these 7 Habits to our everyday life is helpful for us as individuals, and will be helpful to a new generation of believers striving to mature in their faith. The content, practicality, and arrangement of the materials provides a great service, one that is needed in the church today. I look forward to seeing how *The 7 Habits of Jesus* becomes a transformational tool for Christ's church."

Rev. Gregory S. Walton, *President*
Florida-Georgia District, LCMS

"Discipleship and faith formation is the means to grow people in the faith from infancy to maturity, from those who only receive to those who recognize they have received something so precious they are compelled to share it with others. Jesus used such a process to disciple His first followers. Without a similar commitment to invest ourselves in the lives of others the Church will only become weaker and less effective. *The 7 Habits of Jesus* provides a highly relational process that is focused on Christ, the Scripture and faithful Lutheran confessional theology. The insights it provides will bring transformation to individual lives and renewal for the congregation. It is an excellent first step in the pursuit of the Great Commission, making disciples, a resource that should be implemented by any Lutheran leader who takes seriously Jesus' mission and command."

Rev. John F. Bradosky, *Bishop*
North American Lutheran Church

"Many would agree that we are witnessing the emergence of a new church. The critical shift of this new church will be the focus of transforming people's lives in the image of Jesus. In this transformational process we need tools like *The 7 Habits of Jesus.*"

Rev. Larry Klinker
Pastor, Zion Lutheran- New Middletown, OH

"I am grateful for the missionary experience and spirit in which this book was written. I appreciate that the authors have introduced a discipleship model and resource for ministry focused on Christ's mission of reconciliation to unite all people to God and to one another. It was refreshing to see a work that leads others to God's grace and wisdom with purpose."

Rev. Dr. Rick Armstrong
Executive Director, Lutheran Counseling Services

"*The 7 Habits of Jesus* provides a comprehensive and accessible way for churches to actually get (back) into the business of making disciples. A particular strength of *The 7 Habits of Jesus* is the method of combining the three dimensions of engagement: self-study, fellowship groups, and partnerships. If you want real and enduring change in your relationship with Jesus for the sake of God's mission in the world, use the tool *The 7 Habits of Jesus.*"

Rev. Dr. Johan Bergh
Pastor, Coordinator for Coaching, ELCA

"*The 7 Habits of Jesus* is a triumph in Lutheran faith formation and praxis. Birthed from over 20 years of mission experience in Kenya, Pastor Schmalzle successfully presents a user friendly model of discipleship which guides us into the realm of personal and communal transformation. It's simply accessible and incredible!"

Rev. Dr. Nathan Swenson-Reinhold
Lead Pastor, St. Stephen- Longwood, FL

"Martin Luther spoke multiple languages. Best of all he spoke the language of the heart in its longing and struggle to experience God. Through *The 7 Habits of Jesus*, Pastor Schmalzle shows Luther jumping centuries to guide our hearts in discipleship. This book will help you find a faith that succeeds where others fail."

Rev. Dr. Russell L. Meyer
Executive Director, Florida Council of Churches

"*The 7 Habits of Jesus* lives up to its title as a Handbook on Discipleship. It is inspiring, insightful, and instructional. It invites readers into an interactive process of listening, sharing, learning, and leading into deeper relational connections to Jesus, neighbor and to the world. It is a practical and comprehensive discipleship development handbook that I'm eager to use in the congregational setting and commend it for your use in faith formation and growing disciples."

Rev. Dr. Rita Gardner Tweed
Pastor, Spirit of Grace- Hudson, FL
former Director for Evangelical Mission, ELCA

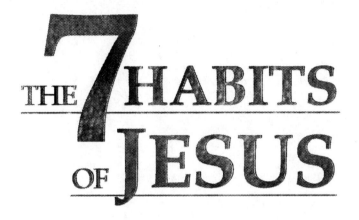

THE 7 HABITS OF JESUS

Faith Formation
Handbook for Discipleship

Robert Schmalzle
with
Aaron Schmalzle

Dedicated to...
"Our Lord Jesus Christ
through whom we have
now received reconciliation"
Romans 5:11

The 7 Habits of Jesus
Faith Formation Handbook for Discipleship
First Printing, 14 September 2014, *Holy Cross Day*

Large-quantity purchases and custom editions of this book are available for a discount. For information: www.7habitsofjesus.com/about-the-book

Scripture quotations in this publication are from the *"The Message: The Bible in Contemporary Language"* © 2002 by Eugene H. Peterson; and, the "New Revised Standard Version" (NRSV) © 1989, of the Bible. All rights reserved.

The reference *"LW"* refers to the American Edition of *"Luther's Works,"* Philadelphia: Fortress; St. Louis: Concordia, 1955-86.

Used with permission: *"Christians Organized for Mission,"* Dr. Herbert T. Mayer, Morse Press, Medford, Oregon, 1992.

Used with permission: *"The Doctrine of Martin Luther's Small Catechism,"* Dr. Herbert M. Zorn, Lutheran World Federation Publications, 1997.

Illustrations by Mark Kloess used with permission, *"Currents in Theology and Mission,"* Chicago, Illinois.

Edited for publication by the Rev. Omar Stuenkel

Library of Congress Cataloging-in-Publication Data
Schmalzle, Robert.
    The 7 Habits of Jesus: Faith Formation Handbook for Discipleship / Robert Schmalzle with Aaron Schmalzle.
        p. cm.
ISBN 978-1-4841-9073-9 (alk. paper)
 1. Discipling (Christianity). 2. Christian life. 3. Church renewal—Lutheran Church. 4. Spiritual formation. I. Title. II. Schmalzle
BV4520. 2014
248.5 – dc23   **2014921711**
CreateSpace Independent Publishing Platform, North Charleston, SC

The paper used in this publication meets the minimum requirements of the American National Standard for Information Sciences—Permanence of Paper for Printed Library Materials, ANSI Z329.48-1984.

    2   4   6   8   10   9   7   5   3   1

CONTENTS

Seven Habits of Jesus

Acknowledgements 17

Preface 19

Introduction 23

Being Disciples	23
Origin of the Habits	24
History of the Habits	25
Why Habits	25
Lifestyle Habits	26
Purpose of the Habits	27
Simple yet Profound	27
Signs of a Disciple	28
Christ's Cross	29
Become Christ-Like	30
Christ's Mission	31
The Seven Habits of Jesus	32
Memory Device	35
Important Suggestions	36
Discipleship Training	37
Discipleship Group Names	41
Hymn: Gather Us In	42

1a. Remembering   45

Remembering Goal	45
Salvation	46
Water and Salvation	47
Cleansing and Remembering	48
Baptism Defined	49
Unconditional Birth & Rebirth	50
Ten Blessings of Baptism	50
Lifelong Process	51
St. Paul on Baptism	52
Baptized into Christ	55
Remembering Christ's Indwelling	55
Attitude of Gratitude	57
Hymn: Baptized in Water	59
Insights	60

1b. Remembering   63

Remembering Goal	63
The Apostles' Creed	64
Baptized into the Trinity	67
Luther on Baptism	68
Confession and Forgiveness	70
Remembering Our Baptism	72
Ways of Remembering	73
Internal Self-Talk Phrase	76
Creating Self-Talk Phrases	79
Hymn: Baptized in Water	81
Insights	82
Self-Study for Remembering (1a)	84
Self-Study for Remembering (1b)	85
Make it my HABIT Worksheet	86

2a. Listening   89

Listening Goal	89
Listening with Fluency	90
The Word of God	92
Ignoring God's Voice	93
Listening to God's Voice	94
Law & Gospel Voice	95
Law & Gospel Bible Reading	100
Using a Law & Gospel Worksheet	103
Hymn: Listen, God is Calling	105
Insights	106

2b. Listening   109

Listening Goal	109
God's Voice in Worship	110
God's Voice Penetrates the Soul	112
Identifying God's Law Voice	114
Listening to God's Law Voice	115
Identifying God's Gospel Voice	116
Listening to God's Gospel Voice	117
Using a Law & Gospel Worksheet (O.T.)	118
Using a Law & Gospel Worksheet (N.T.)	119
Hymn: Listen, God is Calling	121
Insights	122
Self-Study for Listening (2a)	124
Self-Study for Listening (2b)	125
Make it my HABIT Worksheet	126

3a. Praying   129

Praying Goal	129
Praying to God	130
The Lord's Prayer	132
Praying the Lord's Prayer	133
Unceasing Prayer	134

An Obstacle to Praying   135
The A.B.C.'s of Praying   137
The Lord's Prayer: Nine Parts   137
I Cannot Pray   147
Hymn: What a Friend We Have in Jesus   149
Insights   150

3b. Praying   153

Praying Goal   153
Anticipation   154
God Answers Prayer   155
God's Answers   156
God Dwells Within   158
Meditative Prayer   159
Meditative Prayer Explained   160
Listening to God's Voice   162
Solitude and Prayer   166
Fasting and Prayer   167
Praying with Others   168
Prayers Written by Others   168
Spontaneous Prayers   170
Praying in Jesus' Name   170
Close Your Eyes   171
Amen!   171
Hymn: What a Friend We Have in Jesus   173
Insights   174
Self-Study for Prayer (3a)   176
Self-Study for Prayer (3b)   177
Make it my HABIT Worksheet   178

4a. Preparing   181

Preparing Goal   181
Worship Expectations   182
Preparing for Worship   183
Worship is God-centered   184
Three Means of Grace   185
Word & Sacrament Worship   186
What is a Sacrament?   187
Why is it a Sacrament?   187
Listening to God's Voice through
    Baptismal Renewal   190
Chosen in Baptism   191
Our Response   192
Daily Renewal   192
Baptismal Renewal   193
Listening to God's Voice through
    the Scripture readings & Sermon   194
Listening to the Sermon   195
Listening to God's Voice through
    Holy Communion   197
Hymn: All are Welcome   201
Insights   202

4b. Preparing   205

Preparing Goal   205
Worldly Forgiveness   206
A Process of Forgiveness   208
Stories of Forgiveness   211
Natural Moral Law   213
Seven Sinful Habits   215
Ten Commandments   216
Hymn: All are Welcome   219
Insights   220
Self-Study for Preparing (4a)   222

Self-Study for Preparing (4b) 223
Make it my HABIT Worksheet 224

5a. Returning 227

Returning Goal 227
Returning 228
Returning our Offering to God 228
The Rich Fool 230
Wealth 231
Ten Principles 233
Hymn: We Give Thee But Thine Own 239
Insights 240

5b. Returning 243

Returning Goal 243
The A.B.C.'s of Tithing 244
Tithing Helps Us 246
Money Management 247
10-10-80 Money Mgmt. Plan 248
More Blessed to Give 249
Giving From Love 250
Take Care 251
Discipleship 251
A.B.C.'s of Sacrificial Giving 252
Seven Offering Myths 253
Hymn: We Give Thee But Thine Own 255
Insights 256
Self-Study for Returning (5a) 258
Self-Study for Returning (5b) 259
Make it my HABIT Worksheet 260

6a. Inviting — 263

Inviting Goal	263
Lifesaving Station Parable	264
Lifesaving Parable	266
Becoming a Christian	267
Being a Christian	269
Christ's Death	269
Christ's Resurrection	270
Christ's Great Commission	271
Being an Evangelist	272
Baptism: God's Action	274
Baptism as Adoption	275
Baptismal Salvation	276
Family of God	276
Baptizing Infants	277
Unconditional Birth & Rebirth	279
Ten Blessings of Baptism	279
Through your Baptism	280
Baptismal Descriptions	280
Mission of Reconciliation	281
Hymn: I Love to Tell the Story	283
Insights	284

6b. Inviting — 287

Inviting Goal	287
Baptismal Salvation	288
Baptismal Invitation	289
The Unbaptized	290
Help for Inviting	292
Believing	294
Faith Alone	294
Scripture on Believing	295
Baptismal Invitation	298
Roadblocks and Responses	299

Reasons for Considering Baptism 300
Listening 301
The Four P's 302
Christian Conversion 303
Hymn: I Love to Tell the Story 305
Insights 306
Self-Study for Inviting (6a) 308
Self-Study for Inviting (6b) 309
Make it my HABIT Worksheet 310

7a. Caring 313

Caring Goal 313
Caring for Others 314
The Way to Love 316
Christ's Love Compels Us 317
Called to Care 318
Christian Caregiving Principles 319
Jesus' Habit of Caring 320
Three Spheres of Caring 321
First Sphere of Caring: Family 322
Family & Friends 323
Listening 323
Listening Basics 324
Listening with Love 325
Listening Feedback 326
Forgiving 327
Forgiveness Is Not 328
Forgiveness Is 328
Unforgiving 329
How we Forgive 330
Forgiven to Forgive 331
The World's Way 333
Christ's Way 333
Resolving Relationship Conflicts 334
A.B.C.'s of Matthew 18:15 334

Praying, Listening, and Forgiving   337
Hymn: Jesu, Jesu, Fill us with your Love   341
Insights   342
Self-Study for Caring (7a)   344
Make it my HABIT Worksheet   346

7b. Caring   **349**

Caring Goal   349
Caring through Work   350
Made to Work   351
Luther on Work   353
Gifted with a Talent   354
Discovering Our Talent   355
Preferred Preferences   355
Four Preferred Functions   356
Talent Indicator   357
Identifying Your Preferred Preference   363
Type Charts   364
Do Not Use Your Type to:381
Use Your Type to:381
Hymn: Jesu, Jesu, Fill us with your Love   383
Insights   384
Self-Study for Caring (7b)   386
Make it my HABIT Worksheet   388

7c. Caring   **391**

Caring Goal   391
Caring for Creation   392
God Loves the World   393
Mission of Reconciliation   394
How We Care for Creation   396
Responding to Poverty   399
Crises of Creation   401
Crisis 1: Population Growth   402

Crisis 2: Climate Change   404
Crisis 3: Resource Consumption   406
Crisis 4: Water   409
Crisis Management   410
More Simple Lifestyle   412
Hymn: Jesu, Jesu, Fill us with your Love   417
Insights   418
Self-Study for Caring (7c)   420
Make it my HABIT Worksheet   422

Post Script   **425**

Appendix   **431**

Utilizing the Companion Website   431
Christian Glossary   432
The Science of Forming Habits   436
Discipleship/ Faith Formation Bibliography   441
Notable Saints Triumphant   443
Revised Common Lectionary   445

Hi, my name is Mousie. My family comes from a long line of church mice. A church mouse lives in church buildings to be closer to God. Martin Luther often referred to us.

ACKNOWLEDGEMENTS

Seven Habits of Jesus

In 1979, I was sent to Kenya in East Africa as a missionary of the Association of Evangelical Lutheran Churches (AELC). It was an incredible adventure for my wife Denise and me. We had the good fortune to witness the beginning of Christianity's rapid growth in sub-Saharan Africa. It was no doubt providential that I was welcomed to Kenya by three missionaries who were about to return to the States for retirement. These pastors all had a lifetime of experience as Lutheran missionaries. Quite frankly, I welcomed their mentoring because I had not a clue as to what to do! So, these kind pastors, whose lives were dedicated to Christ's mission, took me under their wings. Most importantly, they steered me away from making ministry to the congregation the focus. Instead, they taught me to make Christ's mission to the world the congregation's primary focus. **These pastors taught me that discipleship training was the critical way for believers to experience a relationship with Christ in their daily lives.** They taught me how a congregation, through discipleship training, can turn away from an inward, self-serving focus, toward an outward focus on Christ's reconciling world-wide mission. Thank you Pastors Jim Dretke, Paul Volz, and Bob Ward! These pastors taught me that being a disciple of Christ cannot be limited to activity within the institutional church. The Seven Habits of Jesus teach us how to be disciples both in the church and in our daily lives.

The purpose of *The Seven Habits of Jesus* is to provide a practical way for us to learn and re-learn faith formation from Jesus and to grow in our openness to his presence, power, and promises in our daily lives.

PREFACE

"Pastor, what has happened to our congregation? We used to be so active, and now there's talk about merging."

There is no way to sugar-coat it; Protestant congregations are now experiencing very serious difficulties. The model of congregational ministry that so successfully evolved after World War II seemed invincible. This model of ministry, that many now refer to as the *membership model,* produced unprecedented growth in Protestant congregations for more than half a century. For a variety of reasons, this model is no longer *working* and many pastors and lay leaders now seek ways to grow healthy congregations. Sadly, a record number of pastors and dedicated lay leaders are becoming *burned-out* and leaving their congregations.

Congregations are looking for innovative ways to be faithful to God that will energize their ministry. Those congregations that seem to be weathering the storm have engaged in a discipleship model of ministry. A discipleship model of ministry is focused on Christ's mission of reconciliation to unite all people to God and to one another. Without discipleship training Christ's mission is too often limited to the confines of the congregation and does not relate sufficiently to one's daily life, let alone to one's encounter with the world.

The *Seven Habits of Jesus* serves as a discipleship training resource through which the followers of Jesus may experience the benefits of living each day with him. When discipleship training occurs within a congregation, the mission and ministry of that congregation are given new impetus toward Christ's mission of reconciliation, that it may be experienced around the world today in an unprecedented manner!

Within the past several decades an ever-present *buzz word* among Christians has been **discipleship**. We now realize that not all ideas about discipleship are the same, or even similar. It is important therefore, to know that the understanding of discipleship within *The Seven Habits of Jesus* is rooted in the teachings of Martin Luther (Seven Marks of the Church, Luther's Works Vol. 41, pp 148-168).

Martin Luther rejected both the medieval Roman Catholic approaches and the practices of the renewal movements initiated by the Protestant Reformers. Luther's great insight about discipleship was based upon his discovery that God's righteousness is a gift, not a demand. For some Christians discipleship training is all about acquiring spiritual techniques that will help them experience an emotional closeness to the Lord Jesus. However, *The Seven Habits of Jesus* approach is quite different.

Seven Habits offers an understanding of discipleship training as God/grace-centered rather than people/works-centered. A God/grace-centered approach to discipleship training is based upon the tradition of Isaiah and Jeremiah. In Isaiah (Ch 55), God freely offers the gift of abundant life. In Jeremiah (Ch 18), God is likened to a potter with clay. The work of faith formation is God's work, not ours. Discipleship training is not about our ascent to God, but rather God's descent to us. Luther describes this in his Galatians commentary (Gal 3:14), *It is not our invitation of Christ that makes us sons; it is the Sonship of Christ that makes us imitators.* Luther brought to light a new way to be a disciple with his understanding of salvation by grace. God's grace keeps us from a two-tiered hierarchy associated with most discipleship training programs, which make a distinction between a *nominal* disciple and a *spiritual* disciple. We are disciples because we are dependent upon the wonder and power of God's Word. Our discipleship is cross-centered, and trusts that Christ died not only for his followers, but for the whole world. Luther said, *This life is not about being righteous, but growth in Christ's righteousness.* Luther brought the disciplines (habits) out of the prayer closet and into our everyday lives in the world. He taught: *As you go throughout the day and discover the devil whispering in your ear, you only need to shout: I AM BAPTIZED!* He also brought the Lord's Prayer into our daily lives. As we go about each day, he instructed, *Pray the Lord's prayer all the way through, until it brings forth in your heart a prayer for what you need the most at that very moment.* **Luther has suggestions for bringing all seven habits/disciplines into our daily lives. The Seven Habits of Jesus also attempt to bring all seven habits/disciplines into our daily lives. To be a follower of Jesus is not about *doing* something, or *practicing* certain habits. Too many followers have stopped following because they thought they could force themselves into a certain lifestyle or daily discipline. No one can *will* themselves into being a follower of Jesus. Instead, we become followers of Jesus when we accept Christ's present in our hearts, and welcome a relationship with him. It's not a matter of what we *do*, it's all a matter of *being* in a relationship with Christ Jesus and recognizing that he pursues a relationship with all the baptized. *The Seven Habits of Jesus* are intended to strengthen our heartfelt relationship with Christ Jesus so that our lifestyle may facilitate Christ's Mission of Reconciliation in the world.**

Being a disciple is not something that is widely discussed or witnessed in the church today. Nevertheless, transformation is not only possible, but has actually occurred to a significant degree in the everyday lives of countless Christians since the time of Jesus. With God all things are possible.

Bonhoeffer, *Ethics*

If you look inside a Christian you will find the very form and shape of Christ...All this is to say, the life I now live is not my own, it is his own life.

Luther, LW 26

My wife's family came from the Castle Church in Wittenberg, Germany where Martin Luther launched the Reformation. They are really proud of that!

INTRODUCTION

The Seven Habits of Jesus

hab·it (n)

1. unconscious behavior acquired by repetition.
2. spiritual discipline of faith formation.
3. faith nurturing practice of the church.

Opening Prayer

May God the Father, and the ever living high priest Jesus Christ, strengthen us in faith, truth, and love; and give to us our portion among the saints with all those who trust in our Lord Jesus Christ. We pray that our fruit may abound and that we might be made complete in Christ Jesus our Lord. Amen.

Polycarp (69-155)

Being Disciples

The challenge now facing the Church is to share the gospel of Jesus Christ beyond the confines of a congregation. This is not a challenge that will cost money or require much effort. However, it is a shift that challenges the baptized to live their daily lives as disciples and followers of Christ Jesus. Through a discipleship model Christians are being invited to daily participate in the Church's first model of ministry: living each day with Christ. Today, Christians are being challenged to a renewed understanding of what it means to be a follower of Jesus. The *Seven Habits of Jesus* teach us how to be disciples both in Christian community and in our daily lives.

Origin of the Habits

Jesus tells us in the twenty-eighth chapter of Matthew's Gospel...*All authority has been given to me. Therefore, go and make disciples of all nations, <u>baptizing</u> them in the name of the Father, and the Son, and the Holy Spirit, and <u>teach</u> them to obey everything that I have commanded you. And remember, I am with you always, even to the end of the age* (Matt 28:18-20).

<u>Christ's Great Commission</u>
+**Baptize** all people
+**Teach** the baptized

Baptize: *Christians are made, not born*, Tertullian taught. Through the act of baptism God makes us Christians and adopts us into his eternal family. Christ's Spirit, is baptized into us so that we might participate into his mission of reconciliation to *make all things new*.

Teach: The baptized learn how to be disciples by practicing the seven habits Jesus taught. These seven habits feed the faith of the baptized, which is referred to as faith formation.

The first three habits are foundational: **Remembering** our baptismal adoption into God's family; **Listening** to God's law and Gospel voice in Scripture; **Praying** for God's help with all our daily needs. The last four teachings of **Preparing**, **Returning**, **Inviting**, and **Caring** each build upon the foundation of the first three habits.

History of the Habits

Throughout the ages, Christians have participated in seven habits that were taught by Jesus, passed on to his disciples, and now given to us as a way to grow in our openness to Christ's loving presence in our daily lives. These seven habits of Jesus have become the most important habits, or routines, in the daily lives of Christians. Martin Luther was a strong proponent of these seven habits and cautions us, not to make up new ways of being a Christian (LW 41, p.164). We are told, *Take on a new life, a God-fashioned life, a life renewed from the inside as Christ reproduces his character within us* (Eph 4:22). This new life is what the Seven Habits of Jesus offers us. Although these seven traditional habits of Jesus seem to describe what we do, in reality, they describe *how* Christ effectively breaks into our daily lives to transform us into his disciples. We do not become the disciples Christ intends us to be by our mastery of the habits, or by anything we are able to accomplish on our own. Becoming a disciple is the work of Christ's own Spirit within us, which gives us the capacity (ability) to recognize and participate in Christ's mission to restore and return the creation back to its Creator.

Why Habits

Why refer to the *traditional disciplines* of Jesus as the *habits* of Jesus? The word *habit,* as a daily behavioral pattern, is better understood and does not have all the negative baggage we often associate with the word discipline. Also, the word *habit* describes a behavioral pattern that is acted-out in a way that requires more than our conscious efforts (**See the Appendix:** *Forming Habits*). When we participate in Jesus' seven habits it is Christ Jesus alone who empowers us to experience a new relationship with God and one another. We are acting out behaviors that don't depend simply on our own efforts, but instead upon the transforming power of Christ's death and resurrection within us. The Apostle Paul put it this way, *It is no longer I who lives, but it is Christ who lives within me* (Gal 2:30). To become more like Christ is not about trying to **change our lives**, but allowing Christ to **exchange his life** for ours (2 Cor 5:17).

Lifestyle Habits

When the seven habits of Jesus become part of our daily lives, we can expect to experience the benefits of living each day in union with Christ. These seven habits are not intended to be a measure of our piety or sincerity, nor do they have the merit to earn God's favor. And yet, it is through these habits of Jesus, that Christ draws us into his redeeming presence. The goal of a Christian's daily life is to be an *apprentice* of Jesus. The New Testament does not actually describe any other type of lifestyle apart from putting

into practice the *habits* Jesus taught. **What is it like to live our lives with God? He gives us the character of Christ, much the same way that fruit appears on a fruit tree** (Gal 5:22).  The daily lifestyle of Christians has been clearly laid out in the *habits* that Jesus passed on to his disciples. This means that there is a straightforward way to live each day with Christ and participate in his mission to the world. Through these seven habits of Jesus we begin to experience life, not in a me-centered way which is our natural tendency, but in a Christ-centered way.

Purpose of the Habits

The purpose of Jesus' habits has always remained the same. We have been invited into God's family through baptism, and the habits teach us how to participate in Christ's eternal kingdom. Discipleship training is not intended to simply be a way of becoming *more religious* or *more spiritual*. Discipleship training is about being more engaged in Christ's redeeming kingdom in the world. The seven habits open our hearts to the wonder and mystery of Christ's redeeming work in our lives, in our faith community, neighborhood, society, and in the world. The seven habits of Jesus give us his own capacity to celebrate the love, joy, peace, justice and hope he has brought into the world. The habits of Jesus help us to discern and celebrate that Christ is *making all things new.*

Simple yet Profound

The seven habits of Jesus are by no means an exhaustive list of all the habits, routines, disciplines, or faith-nurturing practices that Christians have used throughout the ages. However, these seven habits of Jesus can be considered to be the essence of our new life with Christ. On the surface, these seven habits may seem elementary. But, do not be deceived! They are simple, and yet profound. These seven habits of Jesus are not intended to be unpleasant. For various reasons, many in the church find some of these habits, like reading the Bible and prayer, to be routines that are easily neglected. And yet, through the practice of his seven habits, Christ produces within us a profound connection to the triune God that is rarely experienced in our world today.

Signs of a Disciple

+ Trusting God's presence in difficult times
+ Becoming more forgiving; letting go of anger
+ Learning more easily from mistakes
+ Accepting that everything in life is a gift from God
+ Less inclined to try and control others
+ Less judgmental of different people
+ Much more generous with money
+ Knowing the difference between happiness and joy
+ Accepting that life is in God's hands
+ Trusting that God values each person's life
+ More committed to self-care and family care
+ Having more experiences of love, joy, and peace
+ Looking forward to worship and fellowship
+ Praying as a first response to human disaster
+ Feeling more confident about eternal life
+ Having a clear understanding of Christ's mission of reconciliation in our world

We mice regularly have home fellowships for training on how to be the mice God intends us to be.

Christ's Cross

Becoming a disciple of Christ is not about trying to *change* our lives, but about realizing that Christ has already *exchanged* his life for ours through his death on the cross. A unique and probably the most important emphasis of Christianity says that Christ's sacrificial death on the cross made it possible for him to *exchange* our broken relationship to God with his own relationship to God. Through this *great exchange,* our broken relationship to God has been *reconciled* and made whole. Christ Jesus died *on our behalf, in our place, for our punishment, to reunite us to God, to exchange his life for ours.* Becoming a disciple of Christ is a life-long process of accepting that Christ reconciled (reunited) us to God, to each other, and to God's Creation. *Because of Christ's sacrificial death, we are no longer at odds with God* (Rom 5:10). *Our old life is gone; we now have a new life with God who put the world right with himself through his Son, the Messiah* (2 Cor 5:18).

Becoming Christ-Like

Becoming Christ-like is God's desire for our lives. Jesus passed on to his disciples the *seven habits* so that they might become more like him. The Apostle Paul explains, *It is no longer I who lives, but Christ who lives within me* (Gal 2:20). Martin Luther explains, *We have all been invited by God to become little Christs*. To this end, we daily participate and depend upon the *seven habits* Christ has given us. *It is God himself who plants the Spirit of his Son within us to begin our transformation into Christ's own image* (2 Cor 5:17). Too often, Christians believe that what they *do* is more important than *who* they are in Christ. God is certainly concerned about what we do and don't do. However, God's greatest desire is for us to recognize and celebrate his Son's indwelling presence. Martin Luther said, ***If you look inside a Christian you will find the very form and shape of Christ. The life I now live is not my own, but his!*** Dietrich Bonhoeffer said, *To be a Christian is to participate in a lifelong process by which confession, prayer, study of Scripture, worship, service, and the like, focus us upon the very life of Christ.*

Christ be with me, Christ within me,
Christ behind me, Christ before me,
Christ beside me, Christ to win me,
Christ to comfort and restore me.
Christ in quiet, Christ in danger,
Christ in hearts of all that love me,
Christ in the stranger and friend.
St. Patrick (389-461)

Christ's Mission

So if anyone is in Christ, there is a new creation, the old has passed away; everything has become new! All this is from God, who reconciled us to himself through Christ, and has given us the ministry of reconciliation; that is, in Christ, God was reconciling the world to himself, not counting their trespasses against them, and entrusting the message of reconciliation to us. So we are ambassadors for Christ, since God is making his appeal to the world through us. We entreat you on behalf of Christ, be reconciled to God. For our sake God made Christ to be sin who knew no sin, so that in him we might be the righteousness of God (2 Cor 5:17-21).

Christ's Mission of Reconciliation

+Reconciliation is defined as turning a broken relationship into a harmonious relationship

+Christ's reconciliation comes from his death on the cross which gives us a renewed and restored relationship with God and one another.

+Christ's mission of reconciliation begins at the cross. The vertical beam of Christ's cross can remind us that Christ's death brought death to our own broken relationships with God. The horizontal beam of Christ's cross can remind us that Christ's death brought death to our own broken relationships with one another. Christ's resurrection gives us a renewed and redeemed relationship with both God and one another. Through Christ's sacrificial death on the cross, his own capacity to relate to God has been given to us just as his own capacity to relate to others has also been given to us.

The Seven Habits of Jesus

Remembering *our adoption in God's family*

The daily habit of *remembering* helps us to recall and reclaim the greatest gift God will ever give us: eternal life through baptism! St. Paul explains that through the renewal of baptism, *Christ's death brings death to our sinful self-centeredness, while Christ's resurrection brings new life to Christ's presence in our hearts.* (Rom 6:2-18)

Listening *to God's voice in Scripture reading*

The daily habit of *listening* to God's voice in Scripture fills our hearts with his love. Allowing God's *voice* of love to penetrate the depths of our being through Scripture reading is the most essential habit needed if we are to live our lives with Christ. The most reliable way for us to listen to God's voice in Scripture reading is to identify God's two major themes: law & Gospel.

Praying *for God's help with our daily needs*

The daily habit of *praying* provides us with the opportunity to ask for God's help with our needs. As the old favorite hymn tells us: *What a friend we have in Jesus, all our sins and griefs to bear! What a privilege to carry everything to God in prayer! Oh, what peace we often forfeit, oh, what needless pain we bear. All because we do not carry, everything to God in prayer!* Most prayer is experienced through spontaneous petitions we pray throughout each day.

Preparing *to hear God's voice in worship*

The habit of *preparing* for worship involves our intent to bring a specific sin, or broken relationship to worship for forgiveness. God's forgiveness breaks into our lives most powerfully through his means of grace: Baptism, Bible, and Communion; which are provided within a weekly liturgical worship service of Word & Sacrament.

Returning *a percentage of what God gives us*

The offering we give to God represents a small portion of all that God has first given us, which is our time, talents, and treasure! Giving (more accurately *returning*) helps us to recognize that everything in our world, including all that we have, is a gift from God. The tithe (10%) offering has been the standard offering for Christians throughout the ages. Returning a tithe offering to God, helps us to experience a renewed sense of gratitude for all that God has given us.

Inviting *others to baptism & Christ's mission*

The ascended Lord gave his disciples the *Great Commission: Go out and invite everyone into a new life with God by baptizing them in the name of the Father, Son, and Holy Spirit. Then our Lord instructed them in the practice of all that he commanded.* (Matt 28:18-20). Jesus instructed his disciples through the seven habits as a means to participate in the expansion of his Kingdom to all people.

Caring *for others & creation with Christ's love*

The true meaning and purpose of our lives is to recognize that God has put us on earth to join in Christ's mission of love. Our love for God is revealed in our capacity to love others in our family, at work, and in the world. We do not love others by our own will or determination, but by Christ's love and forgiveness, which has been planted in our hearts.

> I've been told that these are the original seven habits of Jesus' disciples, which have passed the test of time. WOW!!!

THE SEVEN HABITS OF JESUS GIVE THE CAPACITY FOR US TO EXPERIENCE THE FATHER'S LOVE, THE SON'S JOY, AND THE HOLY SPIRIT'S PEACE AS WE JOIN IN CHRIST'S MISSION TO MAKE A NEW HEAVEN AND A NEW EARTH.

THE SEVEN HABITS OF JESUS

1. **REMEMBERING**......our baptismal adoption into God's family

2. **LISTENING**..............to God's law & gospel voice in Scripture

3. **PRAYING**.................for God's help with all of our daily needs

4. **PREPARING**...…........to hear God's forgiving voice in worship

5. **RETURNING**.............a percentage of what God has given us

6. **INVITING**...................….others to baptism and Christ's mission

7. **CARING**..................for others and creation with Christ's love

Memory Device

A helpful way to remember the seven habits of Jesus is to use a memory device. Memory devices are learning techniques that help us with information retention. They translate information into a format that our brains can easily recall. A helpful memory device is to use the first letter in each of the seven habits to construct a catchy (somewhat bizarre!) story:

Seven Habits	Sample Story	Your Story
Remembering	**R**eally	R...............
Listening	**L**arge	L...............
Praying	**P**urple	P...............
Preparing	**P**lums	P...............
Returning	**R**ot	R...............
Inviting	**I**n	I...............
Caring	**C**ars	C...............

Important Suggestions

If you are reading this book by yourself, because you would like to better integrate the habits of Jesus into your daily life, you will most likely be disappointed. Throughout the generations, Christians have discovered that discipleship training is best experienced with either a mentor or a partner. Discipleship training, or faith formation as some call it, is best experienced in a partnership where two people are concerned about each other, and pray for each other daily. It is additionally helpful if your partnership is within the context of a small group (under 20 people) of other people who regularly meet together to share food, fellowship, fun, and the challenges of discipleship training.

Also, in the appendix there is:

- Instructions for utilizing the *smart phone* icons, that are located in the margins, in conjunction with the *7 Habits of Jesus* mobile-friendly companion website www.7HabitsofJesus.com
- A list of common vocabulary words associated with discipleship training that you may find helpful
- Information about the science of habit formation
- A bibliography of discipleship training resources
- A list of Saints Triumphant
- The three year Revised Common Lectionary list of Scripture readings that may provide you with a convenient reference for Bible study

We mice sure do like it when Christians get together to share food!

Discipleship Training

<u>Old Paradigm</u>: Creating more members for the church, and strengthen those *tired* members.

<u>New Paradigm</u>: Training the baptized *how to* be disciples and *how to* make disciples so that they may eventually participate in Christ's mission of reconciliation in their daily lives.

Throughout the ages Christian discipleship training has occurred most successfully within three intersecting training opportunities: **fellowship groups, partnerships,** and **self-study**. To get the most out of the seven habits discipleship training process, it is best to be involved in all three opportunities at the same time:

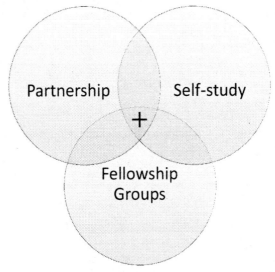

Do not overlook the importance and significance, indeed the necessity, of living out all three dimensions at the same time. You may do one or two together and reap some benefit, but the power will come when all three are combined.

Rev. Dr. Johan Bergh

Fellowship groups –provide the kind of support and accountability that disciples need for growth and maturity. Fellowship groups are a relational way to learn and promote a sense of trust and open discussion in connecting disciples to Christ's Kingdom in their daily lives.

+ Meet each month at one centralized home is desirable
+ Fellowship groups should not exceed 20 participants
+ A shared pot-luck meal helps to build fellowship
+ Participants read over material before each meeting
+ To begin the group session, the opening prayer is read aloud
+ Utilize several reading volunteers to read all material aloud
+ Do not talk negatively about people or your congregation
+ Be positive. Guard against hear-say and rumors
+ Group members are encouraged to share their answers for the *Write & Share with the Group* exercises. (Allot ten minutes)
+ Answers for the *Write & Share with a Partner* exercises are only shared between partners. (Allot five minutes)
+ *Let's give others a chance,* is useful for hearing everyone
+ Asking, *Would you like to share?*, encourages the quiet voices
+ The group meeting ends with singing the hymn found at the end of each session and praying the Lord's Prayer aloud
+ Each group is best led by two co-leaders
+ The host should not be expected to be a leader
+ Most groups only meet during the school year calendar
 + Meeting monthly (not including school breaks) takes most groups eighteen months to complete this process
+ Allow 90 minutes to cover half of a Chapter (i.e. 3b)
+ Allow 30 minutes at the beginning for a simple meal
+ Benefits include friendships, experiences/insights of others, and serving together

They went to the upper room they had been using as a meeting place.... They agreed they were in this for good, completely together.

Acts 1:13-14

Partnership –is a process through which two people work together to reflect, practice, refine, and build new skills by sharing ideas and teaching one another. Disciples have always been given a partner in working through discipleship training. A partner can also be referred to as a peer coach or a mentor.

+ It is important for you and your discipleship training partner to be in the same fellowship group in order to share the exercises designed for partner sharing
+ Partners are usually the same sex; similar ages; both quiet or both talkative; and both partners have a desire to be mature disciples
+ Partners meet once or twice between the monthly group meetings for one hour (often for coffee or lunch) to share reflections from the previous group meeting and to discuss how the material relates to their daily lives as disciples
+ Partners may choose to share their insights and answers from the *self-study questions* found after each paragraph
+ Partners may also want to review the extra *self-study* activities found in each chapter
+ Electronic communication can be used to enhance the partnership, but is usually no match for a face to face meeting
+ Keep the focus of your partnership meetings on faith formation and becoming mature disciples in Christ, not other subjects
+ Never talk about other people. Keep the focus on shared concerns for each partner's discipleship training process
+ Never share your partner's confidential conversation with anyone else (this includes your family and friends)
+ Benefits include particular/personal support and accountability

Jesus called the Twelve to him, and sent them out in pairs. He gave them authority and power to deal with the evil opposition.

Mark 6:7-8

<u>Self-study</u> –helps with memory retention and better comprehension of new information about each of the habits. Our own self-study time will eventually become one of the most important ways to grow as a disciple and experience Christ in our daily lives. Each week set aside five, 30 minute blocks of time to review the material from the chapter in the workbook, which your small group is covering.

+ Answer the questions at the end of each paragraph
+ Review and reflect upon your *Write & Share with a Partner* comments
+ Complete the two *Self-Study* exercises at the end of chapters
+ Make notes on the *Insights* page at the end of each session
+ Complete the *Habit* worksheet located at the end of each chapter to help make new and lasting habits

+ Explore the **7HabitsofJesus.com** website for media links and references, supplemental information, and other materials: **www.7HabitsofJesus.com** Refer to the Appendix for information about logging on to use the companion website
+ As you become more familiar with the habits, your self-study will eventually become time for practicing the habits
+ Disciples often find that some of the habits come easier than the others, but it is important to regularly practice and grow into all of the habits.
+ The chapters on **Remembering** (Ch 1), **Listening** (Ch 2), and **Praying** (Ch 3) serve as a foundation upon which the other four habits are built. There are additional exercises that you are encouraged to practice and implement
+ Benefits include honest reflection and deep learning

May our dependably steady and warmly personal God develop maturity in you so that you get along with each other as well as Jesus gets along with us all.

Romans 15:4

Discipleship Group Names

Traditionally, Christians have named their discipleship groups after one of Jesus' Twelve Disciples (Matthew 10:2; Luke 22:14; Acts 1:2). Use this list of the twelve disciples to help you in naming your discipleship group:

Simon Peter (son of John)	*The Rock*	Matt 4:18-20
James (son of Zebedee)	*Sons of Thunder*	Mark 3:17
John (son of Zebedee)	*Sons of Thunder*	Mark 1:19
Andrew (Peter's brother)	*Fisher of Men*	Matt 4:18-20
Philip (Apostle)	*Inquirer*	Matt 10:3
Bartholomew	*Honest One*	Mark 3:18
Matthew (Levi)	*Follower*	Matt 9:9-13
Thomas (the twin)	*Doubting*	Matt 10:3
James (son of Alphaeus)	*Disciple*	Matt 10:3
Thaddaeus (son of James)	*Learner*	Matt 10:3
Simon the Zealot (the less)	*Patriot*	Matt 10:4
Matthias (the seventy)	*Chosen*	Acts 1:15

Explore the website for media links and references, supplemental information, and materials: **www.7HabitsofJesus.com** Refer to the Appendix for information about logging on to use the companion website for self-study and fellowship enhancement.

♫♫♫♫♫♫♫♫♫♫♫♫♫♫♫♫♫♫♫♫♫♫♫♫♫♫♫♫♫

Gather Us In

Here in this place new light is streaming,
now is the darkness vanished away;
see in this space our fears and our dreamings
brought here to you in the light of this day.
Gather us in, the lost and forsaken,
gather us in, the blind and the lame;
call to us now, and we shall awaken,
we shall arise at the sound of our name.

We are the young, our lives are a mystery,
we are the old who yearn for your face;
we have been sung throughout all of history,
called to be light to the whole human race.
Gather us in, the rich and the haughty,
gather us in, the proud and the strong;
give us a heart, so meek and so lowly,
give us the courage to enter the song.

Here we will take the wine and the water,
here we will take the bread of new birth,
here you shall call your sons and your
daughters,
call us anew to be salt for the earth.
Give us to drink the wine of compassion,
give us to eat the bread that is you;
nourish us well, and teach us to fashion
lives that are holy and hearts that are true.

Not in the dark of buildings confining,
not in some heaven, light years away —
here in this place the new light is shining,
now is the kingdom, and now is the day.
Gather us in and hold us forever,
gather us in and make us your own;
gather us in, all peoples together,
fire of love in our flesh and our bone.

Marty Haugen (b.1950)

 We end our session by joining hands in a circle to pray together the Lord's Prayer.

THE SEVEN HABITS OF JESUS

1. **REMEMBERING**......our baptismal adoption into God's family
2. **LISTENING**..............to God's law & gospel voice in Scripture
3. **PRAYING**................for God's help with all of our daily needs
4. **PREPARING**.............to hear God's forgiving voice in worship
5. **RETURNING**........... a percentage of what God has given us
6. **INVITING**...................others to baptism and Christ's mission
7. **CARING**................. for others and creation with Christ's love

1a. REMEMBERING

Remembering Our Baptismal Adoption

re·mem·ber·ing (vb)

1. the act of recollecting a past event.
2. recalling the benefits of our baptismal adoption.
3. the experience of reliving the past as a present reality.

Opening Prayer

Grant us grace to see what we can do, but also to know what are the limits of our powers, so that courage may feed our trust in you, who is able to rule and overrule the angry passions of men and make the wrath of men to praise you. Amen.

Reinhold Niebuhr (1892-1971)

Remembering Goal

The daily goal of remembering our baptism can be summed up by Martin Luther, *So truly, a Christian life is nothing other than a daily remembering of our baptism, once begun and ever to be continued. For this must be done without ceasing, that we always keep purging away whatever belongs to our old nature, through the power of Christ's death. Then what belongs to our new nature, through the power of Christ's resurrection, may come forth.*

Write & Share with the Group...

What do you know about the When, Where, and Why of your baptism?

When...

Where..

Why..

Salvation

In our society there is a common misunderstanding that salvation is all about what we *do* and *how* we live our lives. Salvation is often misunderstood as something we are able to secure for ourselves. However, this model of do-it-yourself salvation is not the Biblical model. Jesus told Nicodemus that, unless he was born anew from above by God's power, he would not be able to save himself (John 3:3). Paul tells us that, just as none of us are complete when we emerge from the womb, God's design and plan for each of us is to be a never ending work in progress. Daily we turn to God who first turned to us in our baptism. Daily we make an effort to accept God's plan for our lives. It takes a lifetime of repentance and forgiveness for us to recognize our eternal inheritance in God's eternal family through baptism. This is why we daily remember our baptism!

What is society's idea of salvation?

Water and Salvation

All world religions use water rituals as a means to connect people to God. Water rituals are symbolic of one of life's most essential compounds: water. The ancient Hebrews (Israelites, Jews), the ancestors of Christians, practiced a number of water rituals to recall their liberation from slavery in Egypt through the waters of the Red Sea (Exodus 14); which reminded them of their connection to God.

Jesus established the water ritual of baptism as the way for us to pass from our slavery to *sin, death, and the devil,* into the freedom of God's eternal family; to remind us of our connection to God. The followers of Jesus, empowered by the Holy Spirit, went to all the nations of the world baptizing people into God's family with water and the Word (Acts 2:37-47; John 1:12-13). Jesus made baptism the way to be adopted into God's eternal family (Eph 1:35; Gal 3:25-29; Romans 8:14-17).

As unlikely as it may seem, our relationship with God is a free gift and has nothing to do with what we have achieved before we are baptized, as well as anything we will do after we are baptized. Once we are given God's free gift of salvation through baptism, we are given the Trinity's own capacity to share the:

+**Father's love** for all people, especially the poor and the hurting of the world.

+**Son's joy** of living life in all of its fullness as the Creator had intended.

+**Spirit's peace** to experience inner serenity by trusting the Creator to sustain our lives, now and into eternity.

How does knowing salvation is a free gift make a difference to you?

Cleansing and Remembering

Scripture does not *sugarcoat* our lives. We are sinners that fail to live by God's moral demands. As C.S. Lewis said, *Perhaps humanity's greatest problem is believing they have no problem with God.* And yet, Scripture tells us that our sin is so impossible to overcome by our own efforts, that we need God's help to redeem the destructive effects of our own sinful nature. To make matters worse, our problem is not limited to the sins we commit. Our greatest problem is that our nature (being) is infected by satan's evil, which Scripture teaches us we inherited from our first parents. Like them, after the fall, we initially approach every aspect of life in a sinful way. The result is a broken relationship with God and one another. St. Paul taught that, *the evil I am doing, I believe to be good* (Rom 7:19). We need God's help to limit the destructive effects of our sinful nature. Therein lies our need to be cleansed by the waters of baptism. For the very first Christians baptism was, above all else, a cleansing bath of total immersion to drown one's sinful nature. But, that's not all that baptism does! It not only pronounces a death sentence on our sinful nature, baptism also blesses us with the indwelling of Christ's own presence. Luther said, *baptism begins our dying to sin and our rising with Christ.* Through baptism the image of God, in which we were created, is restored. **Just because our old inclination to sin remains, we should rely on Christ's own Spirit which now lives within us because of our baptism. Every day is a new opportunity to remember and celebrate the blessings of our baptism. Every day is a new opportunity to commit ourselves to a renewed relationship with Christ and a greater participation in Christ's mission of reconciliation to restore our relationship with God and one another.**

Does it make sense to you that humans are infected by sin?

> *Through baptism you were washed, you were justified in the name of the Lord Jesus Christ and in the Spirit of our God.*
>
> (1 Cor 6:11)

Baptism Defined

Just as every child must be *born from a woman,* every child of God must be *born from above through the water and Spirit* of baptism **(John 3:3)**. The word *baptism* (*baptizein,* Gk.) means to *wash.* When the Church *washes* a person with water, and repeats aloud the command of our Lord Jesus *to baptize in the name of the Father, the Son, and the Holy Spirit,* that person becomes a newly adopted child in God's eternal family (Matthew 28:18-20). At the moment of Christian baptism, our sinful separation from God is *washed* clean. The Holy Spirit plants the seed of faith within us; Christ begins to dwell within us; and, eternal life is promised by the Father. Like our physical birth into life, our spiritual birth into a new life with God is experienced as a passive recipient of an act of *the Triune God.* (2 Cor 5:17; Gal 6:15; Col 2:12). There is nothing we can do to baptize ourselves. St. Paul explains, *It was not because of any good deeds that we ourselves have done, but because of his own love that he saved us, through the Holy Spirit, who gives us a new birth and a new life by washing us (Titus 3:5).* **Christianity is the only religion that has ever offered eternal salvation as an entirely undeserved gift from God. The habit of remembering helps us to daily remember and give thanks to the Trinity for the blessings of our baptismal adoption into God's eternal family.**

How often do you focus on Remembering your baptism?

Unconditional Birth & Rebirth

God's saving work in baptism is not dependent upon our cooperation. Scripture teaches us that both our lives and our salvation are gifts given to us by God alone. There is no more beautiful or powerful statement of salvation than God's saving action in baptism. Baptism is the Church's proclamation that we are who we are, **not** because we decided to believe in God, but because God has chosen us to be in his eternal Kingdom. Christianity is not, and can never be, a do-it-yourself religion. In the same way we are unable to give birth to ourselves, we are also unable to be *born from above as a child of God* (John 3:3).

How does your Baptism as a gift define you?

Ten Blessings of Baptism

+ Our original sinful nature is washed clean (1Cor 6; Acts 2)
+ The seed of faith is planted in us by the Holy Spirit (Titus 3)
+ We are given power over our old sinful nature   (1Cor 10)
+ The Holy Spirit becomes involved in our daily lives   (Col 2)
+ The real presence of Christ begins to live within us   (Gal 2)
+ We are given the *love, joy, and peace* of the Trinity (Gal 5)
+ Spiritual gifts are given for Church growth & unity (Rom 12)
+ The Lord gives power to resist satan's temptations (Matt 4)
+ The righteousness of Christ is imprinted upon us   (Rom 6)
+ God gives eternal life to us as an unearned gift   (Mark 16)

Christians sure are fortunate to have all those ten blessings through Baptism!

Write & Share with a Partner...

Which blessing of baptism best describes
the blessing of your baptism? Why?

....

....

....

....

Lifelong Process

Baptism is not a one time event, but the beginning of a special lifelong relationship with God. No one would ever expect a newborn to physically remain a baby. Likewise, God does not expect the baptized to spiritually remain the same. Our baptism is not an isolated event, but a lifetime of renewals and rememberings that strengthen our relationship with God. God promises each of us, at the font, that he will be with us every day until we reach our heavenly home. God, therefore, expects that every day we would turn away from our relationship to our old nature in order to turn toward our new nature with Christ. Daily, the Holy Spirit within us is stirred up in order to renew our relationship with Christ. It is the daily work of the Holy Spirit that gives us the ability to respond to God's gift of Christ within our souls. Day after day, we can grow in recognizing God at work within our daily lives. As we daily remember our baptism we grow in our ability to recognize the Spirit at work with our lives. Some days, the Spirit's work in our lives is obvious and meaningful; some days it is not. Nevertheless, the work of the Holy Spirit that began in our baptism remains a powerful presence in our lives. As the Spirit conforms our faith to Christ, we are able to participate in Christ's mission of redemption to *make all things new*. In his Small Catechism, Luther describes what baptism means for daily living: *It means that our old sinful self, with all its evil deeds and desires, should be drowned through daily repentance; and that day after day a new self should arise to live with God in righteousness and purity forever.* When we invite the Holy Spirit to drown our old nature of sin, with all its evil deeds and desires, we are saying, *I can't save myself, I need your help!* We never get too old or too righteous to not depend upon the Spirit's help to die to self and rise to a new life with Christ. Baptism is a once-and-for-all act of God, which takes one's whole life to finish.

Is your baptism a lifelong process?

St. Paul on Baptism

In the sixth chapter of the book of Romans, St. Paul describes baptism as a process of death and rebirth: *Baptism into the life of Jesus means that when we are lowered into the water, it is like the burial of Jesus; when we are raised up out of the water, it is like the resurrection of Jesus.* Each of us is

HIS DEATH BRINGS DEATH TO SIN

raised into a light-filled world by our Father so that we can see where we're going in our new grace-filled world. Could it be any clearer? Our old way of life was nailed to the cross with Christ, a decisive end to that sin-miserable life—no longer at sin's every beck and call! What we believe is this: If we get included in Christ's sin-conquering death, we also get included in his life-saving resurrection. We know that when Jesus was raised from the dead it was a signal of the end of death-as-the-end. Never again will death have the last word. When Jesus died, he took sin down with him, but alive he *brings God down to us. From now on, think of it this way: Sin speaks a dead language that means nothing to you; God speaks your mother tongue, and you hang on every word. You are dead to sin and alive to God. That's what Jesus did. That means you must not give sin a vote in the way you conduct your lives. Don't give it the time of day. Don't even run little errands that are connected with that old way of life. Throw yourselves wholeheartedly and full-time—remember, you've now been raised from the dead!—into God's way of doing things. Sin can't tell you how to live. After all, you're not living under that old tyranny any longer. You're living in the freedom of God. So, since we're out from under the old tyranny, does that mean we can live any old way we want? Since we're free in the freedom of God, can we do anything that comes to mind? Hardly. You know well enough from your own experience that there are some acts of so-called freedom that destroy freedom. Offer yourselves to sin, for instance, and it's your last free act. But offer yourselves to the ways of God and the freedom never quits. All your lives you've let sin tell you what to do. But thank God you've started listening to a new master, one whose commands set you free to live openly in his freedom!* (Rom 6:2-18).

HIS LIFE BRINGS US LIFE

What do you think about Paul's description of your Baptism?

Martin Luther explains in his *Large Catechism* how difficult it is for us to accept that something as simple as baptism has adopted us into God's eternal family without any involvement on our part

The significance of baptism is a blessed dying unto sin and a resurrection in the grace of God, so that the old man, which is conceived and born in sin, is therefore drowned, and a new man, born in grace, comes forth and rises. Thus, St. Paul in his letter to Titus, calls baptism a "washing of regeneration," since in this washing many are born again and made new. As Christ also says in John's Gospel, "Unless you are born again of water and the Spirit of grace, you will not enter into the Kingdom of Heaven." For just as a child is drawn out of its mother's womb and born, and through this fleshy birth is a sinful person and a child of wrath, so all people are drawn out of baptism and spiritually born, and through this spiritual birth become children of grace. Therefore, our lives are nothing else than a spiritual baptism which does not cease till death, because all who are baptized are condemned to die; so then, the life of a Christian, from baptism to the grave, is nothing else than the beginning of a blessed death, for at the Last Day God will make us altogether new.

Martin Luther (1483-1546)

Baptized into Christ

Paul's teaching in the sixth chapter of his letter to the church in Rome explains what happens when we are baptized. Through baptism we are filled with the supernatural, spiritual power, of both Christ's death and his resurrection. In other words, with the power of Christ's death within us, we have his own power over *sin, death, and the devil* (Luther).

With Christ's power of resurrection within us, we have his own power to be loving, forgiving, and trusting in eternal life. We don't always feel, act, or look like someone with Christ's own power. Nevertheless, Christ's own Spirit is fully alive within us through our baptism. That is the greatest miracle of our salvation!

What may we expect from Christ's own Spirit living within us?

Remembering Christ's Indwelling

Even though the act of baptism is a once-and-for-all paramount act of God, it takes a lifetime to move to greater completion. When we were baptized, a lifelong process of transformation was set into motion to move us away from our sinful identity, toward a new life with God. It is primarily through the daily remembering of our baptismal adoption that this transformation occurs within us. Daily remembering our baptism should permeate all of the activities that are accompanied with the sign of the cross. When we remember the baptismal covenant God has made with us, we allow Christ to freely live within us.

Through Christ's death and resurrection, God sets into motion a daily process to transform us so that we will become the children he intends us to be. This transformation is made possible because at the moment of our baptism Christ begins living within us, making *our bodies his temple.* Although Christ lives within us through Baptism, he never forces his presence upon us. And yet, when we acknowledge Christ, through a process of remembering our baptism, it is then that his life truly becomes our life.

When Christ lives within us the two most important aspects of Christ's life become a part of our daily lives: his death and his resurrection. By his death, Christ brings death to our self-centered, sinful ways of living.

Through our baptism, we are given Christ's own capacity to bring death to the most destructive and evil force within us: our own self-centeredness and rebellion against God. The power of Christ's death that we receive in baptism is the power that breaks the sin we inherited from our *first parents.* Christ's death, at work within us, brings death to our inner connection to sin, death, and the devil's evil ways.

Through the power of his resurrection, Christ brings a new way to live in our relationship with God and with others. Through our daily remembering, our sinful ways are *drowned* and our new life with Christ is *raised up* just as it was on the day of our baptism, and just as it will be at the end of all time.

Through our baptism, we are given Christ's own capacity to bring about a new way to live and relate to God and to one another. The power of Christ's resurrection, which we received in baptism, is the power to bring about love and forgiveness to our relationship with God and our relationships with others.

How is Christ's death and resurrection at work within you?

Attitude of Gratitude

When we daily remember our baptism, we are remembering a powerful act of God, which cannot be captured in a video recording. When we recall how God has transformed our lives through baptism, a sense of gratitude spontaneously wells up within us. Gratitude is one of the greatest virtues in shaping our new life with Christ. Martin Luther referred to gratitude as, *the basic Christian attitude and the very heart of the gospel.* There is a large body of research to indicate that grateful people are happier, less depressed, less stressed-out, and more satisfied with life.

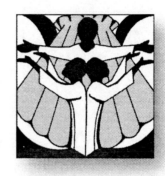

What is your experience with an attitude of gratitude?

The blessings of baptism are so boundless that if our timid human nature considers them, it may doubt whether they could all be true. No greater jewel can adorn our body and soul than baptism, for through it we obtain perfect holiness and salvation. Baptism is so full of comfort and grace that heaven and earth cannot contain it.

Martin Luther (1483-1546)

Write & Share with a Partner...

*How does (would) remembering your baptism
help you start each day more cheerfully?*

....

....

*How does (would) remembering your baptism
throughout the day help you grow in faith?*

....

....

*Would you know who is the greatest of the
saints? It is not he who studies the Scriptures
and prays the most; it is not he who tries to be
loving and kind to all; it is not he who has even
temperance; it is also not he who fights for
justice and sacrifices his life for a cause; it is not
he who is the most faithful in worship; it is not
he who humbles himself through confession;
but, it is he who is always grateful to God and
who receives everything in life as an instance of
God's goodness.*

William Law (1686-1761)

♫♫♫♫♫♫♫♫♫♫♫♫♫♫♫♫♫♫♫♫♫♫♫♫

Baptized in Water

Baptized in water, sealed by the Spirit,
*   Cleansed by the blood of Christ our king;*
Heirs of salvation, trusting his promise,
Faithfully now God's praise we sing.

Baptized in water, sealed by the Spirit,
*   Dead in the tomb with Christ our king;*
One with his rising, freed and forgiven,
Thankfully now God's praise we sing.

Baptized in water, sealed by the Spirit,
*   Marked with the sign of Christ our king;*
Born of the Spirit, we are God's children,
Joyfully now God's praise we sing.

Michael Saward (b.1932)

 We end our session by joining hands in a circle to pray together the Lord's Prayer.

Insights for developing my Remembering HABIT:

*How will the habit of remembering my baptism **help** me live a more Christ-centered life?*

....

....

....

....

....

....

....

....

*How often will I **attempt** to remember my baptism?*

....

....

....

....

....

....

....

....

....

....

*How will the habit of remembering my baptism **become** a part of my life?*

....

....

....

....

....

....

....

*How is remembering my baptism **important** to my maturity as a disciple of Christ?*

....

....

....

....

....

....

....

*What is the **timeframe** to make remembering my baptism a habit?*

....

....

....

....

....

THE SEVEN HABITS OF JESUS

1. **REMEMBERING**......our baptismal adoption into God's family

2. **LISTENING**.............to God's law & gospel voice in Scripture

3. **PRAYING**.................for God's help with all of our daily needs

4. **PREPARING**.............to hear God's forgiving voice in worship

5. **RETURNING**........... a percentage of what God has given us

6. **INVITING**..................others to baptism and Christ's mission

7. **CARING**................. for others and creation with Christ's love

1b. REMEMBERING

Remembering Our Baptismal Adoption

re·mem·ber·ing (vb)

1. the act of recollecting a past event.
2. recalling the benefits of our baptismal adoption.
3. the experience of reliving the past as a present reality.

Opening Prayer

O eternal Trinity, my sweet love! You, supreme strength, strengthen us. Today, eternal God, let our cloud be dissipated so that we may perfectly know and follow your truth in truth, with a free and simple heart. God, come to our assistance! Lord, make haste to help us! Amen.

Catherine of Sienna (1347-1380)

Remembering Goal

The daily goal of remembering our baptism can be summed up by Martin Luther: *So truly, a Christian life is nothing other than a daily remembering of our baptism, once begun and ever to be continued. For this must be done without ceasing, that we always keep purging away whatever belongs to our old nature through the power of Christ's death in us. Then what belongs to our new nature in Christ, through the power of his resurrection, may come forth.*

Write & Share with the Group...

What does it mean for you to be baptized
and adopted into the Trinity?

....

....

....

The Apostles' Creed

The Apostle's Creed is based on a short description of the Triune God in whom we were baptized. The Apostle's Creed was developed from a series of questions originally asked of a person (or a child's sponsor) prior to Baptism. Its oldest origin occurs in the first century.

The First Part: God the Creator

I believe in God, the Father almighty,
    creator of heaven and earth.

Luther's explanation: *I believe that God has created me together with all creatures. God has given me and still preserves my body and soul; eyes, ears, and all limbs and senses; reason and all mental faculties. In addition, God daily and abundantly provides shoes and clothing, food and drink, house and home, spouse and children, fields, livestock, and all property—along with all the necessities and nourishment for this body and life. God protects me against all danger and shields and preserves me from all evil. God does all this out of pure, fatherly, and divine goodness and mercy, without any merit or worthiness of mine at all! For all of this I owe it to God to thank and praise, serve and obey him.* **This is most certainly true.** (Psalm 8)

The Second Part: God the Redeemer

I believe in Jesus Christ, his only Son, our Lord.
He was conceived by the power of the Holy Spirit
and born of the virgin Mary.
He suffered under Pontius Pilate,
was crucified, died, and was buried.
He descended into hell.
On the third day he rose again.
He ascended into heaven,
and is seated at the right hand of the Father.
He will come again to judge the living and the dead.

Luther's explanation: *I believe that Jesus Christ, true God, begotten of the Father in eternity, and also true human being, born of the virgin Mary, is my Lord. He has redeemed me, a lost and condemned person. He has purchased and freed me from all sins, from death, and from the power of the devil, not with gold or silver but with his holy, precious blood and with his innocent suffering and death. He has done all this in order that I may belong to him, live in his kingdom, and serve him in eternal righteousness, innocence, and blessedness, just as he is risen from the dead and lives and rules in eternity. **This is most certainly true.*** (Luke 23:39-46)

We mice were in the stable where Jesus was born. How wonderful is that!

The Third Part: God the Sanctifier

I believe in the Holy Spirit,
> *the holy catholic church,*
> *the communion of saints,*
> *the forgiveness of sins,*
> *the resurrection of the body,*
> *and the life everlasting. Amen.*

Luther's explanation: *I believe that by my own understanding or strength I cannot believe in Jesus Christ my Lord or come to him, but instead the Holy Spirit has called me through the Gospel, enlightened me with his gifts, made me holy, and kept me in the true faith, just as he calls, gathers, enlightens, and makes holy the whole Christian church on earth and keeps it with Jesus Christ in the one common, true faith. Daily in this Christian Church the Holy Spirit abundantly forgives all sins—mine and those of all believers. On the last day the Holy Spirit will raise me and all the dead and will give to me and all believers in Christ eternal life.* **This is most certainly true.** (Acts 2)

How can we best share the meaning of the Creed with others?

Baptized into the Trinity

When we are baptized into the Triune God, the Father, Son, and Holy Spirit, we are baptized into the mission of the Trinity in the world (Matt 28:18-20). The mission of the Trinity in our world is most often referred to as Christ's mission—Christ's mission of reconciliation. Through our baptism into the death and resurrection of Christ we become full participants in his mission.

Through our baptism into Christ's ongoing mission of reconciliation, our broken relationships with God, others, and the world are in the process of being made whole...reconciled. Through our baptism into the life of Christ and his mission of reconciliation, God promises us that we will be reconciled (united) with the family of the Trinity, the human family, and the world into eternity. To reconcile is to have a relationship free of conflicts, differences, or divisions; one united in harmony. In the New Testament two terms are used to describe our reconciliation with God: *adoption* and *access*.

<u>Adoption</u> The Father sent his Son on a mission in which the Holy Spirit adopted us into the family of the Trinity. John tells us that we become the adopted children of the Trinity through baptism. Paul tells us that through baptism we have become *children of the Father* and *heirs* (inheritors) of God (Gal 4:5). Jesus, who regularly addressed God as *Father*, invites us to do the same. We are to approach our heavenly Father affectionately, as we would our own earthly father (Abba/Daddy).

Access St. Paul tells us that we have access through our baptism into the fellowship of the Trinity. We have access to the Father, through the Son, by the Holy Spirit (Eph 2:17-18), to effect Christ's mission of reconciliation in our world. *Since we have access to the most holy place by the blood of Jesus, let us draw near to God with a sincere heart* (Heb 10:19-21). Through Christ's death on the cross, he has united us with God into a new and reconciled relationship which transcends death and offers eternal life to all in his family.

Christ's gift of reconciliation has both a vertical relationship to God, as well as a horizontal relationship to people. Paul teaches that *Christ has removed the barriers that divide us* (Eph 2:14). And, the power of his reconciliation extends throughout the Church, society, creation, and even the entire universe (Col 1:15-20).

Are you familiar with what the Bible teaches about the Trinity?

Luther on Baptism

Luther said... **Never adopt the opinion that your baptism is something that happened in the past and cannot be used in our present life. Baptism is not a one-time action, but a truly splendid on-going act of God. Everyone should therefore look upon baptism like the** clothes we put on every day. We should at all times be clothed in the blessings of baptism. We must every day remember our baptism so that our old nature is suppressed and our new nature in Christ would be allowed to grow toward maturity.

Martin Luther was fond of saying...*I am baptized* (using the present passive verb) rather than, *I was baptized* (the past perfect tense verb). With this emphasis, Luther describes baptism as an ongoing condition before God. Baptism is not just a past event, but defines both who we are and what we will become. When Scripture invites us to *remember* (*anamnesis*, Greek), it is not an invitation to merely reflect on something that happened in the past. The word *remember*, as it is used in Scripture, is a reliving of a past event in such a way that it becomes a powerful and living present experience. Therefore, remembering our baptism is a similar, yet positive, experience to that of a veteran reliving a past event through post-traumatic stress disorder (PTSD).

Martin Luther said...*Baptism is the greatest event in our lives; nothing else in all of life can begin to compare to the significance and importance of God's gift of a new and eternal life through baptism. If there is anything we should daily* *remember, if there is anything we should keep from forgetting, it would most certainly be our baptism! The act of baptism is quickly over as we can plainly see. But, the drowning of sin and our rising to a new life lasts throughout our whole life. Therefore, the life of a Christian, from our beginning in baptism to the grave, is nothing else than a series of deaths and risings to prepare us for our final day when God will make us altogether new.*

How do you feel about what Luther said regarding Baptism?

The mice that knew Martin Luther said he always talked about Baptism.

Confession and Forgiveness

In many respects the daily renewal of baptism is a process of confession and renewal. According to Scripture (Acts 2:38, 17:30), if we are to receive God's renewing forgiveness we must first confess our sins. *If we claim that we're free from sin, we're only fooling ourselves, which is nonsense. On the other hand, if we admit our sins he won't let us down; he'll be true to himself. He'll forgive our sins and purge us of all wrongdoing* (1 John 1:9).

+ **It is necessary to reflect upon the *thoughts, words, and deeds* that we have committed, which do not reflect our status as a baptized child of God.** It can be helpful to reflect upon the Ten Commandments (See chapter *4b. Preparing*), to identify how we have sinned. Another similar resource to consider is the *seven deadly sins* (pride, anger, lust, envy, greed, sloth, and gluttony), that we have committed. It is necessary that we be specific in our confession. For example: *I need to stop lying to my boss*, instead of, *I need to be more honest.* Our confession needs to be specific about what we have actually done, or left undone.

+ **After we have identified a particular sin that we have committed, we next need to ask: *Why did I commit that sin*?** The answer to this question is critical because sin is often an attempt to meet a legitimate need in an illegitimate way.

+ **Next, we want to ask, *What has happened as a result of my sin*?** In other words, *What are some of the negative consequences of my sin?* For instance, a common consequence is that our sin of lying can evolve into a chronic pattern of lying.

+ **It is helpful to recognize that often our sinning has hurt others in our lives.** If we have hurt another person we need to seek reconciliation with them (Matthew 18:15)

+ **Confession is not just about recognizing what we have done, but how we will need to change in order to avoid a repeating pattern of sin.** This involves trying to set right what we did wrong, in a very intentional manner, so that a pattern of sinning is not established.

+ **The most important reason to confess our sins is to receive God's forgiveness. When God forgives us of our sins, he forgives all of our sins. An important way to recognize God's complete forgiveness of our sins is to make the sign of the cross upon our forehead or chest, which affirms God's unconditional forgiveness for the baptized and adopted children in his family.**

+ **Read aloud Psalm 51:1, 10-12 or Psalm 103:8-13, for the assurance of God's loving forgiveness.**

How often do you participate in confession?

Write & Share with a Partner...

Why do you think God wants us to confess our sins before he forgives us?

....

....

> *I bind unto myself the name,*
> *The strong name of the Trinity;*
> *By invocation of the same,*
> *The Three in One, the One in Three,*
> *Of whom all nature hath creation;*
> *Eternal Father, Spirit, Word,*
> *Praise to the Lord of my salvation,*
> *Salvation is of Christ the Lord.*
> *Amen.*
>
> St. Patrick (389-461)

Remembering Our Baptism

 Throughout the ages, Christians have remembered their baptismal adoption into God's family in many different ways. Tertullian (AD 211) described a common way to be renewed in our baptism that was popular in his age: *Before we bathe in the morning, as we put on our clothes, whenever we eat, attend to the activities of our daily lives, we, the baptized, trace the sign of the cross upon our foreheads.* Cyprian (AD 250) also taught: *those who have been baptized have the sign of the cross, the sign of blood, marked upon their foreheads at the highest part of the body to recall the lifted-up cross in which we have been baptized.*

Has it been important to you to remember your Baptism?

Ways of Remembering

Some common ways for us to remember our baptism:

A. **We can use a brief order of confession and forgiveness, usually in the morning, as a way to remember our baptism.** Example: *I was baptized in the name of the Father, + Son, and Holy Spirit, and adopted into the eternal family of the Trinity. Merciful God, I confess that I have sinned in thought, word, and deed, by what I have done and by what I have left undone. Forgive me, so that I might be renewed in the covenant of my baptism.*

It is important that we refrain from always using this type of generic confession. More often than not, our confession should reflect self-examination. Most of us are *experts* at examining the sins of others. However, we are much less capable at identifying our own sins. Our confession, to be most helpful, needs to bring before Christ specific sinful thoughts, words, and actions. The traditional word for this is the *examination of conscience.* One way to help us sincerely identify our sins is to review the *Ten Commandments.* Another way to identify our sins that has been helpful to many in the Church is to review the *Seven Deadly Sins.* When we confess our sins there is a need for our sins to be specific. We want to be honest with God, and ourselves, in order to be truly grateful for God's forgiveness.

B. **We can use a verbal acclamation of thanksgiving to remember our baptism. Luther was known to have frequently said out loud, *I am baptized!*** As we go through the day we can use water as a helpful *trigger* for a baptismal acclamation of thanksgiving. Example: I am baptized... Christ is with me!

C. **We can remember our baptism throughout each day by singing a renewal of baptism to a favorite piece of music.** Example: Remembering our baptism may be easily put together with a familiar tune like *Amazing Grace*: Bap-tized and a-dopted in God's fam-ily. God is my fa-ther now. Je-sus has be-come the Lo-rd of my life. The Holy Spir-it lives in me.

D. **Whenever we see water we can give thanks to God for our baptism**. When we wash up with water in the morning it is an excellent time to renew our baptismal identity as a child of God. A helpful way to renew our baptism is with a prayer of thanksgiving as we make the sign of the cross upon us. Example: **In the name of the Father, Son, and Holy Spirit, I am an adopted child in God's eternal family!**

I like to hear Christians sing about being baptized!

E. **Wearing a cross can become a trigger that encourages us to thank God for our baptism and ask him to allow us to become more like Christ.** Similarly, wearing a military style *dog tag* can also be a visual reminder of *who's* we are as a result of being baptized. It is also popular to hang a baptismal *dog tag* on a bed post, or a shower head, to help trigger the remembering of our baptism. Dog tags can be inexpensively customized on the internet with a message like: I'm a baptized and adopted child in the eternal family of the Trinity.

F. **Like the Christians in Cyprian's day, we can trace a cross upon our foreheads to recall being baptized into Christ's death and resurrection.** We might also want to trace a cross upon the forehead of a loved one to remind them of their eternal adoption into God's eternal family through baptism.

G. **Repeat, throughout each day, your own personal and constructive internal self-talk phrase, which is a powerful way to thank God for all the blessings of our baptismal adoption into his family.** (More info on internal self-talk is provided next on pp. 76-79)

Which of these ways of remembering appeals to you the most?

Internal Self-Talk Phrase

Almost every minute of every day we are engaged with our own internal self-talk phrase. This self-talk phrase, for better or worse, interprets the events of our daily lives.

<u>Mental health research has discovered:</u>
- × EVENTS ALONE DO NOT CREATE GOOD OR BAD EMOTIONS
- ✓ SELF-TALK OF EVENTS CREATES GOOD OR BAD EMOTIONS

We all have negative self-talk statements running through our minds at all times. Our internal monologue is a never-silent stream of self-talk statements, which create either good or bad emotions.

What are some of the negative self-talk phrases that run through your mind when you experience bad emotions?

....

....

....

....

....

....

....

....

....

....

Review the negative statements you have written down to help you determine which of the following ten destructive thought patterns is your most common negative self-talk statement: (Having two or three statements is common)

1. **All or Nothing**. This destructive self-talk states that something is perceived as all good or all bad: *If I don't get an A in math, it's the same as failing.*

2. **Overgeneralization**. Making rules and drawing conclusions to apply to every situation: *Mary didn't want to go to the movies; nobody wants to go on a date with me.*

3. **Ignoring the Positive**. Only paying attention to problems and weaknesses: *My friends tell me I am a good golfer, but they are only trying to make me feel better.*

4. **Inferring**. Thinking another person has negative motives: *The only reason Bobby gave me a hug is because he wants to use my car.*

5. **Mind Reading**. Thinking you know the thoughts and desires of another person: *She told me she's going to visit grandpa but she's really going to visit grandma.*

6. **Magnification**. The pattern of convincing yourself that it's the little things that really upset us: *It was not an innocent mistake, she refused to look directly at me.*

7. **Minimization**. When you ignore positive things as being insignificant: *Well, I got a raise but it's not even close to what I need.*

8. **Infallibility**. The belief that your feelings represent reality: *Ross, nobody thinks Tom insulted you, except you.*

9. **Labeling**. The practice of name-calling with the use of derogatory labels for others: *Mary is the absolute biggest klutz; she breaks everything.*

10. **Fortune Telling**. The false understanding that you are capable of predicting the future: *It won't do me any good to talk to Jane, she just doesn't listen.*

> Even mice have negative self-talk phrases running through our minds every day.

What happens that triggers your negative feelings?

Example: When other people criticize me
....

What was your negative emotional response?

Example: Like everything was going wrong
....

Which of the 10 destructive patterns do you use?

Example: It was #1, something is all good or all bad
....

How is that destructive pattern bad for you?

Example: I'm very "up" or very "down"
....

Recognizing and replacing a negative and destructive self-talk phrase with a positive and constructive self-talk phrase, such as a renewal of baptism phrase, can give us the capacity to feel good and act great.

Destructive Self-Talk	Constructive Self-Talk
Something always goes wrong	The Spirit is my daily guide
I worry about everything	The Father is my provider
He makes my blood boil	Christ empowers me to love
I am usually right	Jesus Christ is my Lord

Creating Self-Talk Phrases

+ Write-out a positive and constructive self-talk phrase (that incorporates a blessing of baptism) one hundred times each day for 21 days.
+ When driving alone, repeat aloud your constructive self-talk baptismal phrase for the next 21 days.
+ Once each day, for 21 consecutive days, participate in meditative prayer (See chapter *3b*. Praying) in which you encounter Jesus in your inner sanctuary and listen to him gently repeat your constructive self-talk phrase.

What keeps you from using more constructive self-talk?

The Lord always watches over me!

The real problem of the Christian life comes where people do not usually look for it. It comes the very moment you wake up each morning. All your wishes and hopes for the day rush at you like wild animals. And the first job each morning consists simply in shoving them all back; in listening to that other voice, taking that other point of view, letting that other larger, stronger, quieter life come flowing in. We can only do it for moments at first. But from those moments the new sort of life will be spreading through our system because now we are letting Him work at the right part of us. We are like eggs at present. And you cannot go on indefinitely being just an ordinary, decent egg. We must be hatched or go bad.

C.S. Lewis (1898-1963)

Write & Share with a Partner...

What are some of the most important insights you discovered in this chapter on Remembering?

....

....

What new way of remembering your baptism will you try to do?

....

....

♫♫♫♫♫♫♫♫♫♫♫♫♫♫♫♫♫♫♫♫♫♫♫♫♫

Baptized in Water

Baptized in water, sealed by the Spirit,
          Cleansed by the blood of Christ our king;
Heirs of salvation, trusting his promise,
Faithfully now God's praise we sing.

Baptized in water, sealed by the Spirit,
          Dead in the tomb with Christ our king;
One with his rising, freed and forgiven,
Thankfully now God's praise we sing.

Baptized in water, sealed by the Spirit,
          Marked with the sign of Christ our king;
Born of the Spirit, we are God's children,
Joyfully now God's praise we sing.

Michael Saward (b.1932)

 We end our session by joining hands in a circle to pray together the Lord's Prayer.

Insights for developing my Remembering HABIT:

*How will the habit of remembering my baptism **help** me live a more Christ-centered life?*

....

....

....

....

....

....

....

....

*How often will I **attempt** to remember my baptism?*

....

....

....

....

....

....

....

....

....

....

*How will the habit of remembering my baptism **become** a part of my life?*

....
....
....
....
....
....
....

*How is remembering my baptism **important** to my maturity as a disciple of Christ?*

....
....
....
....
....
....
....

*What is the **timeframe** to make remembering my baptism a habit?*

....
....
....
....
....

Self-Study for Remembering
Sinners & Saints (1a)

I do not understand my own actions. For I do not do what I want, but I do the very thing I hate (Rom 7:15).

Through our baptism we have become children in God's own family; this makes us saints. At the same time we are sinners. When we say we are sinners, we are talking about our human condition, not just the sins we have committed. Daily we face the old person in us with all our sins and evil desires. Daily we have sorrow for the sinful nature within us. And, daily we confess, we repent, of our sins so that the new person we are in Christ might be experienced in our daily lives. We are not sometimes sinners and sometimes saints. We are always both sinners and saints at the same time.

Exploring Scripture:
John 8:34-36; Acts 10:43; Col 1:13-14; 1 John 1:8-9

What does it mean for you to be a sinner and a saint in your daily life?

. . . .

. . . .

. . . .

. . . .

Self-Study for Remembering
Mission (1b)

Go therefore and make disciples of all nations, baptizing them in the name of the Father and of the Son and of the Holy Spirit, teaching them to observe all that I have commanded you (Matt 28:19-20).

Too often Christians only focus on their own relationship with God. However, being a disciple is also about making disciples. As disciples we want to try to look beyond ourselves in order to share the good news of Jesus (gospel) with other faiths and those with no faith. Our mission to share Jesus occurs wherever people do not know Jesus as Savior. We are all missionaries because we are Christians. Being a Christian is not about how we live our lives, as much as it is sharing the Savior with others.

Explore Scripture:
Luke 4:18-19; Acts 10:34-43; 1 Cor 15:3-4; Eph 2:17-22

What do you think about your ability to invite another to be a disciple of Christ?

....

....

....

....

Use your answers from the Insights questions in parts A and B to help make **REMEMBERING** *a*

Help

Attempt

Become

Important

Timeframe

How will the habit of remembering my baptism **help** me live a more Christ-centered life?

....

....

....

....

How often will I **attempt** to remember my baptism?

....

....

....

....

How will the habit of remembering my baptism **become** a part of my life?

....

....

....

....

How is remembering my baptism **important** to my maturity as a disciple of Christ?

....

....

....

....

What is the **timeframe** to make remembering my baptism a habit?

....

....

....

....

THE SEVEN HABITS OF JESUS

1. **REMEMBERING**......our baptismal adoption into God's family

2. **LISTENING**..............to God's law & gospel voice in Scripture

3. **PRAYING**................for God's help with all of our daily needs

4. **PREPARING**...........to hear God's forgiving voice in worship

5. **RETURNING**........... a percentage of what God has given us

6. **INVITING**...................others to baptism and Christ's mission

7. **CARING**................. for others and creation with Christ's love

2a. LISTENING

Listening to God's Voice in the Bible

lis·ten·ing (vb)
1. to be attentive to hearing
2. to pay attention; to heed; to obey
3. to wait attentively for another's voice

Opening Prayer

O Everlasting God and Father of our Lord Jesus Christ: Grant us Thy grace that we may study Thy Holy Scriptures diligently and, with our whole heart, seek and find Christ therein and through Him obtain everlasting life, through Jesus Christ, our Lord. Amen.

Martin Luther (1483-1546)

Listening Goal

The primary goal of this chapter on listening is to make reading the Bible a meaningful habit, through which we are able to listen to God's Word, his voice, as he speaks directly to each of us. Through our daily Bible reading, God's voice speaks to the depth of our souls a message about our sin (law), and our great need for the Savior (gospel). As Luther said, *From all eternity God has had an active voice, a thought, a conversation, a will, an address within him that he wants to share with us through Scripture.*

> ## Write & Share with the Group...
> *Why do you think so few people in the church read the Bible?*
>
> ....
>
> ....

Listening with Fluency

Few Christians participate in daily Bible reading. Those who have studied this matter have identified a crucial factor. The reason so few Christians read the Bible is because they were incorrectly taught that reading the Bible is a matter of literacy (learning its content), instead of a matter of fluency (learning how to read the Bible). Biblical literacy is limited to remembering and recalling the *who, what, when, where,* and *why* of a Scripture passage. Biblical fluency teaches us that when we read the Bible we are opening ourselves up to God's transforming voice, which speaks directly to our souls. It is God's voice that offers us his own presence, power, and promises. Being fluent in reading the Bible requires a trained ability to recognize God's powerful voice as it breaks into our lives to transform us. When God's voice enters our souls through Bible reading, it does so in two very distinct ways: through God's *law voice* and through God's *gospel voice.* When God's law and gospel voices enter our souls they can be likened to a medical diagnosis and prognosis. First, God's law voice diagnoses our problems. Next, God's gospel voice offers us a prognosis to restore our relationship with God through the Savior. Just as a physical exam with our medical doctor involves a diagnosis and a prognosis for our physical health, the law and the gospel within each passage of the Bible offers God's diagnosis (law) and his prognosis (gospel) for our spiritual health.

Whenever we read a Bible passage we anticipate the passage will offer us two things: First, the passage will tell us how we have been living our lives in a way that is not good for our relationship with God and with others. In theological language this is referred to as God's law. God's law voice tells us what we should, could, or ought to do to improve our relationship with God and others. God's law voice reveals our sinful rebellion against the life God desires for us. God's law voice reminds us that we need the Savior's help.

Second, the passage will most importantly, tell us how God desires us to be connected to the Savior so that our relationship with God and others might improve. In theological language this is referred to as God's gospel. God's gospel voice tells us of the faith, hope, and the love God freely gives us through the Savior. The reason we read the Bible is to let God's voice speak to our souls and transform our lives. When we read a passage of the Bible, we need to do more than just remember the story. For Martin Luther, Jesus' habit of daily listening to God's voice through law and gospel Bible study is essential for a disciple.

Why do you think Biblical fluency is so important to a disciple?

Literacy: Knowing the content and the people.

Fluency: **Knowing how God's law and gospel voice is speaking a specific message to us through our reading of the Bible.**

The Word of God

The *Word of God* is the most ancient name for the Bible because it is a record of God's *voice*, and the life his voice has brought into existence. God's Word is not a *voice* about God, but a *voice* from God. The Lutheran Confessions refer to the Word of God as the *living voice of God.* The Word of God tells us that when God speaks, it is such a powerful force that his *words* created the world out of nothing (Gen 1:3). The prophet Isaiah tells us that whenever God has spoken, his voice has always accomplished the result he intended (Is 45:23; 55:10). It is God's actual *voice* that has shaped history by *conforming everything to his will* (Ps 147). The *Word of God* alone is filled with power to either *bless* or *condemn* (Deut 30:16-20).

How do you describe the power of God's Word, his voice?

From listening in on Bible study groups, I've learned it's a matter of fluency, not literacy.

One does not live by bread alone, but by every word that comes from the mouth of God.

Matt 4:4

Ignoring God's Voice

There are two contemporary ways that distort God's voice and keep us from listening to the voice of God: the *fundamental* and the *liberal* ways of reading the Bible.

The *fundamental* way of reading the Bible claims that by our own reason and personal examination, we are able to accept certain *fundamental truths*, which save us from eternal separation from God. The *fundamental* way of reading the Bible focuses on what we must believe to save ourselves, instead of focusing on the saving power of God's *voice* as it breaks into our lives with the Savior's gift of salvation.

The *liberal* way of reading the Bible claims that by adopting a Biblical social ethic that God expects of us (*i.e. humility and justice*), we can make the world a better place. The liberal way of reading the Bible focuses on how we are to act, instead of focusing on the saving power of God's *voice* as it breaks into our lives with the Savior's gift of salvation.

Both the *fundamental* and *liberal* ways of reading the Bible are based upon Greek philosophy, which has significantly shaped Western civilization. Greek philosophy seeks to identify certain *truths*, which shape our thoughts, beliefs, and behaviors. In contrast, the Judeo-Christian way of understanding a Biblical text is based upon Hebrew thought, which is quite different from Greek thought. Hebrew thought is based upon the ancient understanding that God's *voice* alone has the power to transform us and the world.

Why is it so important for a Christian to know Hebrew thought?

Write & Share with a Partner...
Do you find it difficult to hear God's
voice when reading the Bible?

....

....

Do you read the Bible with a Greek
or a Hebrew understanding?

....

....

Listening to God's Voice

The best way for us to listen to God's *voice* through Bible reading, is to recognize God's two most important themes in the Bible: God's law and God's gospel. God's law voice is about what God wants us to do, but what we are unable to do. God's gospel voice is about what God does for us by freely offering us salvation through his appointed Savior. God's law reveals the sin-filled self-centeredness we inherited from our first parents. Whereas, the transforming power of the gospel speaks to our souls to give us a new relationship with God and others. God's law always demands something from us, while God's gospel always offers us something. The following chart can help us to compare and contrast God's law voice with God's gospel voice in the Bible.

How much experience do you have with law & gospel Bible study?

GOD'S LAW VOICE	⇔	GOD'S GOSPEL VOICE
Tells us what we don't do.	⇔	*Tells us what God will do for us.*
Exposes our sinful nature.	⇔	*Reveals the Holy Spirit within us.*
Attacks our sinful ways.	⇔	*Empowers our Christ-like living.*
Exposes our selfishness.	⇔	*Reveals Christ's love within us.*
Drives us to the Gospel.	⇔	*Creates gratitude toward God.*
Gives the demands of God.	⇔	*Gives the gifts of the Holy Spirit.*
Shows our need for faith.	⇔	*Strengthens our faith in Christ.*

Law & Gospel Voice

The goal of Bible reading is not for us to interpret the Bible, but for God's voice to interpret our lives with his law and his gospel! This is the single most important reason for reading the Bible. When we become aware of both God's law voice and God's gospel voice within a passage, it is then that God's voice becomes for us a transforming power in our lives. In a practical way, while reading the Bible, we need to keep asking ourselves: *Are these words God's law voice, or are these words God's gospel?* Through his law voice, God interprets our lives and describes our chronic connection to *sin, death, and the devil.* Through his gospel voice, God interprets our lives and freely offers us *forgiveness and eternal life.*

As Martin Luther explains...*For us to properly hear God's voice in the Bible requires that we understand God's law, that we understand God's gospel, and that we do not mix them together so that each part remains the clear voice of God.* We read the Bible so that God's voice might speak directly to each of us in a very personal way. Being able to discern God's *law* voice from his *gospel* voice is the critical skill we

need if we are to truly *hear* God's *voice*. **Reading the Bible through the *lenses* of God's law and his gospel is the ancient practice of the church, and is the essential hallmark of Reformation teaching about how to read the Bible.**

Do you expect God's voice to interpret your life in Bible study?

For those new to a Law & Gospel Bible study, it can be helpful to recognize:

> **God's law primarily reveals human sin.**
> **God's gospel primarily reveals the Savior.**

LAW **S**HOWS **O**UR **S**IN
GOSPEL **S**HOWS **O**UR **S**AVIOR

The Bible is the Word of God. He spoke it. It issued from his mouth. We read in 2 Timothy 3:16 that, All Scripture has been breathed out from God's mouth. Hence, the familiar Biblical phrases, The Word of the Lord came to me saying, or, Thus says the Lord.

John Stott (1921-2011)

We mice like listening to Law and Gospel Bible study. It stimulates our minds and interprets our souls!

*Lutherans understand the Scriptures to be the source and norm of the Christian proclamation of God's Word. This Word always exercises one of two theological functions, which we call **Law** and **Gospel**. The theological function of the **Law** is to expose our sin (all have sinned and fall short of the glory of God...Romans 3:23) and drive us to the cross of Christ, which is where the **Gospel** is revealed as the power of God to save us from our otherwise hopeless predicament (...they are now justified by his grace as a gift, through the redemption that is in Christ Jesus...Romans 3:24). Law and Gospel always work together. Law without Gospel is incomplete. Gospel without Law is impossible, like a two-story building without a first floor. In this life, the job of God's Law-Gospel Word is never finished. This living Word is the means for our ongoing dying and rising with Christ.*

Edward Schroeder

God's law is everything in the Bible that reveals God's moral expectation of us, which we cannot achieve on our own. The law tells us what we don't do. God's gospel is everything in the Bible that reveals how God saves us from sin, death, and the devil by the work of the Savior. The gospel tells us what God has done for us in Christ Jesus.

Few believe that God actually speaks through his Word until they experience it. Unless a person has had the opportunity of hearing God's Word, no argument can convince them. The work of the Holy Spirit allows God's voice to be heard. Paul teaches that even faith comes from what is heard. Because much of the church in our country no longer believes in the power of God's Word or expects to hear God speak through Scripture, it is no longer common for Christians to listen to God.

Elizabeth Achtemeir

How does God actually speak to you?

The worst thing that can happen to the Church is to confuse law and gospel. When we soften the law, we never give up on our own attempts to offer our rags of righteousness to God. When we turn the gospel into demands, it is no longer the saving Word of redemption in Jesus Christ alone.

Michael Horton

Before returning to Nazi Germany where he would eventually be sent to a concentration camp and executed, Dietrich Bonhoeffer summarizes American religion as *Protestantism without the Reformation*:

> God has granted American Christianity no Reformation. He has given it strong preachers and churchmen, but no Reformation by the Word of God. The American Church finds it difficult to be criticized by the law and to be saved solely by the gospel. As a result, American Christianity is still essentially religion and ethics, without the Word's law and gospel.

In what ways do you agree with Bonhoeffer?

Law and gospel is very important!

Law & Gospel Bible Reading

Step One: Begin with Prayer

(Sample) *Father, as I read your Word, speak to me. Allow your voice to speak to my heart and the circumstances of my life. Let me be open to hear your law & Gospel voice as I read your Word. Amen.*

Step Two: Read and Re-read the Text

It is helpful to read the text repeatedly until we are able to retell the passage in our own words. As we repeatedly read the text, we want to be attentive to those words which may be law and those words which may be gospel. It can be helpful to <u>underline</u> those law words in the passage which seem to be directing us toward our sin. It can also be helpful to circle those gospel words in the passage that seem to be directing us toward the Savior.

Step Three: Review a Study Bible

A study Bible provides helpful insights into the theological issues of the text. However, do not allow these insights, no matter how interesting, to detract from the identification of God's law voice and his gospel voice. Use any theological insights to help identify our problem with sin and God's solution of the Savior.

Step Four: Identify God's Law & Gospel

A helpful way to identify God's law voice and Gospel voice is to ask one law and one gospel question of each passage. **The law question: *How does this passage reveal our sinful self-centeredness, which is keeping us from depending on the Savior?* The gospel question: *How does this passage reveal God's gift of the Savior, which offers us a new life with Christ?***

Step Five: Meditate Upon God's Gospel

Quieting Our Inner Sanctuary: We quiet our souls by focusing on our breathing. Breathe in slowly while silently spelling the name of Jesus (J-E-S-U-S). Hold your breath as you silently spell Christ (C-H-R-I-S-T). Exhale while silently spelling the Lord (T-H-E-L-O-R-D). Repeat this pattern of breathing until you are relaxed, which takes about ten minutes for most people. You may want to adjust this pattern of breathing so it is comfortable for you. Another way to quiet ourselves is to focus on the temperature of our breath as we inhale and the warmer temperature of our breath as we exhale.

Dwelling within Our Inner Sanctuary: The second part of meditation is to meet the Lord Jesus in the sanctuary of our souls, which we may think of as a place created within our mind's eye to be with the Lord. Using our favorite sights, sounds, smells and feelings, we visualize our inner sanctuary which is a favorite place where the Lord Jesus meets us.

Listening to God's Voice in Scripture Speak to Us through Jesus: As Jesus meets us in our inner sanctuary, we ask him to share God's gospel message of forgiveness and hope from the biblical passage we have just read. Listening to God's gospel voice restores our trust and hope in Jesus' death and resurrection. When God's voice is spoken to us through Jesus, our souls are nourished and refreshed.

(For a more complete description of meditative prayer, refer to Chapter 3b, pp.159-165)

Why do you think mice are better than people at quieting?

We have always been good at quieting and listening to Jesus!

As Bonhoeffer explains: *God's Word seeks to enter our souls and remains with us.* God does all the work of speaking to our souls. Our singular, and yet daunting task, is to be attentive to God's voice. Through meditative prayer, we are given the opportunity to listen to a message that God desires to share with us through Jesus. Jesus said, *my sheep can hear and know my voice* (John 10:11). It is the voice of Jesus that nourishes and refreshes the depths of our being.

What hope does this give you?

Through meditation, God's Word seeks to enter our souls and remains with us. Then the Word will do its work in us, often without our being conscious of it. Above all, it is not necessary that we have any extraordinary experiences in meditation. It is enough for us to ponder God's word as Mary did. There may be times when we will experience spiritual dryness and apathy, even an inability to meditate. Above all, we must not allow these difficulties to turn us away from our meditation upon God's Word, but allow us to adhere to our times of meditation with greater patience and fidelity.

Dietrich Bonhoeffer (1906-1945)

Using a Law & Gospel Worksheet

The most common and basic way to identify God's voice involves answering one law and one gospel question.

Complete this worksheet for the text: Luke 15:1-3, 11-32

Restoring Hope in God's Savior

Law Question:
How does this text reveal my sin (self-centeredness), which is keeping me from depending upon the Savior?

My Answer ....

....

....

Gospel Question:
How does this text reveal God's gift of the Savior, which offers a new life with Christ and his mission of reconciliation?

My Answer ....

....

....

(A completed worksheet for the text: **Luke 15:1-3, 11-32**)

Restoring Hope in God's Savior

Law Question:
How does this text reveal my sin (self-centeredness), which is keeping me from depending upon the Savior?

My Answer . Both sons reveal what happens when our self-centered desires turn us away from our heavenly Father— it often ends in hopelessness and despair.

Gospel Question:
How does this text reveal God's gift of the Savior, which offers a new life with Christ and his mission of reconciliation?

My Answer . The Father does not give what the sons/we deserve. Through Christ's death we are made alive/"found" (vs 24,32). We are reunited to God and one another.

Write & Share with a Partner...

What are some of the most important insights you discovered in this chapter on Listening?

....

....

....

....

I looked it up...
"FLU-ENT" (adj): having mastery in listening to God's voice.

♫♫♫♫♫♫♫♫♫♫♫♫♫♫♫♫♫♫♫♫♫♫♫♫

Listen, God is Calling

Listen, listen, God is calling
through the Word inviting,
offering forgiveness,
comfort and joy. (repeat)

Jesus gave his mandate;
share the good news
that he came to save us
and set us free.

Refrain.

Help us to be faithful,
standing steadfast,
walking in your precepts,
led by your Word.

Refrain.

Tanzanian Trad.

 We end our session by joining hands in a circle to pray together the Lord's Prayer.

Insights for developing my Listening HABIT:

*How will adding the habit of listening to God's voice **help** me to live a more Christ-centered life?*

....

....

....

....

....

....

....

....

*How often will I **attempt** to practice the habit of listening to God's voice in the course of one week?*

....

....

....

....

....

....

....

....

....

....

*How will the habit of listening to God's voice **become** a part of my daily routine (be specific)?*

....
....
....
....
....
....
....

*How is listening to God's voice through a Law & Gospel Bible study **important** to my maturity as a disciple of Christ?*

....
....
....
....
....
....
....

*What is the **timeframe** for me to make listening to God's voice through Law & Gospel Bible study a regular habit?*

....
....
....
....
....

THE SEVEN HABITS OF JESUS

1. **REMEMBERING**......our baptismal adoption into God's family
2. **LISTENING**.............to God's law & gospel voice in Scripture
3. **PRAYING**.................for God's help with all of our daily needs
4. **PREPARING**...............to hear God's forgiving voice in worship
5. **RETURNING**........... a percentage of what God has given us
6. **INVITING**...................others to baptism and Christ's mission
7. **CARING**................. for others and creation with Christ's love

2b. LISTENING

Listening to God's Voice in the Bible

lis·ten·ing (vb)
> 1. to be attentive to hearing
> 2. to pay attention; to heed; to obey
> 3. to wait attentively for another's voice

Opening Prayer

Lord Jesus Christ, with us abide, far it is now toward eventide; And let Thy Word, that light divine, continue in our midst to shine. Thus keep us in Thy Word, we pray, while we continue on our way, and help us, when this life is over, to be with Thee forevermore. Amen.

Martin Luther (1483-1546)

Listening Goal

The primary goal of this chapter on listening is to make reading the Bible a meaningful habit, through which we are able to listen to God's voice as he speaks directly to each of us. Through our daily Bible reading, God's voice speaks to the depth of our souls a message about our sin (law), and our great need for the Savior (Gospel). As Luther said, *From all eternity God has had an active voice, a thought, a conversation, a will, an address within him that he wants to share with us through Scripture.*

Write & Share with the Group...

What has been your experience in doing a law & gospel Bible Study?

....

....

How might a law & gospel Bible study help you get more out of reading the Bible?

....

....

God's Voice in Worship

At no other time or place in our week does God's Word, his voice, break into our lives as forcefully as when we are gathered together in worship. God's transforming power in worship is his voice, which we hear through the Bible and the sacraments. It is important that we prepare to hear God's voice in worship by doing a law & gospel study of the assigned Bible readings for each week. These readings are organized in a three year cycle of readings, called the *Lectionary,* which has been used in varying forms for centuries. Martin Luther described worship as the time when, ***The power of God's Word (voice) must have free course.*** That is to say, we can prepare before worship to listen for God's transforming voice by doing a law and gospel study of the assigned readings so that we will be open to receive the specific message God's voice has for us in worship.

What do you think of Luther's description of worship?

See the Revised Common Lectionary in the Appendix.

When we read the Scriptures we must recognize that the law is a taskmaster, for it demands that we do something and that we give something. In short, the law wants something from us. As we identify the law in the text, we ask, 'What is God's law voice asking of me?', which usually leaves us sad and accused (Rom 4:15; 7:13). The Gospel, on the other hand, never demands, it grants freely; it asks us to hold out our hands to receive a free gift from God. In short, the Gospel invites us to freely receive a multitude of blessings through Christ with whom we always have peace and salvation (Rom 1:1-3). As we identify the Gospel in the text we ask, 'What does God's Gospel voice want to freely offer me now?'

Martin Luther (1483-1546)

We all come to reading the Bible with our own agenda, bias, questions, doubts, concerns, and, unless we are extremely careful, we will impose our own agenda on the Biblical text. We must submit to God's law and his Gospel if we are to truly hear him speak.

John Stott (1921-2011)

God's Voice Penetrates the Soul

We learn from the Bible that our souls are best nourished by the voice of God. This is an important benefit of Bible reading which we cannot underestimate. Jesus said, *What good is it for us to gain the whole world and lose our connection to God through our soul; What can a person possibly get in exchange for their soul?* (Mark 8:36). We lose our souls when we neglect the life giving power of God's *voice*. Tragically, many in our society have become enslaved to the desires of the body (world), ignoring the importance of the soul. The Bible describes the soul as the *command center* which serves to direct our daily lives. A contemporary analogy of the soul is to liken it to the steering wheel in a car. It is the steering wheel (soul) that has the ability to turn in one direction or the other, either toward God or away from God. **Allowing God's voice to penetrate our souls through regular Bible reading and our attention to the proclamation of God's Word in worship is an important and essential habit needed to nourish the soul of a disciple.**

Do you understand your soul as your connection to God?

> *Many people are bothered by those passages in Scripture which they cannot understand; but as for me, I always notice the passages in Scripture that trouble me the most are those which I do understand.*
>
> Mark Twain (1835-1910)

I have heard many good sermons. The best sermons included both the law and the gospel.

If preaching in the Church today is sick it is because preachers do not know how to preach both the law and the Gospel. Preachers are lulling people to sleep with a foreign Gospel of unconditional love (Bonhoeffer called it cheap Grace), instead of arousing them with the law of a wrathful God. Only the law can reveal our problem with sin, satan, God's wrath, and hell. If the Gospel is not placed in bold relief against the background of the law's sin, death, and the devil, the Gospel degenerates into a saccharine message of feel good religion devoid of Christ. In Scripture, Jesus Christ is pictured as the fulfiller of the law's demands, the appeaser of God's wrath, the victor over satan, the conqueror of death, the atoner of sin. When the law is taken seriously, it then has the ability to prepare us to hear the Gospel. For the reformers it was not possible to hear the Gospel apart from the law.

Carl E. Braaten (b. 1929)

Dietrich Bonhoeffer wrote: The main purpose of God's law and gospel, as Luther put it, is for the law to terrify and the gospel to justify. It is only when one submits to the law that one can speak of grace. When we ignore the law we cheapen the gospel.

What type of sermon best nourishes your soul?

Identifying God's Law Voice

The primary purpose of God's law is to reveal the truth that we are incapable of having a relationship with God without the saving work of God's appointed Savior, Jesus. The Bible does not *sugar-coat* the truth that all people are sinners, making themselves enemies of God. In the Bible Paul teaches: *The wages (result) of sin (sinful nature) are death (eternal separation from God)* (Rom 6:23).

- ✓ **We initially identify God's law in a biblical text as it applies to all people.** The reason our law questions are in the third person (our), instead of the first person (my), is to restrain our defensiveness at the law's accusations. If we accept that God's law in a text applies to everyone, it becomes easier to apply God's law to ourselves.

- ✓ **For some it is difficult to identify the consequences of violating God's law.** If a person has not experienced the fullness of God's love, especially as a child, it becomes quite difficult for them to accept that *the result of being a sinner, without the Savior, is death.*

- ✓ **Whenever God's law and our sinfulness is minimized, the ability for us to appreciate Christ's sacrificial death and resurrection for our salvation is also minimized.** When the life and death urgency of God's law is not recognized, the law becomes incapable of leading us to the gospel.

- ✓ **The most common error in a law & gospel Bible study is to attempt to identify God's moral law (i.e. the Ten Commandments) only as rules or a guideline for living, instead of a means to reveal our desperate need for the Savior. Only Christ is able to give us the capacity to live by the great commandment:** *Love God and love your neighbor.*

How do you feel about being an enemy of God without Christ?

Listening to God's Law Voice

- LISTEN for the *should, could, ought, must, have to,* and *shall* words in each Bible text.

- LISTEN for how we regularly violate God's First Commandment: *You shall have no other gods.*

- LISTEN for how we are being asked to think, act or speak in a different way.

- LISTEN for how our sin is drawing us away from a life with God and into a more self-centered existence.

- LISTEN for how God is describing a problem all people share in common.

Write & Share with a Partner...

Why do you think it is important for us to know when we are incapable of having a relationship with God?

....

....

Identifying God's Gospel Voice

✓ **Both the explicit and the implicit examples of the gospel in a text will be a response to our problems with *sin, death, and the devil*.** We want to anticipate that the gospel will be expressed within a given biblical text with a wide variety of words, images, and metaphors. And yet, all of these expressions of the gospel will have either a direct or indirect connection to Christ crucified and risen.

✓ **The core confession of the Christian faith is that the Good News of the Gospel is always connected to the Good News of Christ's death and resurrection.** The gospel is best defined as Christ our Savior. The gospel of Christ Jesus, crucified and risen, is God's only solution to our problem of being estranged sinners.

✓ **Within most texts (even a gospel text) the words *Christ, crucified,* or *risen*, are not present.** And yet, when we examine a text for its gospel content we will often find evidence of the gospel's effectiveness in changing lives. There are times when we will need to borrow a gospel text from a neighboring section of the Bible. Think of the Bible as a large neighborhood with plenty of gospel to share between neighbors.

✓ **For those texts within the Old Testament it may require more effort to identify the gospel.** In the Old Testament there will be no explicit material about *Christ crucified and risen*. Instead, there will be specific references to God's promise of a *Savior*. All those words in the Old Testament that reveal God's promises are considered gospel texts.

Who first told you about Christ being our Savior?

Listening to God's Gospel Voice

- LISTEN for how God is describing his solution for our broken relationships with God and others

- LISTEN for God's promise to help us with our sinful nature that destroys the fullness of life.

- LISTEN for God's free gift of eternal life, which does not involve God's judgment or punishment.

- LISTEN for the phrase *for you*. The Gospel says it straight out: **You** are forgiven, Jesus died to save **You**. Eternal life is God's gift to **You,** given by the Savior.

- LISTEN for the many ways that God's promise of eternal salvation is being offered to us, despite our sinful separation from God.

God always has a gospel voice.

Using a Law & Gospel Worksheet

Complete this Old Testament Sample Text: **Jeremiah 31:31-34**

Restoring Hope in God's Savior

Law Question:
How does this text reveal my sin (self-centeredness), which is keeping me from depending upon the Savior?

My Answer ....
....

....

Gospel Question:
How does this text reveal God's gift of the Savior, which offers a new life with Christ and his mission of reconciliation?

My Answer:
....
....

....

A sample completed worksheet for: Jeremiah 31:31-34

Restoring Hope in God's Savior

Law Question:
How does this text reveal my sin (self-centeredness), which is keeping me from depending upon the Savior?

My Answer .God remembered the people's sin with no..........
............hope of forgiveness (vs 32,34)............................

....

Gospel Question:
How does this text reveal God's gift of the Savior, which offers a new life with Christ and his mission of reconciliation?

My Answer .God promises (gospel) an all-new covenant......
............to forgive sins (Savior) (vs 31,34)......................

....

Using a Law & Gospel Worksheet

Complete this New Testament Sample Text: **Romans 3:19-28**

Restoring Hope in God's Savior

Law Question:
How does this text reveal my sin (self-centeredness),
which is keeping me from depending upon the Savior?
My Answer ....
....
....

Gospel Question:
How does this text reveal God's gift of the Savior, which
offers a new life with Christ and his mission of reconciliation?
My Answer:
....
....
....

A sample completed worksheet for: Romans 3:19-28

Restoring Hope in God's Savior

Law Question:
How does this text reveal my sin (self-centeredness),
which is keeping me from depending upon the Savior?
My Answer All sinners will die under God's death sentence
(v19), which we have been given because of our sin.

Gospel Question:
How does this text reveal God's gift of the Savior, which
offers a new life with Christ and his mission of reconciliation?
My Answer Only God can change his own death sentence on
humanity (v 25). God's Son died in our place so we can
live eternally in his family.

Write & Share with a Partner...

What are some of the most important insights you discovered in this chapter on Listening?

· ·

· ·

· ·

· ·

I love reading the law and gospel worksheets from Bible studies!

♫♫♫♫♫♫♫♫♫♫♫♫♫♫♫♫♫♫♫♫♫♫♫♫

Listen, God is Calling

Listen, listen, God is calling
through the Word inviting,
offering forgiveness,
comfort and joy. (repeat)

Jesus gave his mandate;
share the good news
that he came to save us
and set us free.

Refrain.

Help us to be faithful,
standing steadfast,
walking in your precepts,
led by your Word.

Refrain.

Tanzanian Trad.

 We end our session by joining hands in a circle to pray together the Lord's Prayer.

Insights for developing my Listening HABIT:

*How will adding the habit of listening to God's voice **help** me to live a more Christ-centered life?*

....

....

....

....

....

....

....

....

*How often will I **attempt** to practice the habit of listening to God's voice in the course of one week?*

....

....

....

....

....

....

....

....

....

....

*How will the habit of listening to God's voice **become** a part of my daily routine (be specific)?*

....

....

....

....

....

....

....

*How is listening to God's voice through a Law & Gospel Bible study **important** to my maturity as a disciple of Christ?*

....

....

....

....

....

....

....

*What is the **timeframe** for me to make listening to God's voice through Law & Gospel Bible study a regular habit?*

....

....

....

....

....

Self-Study for Listening
Word of God (2a)

> *Long ago God spoke to our ancestors in many and various ways by the prophets, but in these last days he has spoken to us by a Son (Heb 1:1).*

From the beginning of time God has always had a desire to communicate with us, to tell us who he is and what he is doing. God first spoke into chaos and the result was his creation, revealing that he is a creator of order. Throughout the ages God's Word has been heard through the words of his appointed messengers and through the Scriptures. Through Jesus, we hear God's Word, his own message of forgiveness and reconciliation. When we read the Bible, we do more than learn about God, we are actually hearing God speaking to us. Through Bible reading a relationship with God is established. God's great desire is to speak to us through the Bible in order that we might believe that Jesus is our Savior and Lord.

Exploring Scripture:
Psalm 119:105; Luke 11:28; Rom 1:16; 2 Tim 3:15-17

What do you believe makes it possible for you to hear God's voice when you read the Bible?

....

....

....

....

Self-Study for Listening
Law and Gospel (2b)

For God so loved the world that he gave his only son, so that everyone who believes in him may not perish but have eternal life (John 3:16).

The *Law* represents the demands of God, and the *Gospel* is the promises of God. We encounter God's Word as both law and gospel; we need to hear both. Without the law, we do not know we need the gospel. Without the gospel, the law can only kill. God uses this law in two ways: 1. to keep good order in creation, and 2. to drive sinful humanity to depend on God alone. The law is a gift from God, because it reveals to us that we cannot have a good relationship with God through our own efforts alone. The gospel makes us (sinners who oppose the law) right with God. The gospel is a gift from God because it gives us the heart-felt desire to live our lives as God's law requires.

Explore Scripture:
Deut 4:5-8; Psalm 119:105-112; Matt 5:17-18; Gal 2:16

Which are you most aware of in your reading the Bible: law or gospel?

....

....

....

....

Use your answers from the Insights questions in parts A and B to help make **LISTENING** *a*

Help
Attempt
Become
Important
Timeframe

---

*How will adding the habit of listening to God's voice **help** me to live a more Christ-centered life?*

....

....

....

....

---

*How often will I **attempt** to practice the habit of listening to God's voice in the course of one week?*

....

....

....

....

How will the habit of listening to God's voice **become** a part of my daily routine (be specific)?

....
....
....
....

How is listening to God's voice through a Law & Gospel Bible study **important** to my maturity as a disciple of Christ?

....
....
....
....

What is the **timeframe** for me to make listening to God's voice through Law & Gospel Bible study a regular habit?

....
....
....
....

THE SEVEN HABITS OF JESUS

1. **REMEMBERING**......our baptismal adoption into God's family

2. **LISTENING**.............to God's law & gospel voice in Scripture

3. **PRAYING**................for God's help with all of our daily needs

4. **PREPARING**............to hear God's forgiving voice in worship

5. **RETURNING**........... a percentage of what God has given us

6. **INVITING**...................others to baptism and Christ's mission

7. **CARING**................. for others and creation with Christ's love

3a. PRAYING

Praying to God for Help With Our Needs

pray·ing (vb)
1. to earnestly request help for our needs
2. to address God with our thanks and praise
3. to ask for forgiveness with humility

Opening Prayer

We beg you, Lord, to help and defend us. Deliver the oppressed, pity the insignificant, raise the fallen, show yourself to the needy, heal the sick, bring back those of your people who have gone astray, feed the hungry, lift up the weak, take off the prisoner's chains. May every nation come to know that you alone are God, that Jesus Christ is your Child, that we are your people, the sheep of your pasture. Amen.

Clement of Rome (c.96)

Praying Goal

The goal of praying is to develop an ongoing conversation in Christ's name with our heavenly Father, through which we share the needs of our daily lives. To assist us with our daily conversational prayer, Jesus has given his disciples the *Lord's Prayer,* which encourages spontaneous prayers to God for each of our needs. Our conversations and spontaneous prayer are referred to in the Bible as *unceasing prayer.*

Write & Share with the Group...

Why do you think that so many Christians pray less often than they intend?

....

....

Praying to God

Jesus taught his disciples that they could pray to God for help with all of their daily needs, in much the same way they would share those needs with their parents. As Hallesby explains, *To pray is nothing more than letting God into our lives. To pray is to give God our request to employ his powers to help us with our needs. The result of our praying is, therefore, not dependent upon the power or the length of our prayers. Fervent emotions or a clear expression of the situation are not the reasons that our prayers are answered. The results of our prayers are only dependent upon giving our heavenly Father access to our needs, and imploring him to exercise his power to help us.*

We have all learned how to share our needs and wants with others. As children, we learned to ask our parents for all that we needed, and even all that we wanted. Prayer is simply doing what we already know how to do—asking our parents and others for help—but with God as the one to whom we are asking for help. For many, the real obstacle to praying is fear of not knowing how to share our needs with God. The prayerful conversation we have with God is to be as natural as having a conversation with our loved ones. For this reason, Jesus taught his followers a way in which to pray using the same conversational process we use with our trusted loved ones. **Jesus teaches his followers to pray a conversational style of prayer by using the nine parts of the Lord's Prayer.**

Why do you think Jesus emphasized prayer to God?

Ask, and it will be given you; search, and you will find; knock and the door will be opened to you. For everyone who keeps on asking receives, and everyone who keeps searching finds, and for everyone who keeps knocking, the door will be opened.

Matthew 7:7-8

I've learned that everything I need comes from God.

I pray every day, throughout the day.

The Lord's Prayer

One day Jesus was praying and when he finished, one of his disciples said to him, *"Lord teach us how to Pray."* Then, Jesus said to them, *"When you pray, say:*

Our Father, who art in heaven,
　　hallowed be thy name,
　　thy kingdom come,
　　thy will be done,
　　　on earth as it is in heaven.
Give us this day our daily bread;
and forgive us our trespasses,
　　as we forgive those
　　　who trespass against us;
and lead us not into temptation,
　　but deliver us from evil.
For thine is the kingdom,
　　and the power, and the glory,
　　forever and ever. Amen.
　　　(Matt 6:9-13; Luke 11:1-4)

The *Lord's Prayer* is the prayer Jesus gave to his disciples. No other prayer can equal this prayer because it was given by Jesus to teach his disciples how to pray. It has been prayed countless times by Christians in more situations throughout the ages than any other prayer. It is the prayer we use to teach our children how to pray. It is the one prayer Christians have consistently used in weekly worship throughout the ages. It is the prayer we pray most often when words fail us, especially at the time of death.

The Lord's Prayer is masterfully divided into nine parts with three divisions: give, forgive, and deliver. *These three words define all the prayers we will ever pray,* said St. Augustine.

GIVE: We ask God to give us the basic necessities of life, like *bread.* In his humanity, Jesus experienced how important the basics of life are for all of us, and how God loves to provide all of them.

FORGIVE: God desires to forgive us, more than anything else, says Jesus. God's forgiveness empowers our new life in the kingdom and brings reconciliation into our relationships with him and one another.

DELIVER: This is an essential request of all Christians. We have a daily need to be rescued from the evil one (satan). It is satan who tries to destroy the fullness and meaning of our lives, our families, and most importantly, our relationship to Christ.

Do you agree or disagree that the Lord's Prayer defines all prayer?

Praying the Lord's Prayer

The way in which to pray to God is illustrated by the nine parts of the *Lord's Prayer* itself. To pray with the Lord's Prayer, we commit to memory the nine parts of the *Lord's Prayer.* (There are actually seven parts with an introduction and conclusion). Additionally, it is important to understand the meaning of the nine parts of the Lord's Prayer. Each part of the Lord's Prayer can initiate a spontaneous prayer, which is

relevant for the needs we are sharing with God. As we go through each day, we can pray one of the nine parts. It is not necessary to begin with part one and then sequentially proceed to part nine. For example, our whole prayer might be focused on just one part, such as part eight, *Deliver us from evil.* Having realized the meaning of each of the nine parts, we know that in this eighth part of the Lord's Prayer we are asking God to keep us safe from satan, as well as to rescue us from the evil ways temptation comes into our hearts. We consider how this part can help us compose a prayer to our Heavenly Father for a specific concern or need in our lives. **When we pray the Lord's Prayer we may spontaneously pray a sentence prayer for our most important needs.** For example, *Father, keep my daughter Mary, while she is away at school, safe from satan's temptations. Do not allow the evil one to tempt her.*

How do you feel about praying a spontaneous sentence prayer?

Unceasing Prayer

When we spontaneously pray throughout the day with the Lord's Prayer, it is referred to in the Bible as *unceasing prayer*. The New Testament encourages us to pray with this style of prayer more than any other style of praying. *Paul instructed them to pray without ceasing (1 Thes 5:17). Be patient in suffering, be patient in prayer (Rom 12:12). Pray in the Spirit at all times (Eph 6:18). Do not worry, in everything pray to God (Phil 4:6). Continually pray to God at all times (Heb 13:15). Never lose heart, pray at all times (Luke 18:1).*

Unceasing prayer has a way of speaking peace into the chaos of our lives. Through unceasing prayer we experience the presence of God. As we pray to God without ceasing we may experience peace, stillness, serenity, and a renewed passion for life. Brother Lawrence said, *There is no lifestyle in the world more pleasing or full of delight than a lifestyle of unceasing prayer.* Frank Laubach said, *Unceasing prayer with God is the most amazing thing I ever ran across!*

How could you live a lifestyle of unceasing prayer?

The Lord's Prayer teaches us how to ask for God's help with the specific concerns and needs of our daily lives.

An Obstacle to Praying

It may seem counterintuitive, but one of the greatest failures in our praying is to limit our prayers to just a specific prayer-time each day. Our praying is best done as a repeated, open ended opportunity to share with God our thanks and needs as we go throughout each day. Using the format of the Lord's Prayer is a good way to pray throughout each day. The classic book, *Practicing the Presence of God*, teaches us how to pray throughout the day. It was written by Brother Lawrence in the seventeenth century, whose whole life became a prayer. His key for praying throughout the day was to continuously share with God a short sentence prayer which accompanied all of his activities.

What do you think of sharing short sentences with God every day?

In 1535, Martin Luther wrote a letter to Peter, his barber, entitled *A Simple Way to Pray*. It is a helpful explanation of how we can pray throughout each day by utilizing the format of the *Lord's Prayer*. (The following letter is abridged).

Dear Peter,

I shall try my best to let you know how to go about praying throughout the day by using our Lord's Prayer. May our good Lord truly help you to pray, and do it better than I. It is recommended that you begin with the Lord's Prayer. Repeat each part as many times as you would like. For example, the first part, 'Our Father who art in heaven.' Those words will allow the prayer in your heart to come forth. It might be something like, 'Thank you for being my loving Father and for bringing heaven into my life.' You then go on to another part and so on. Each part of the Lord's Prayer will excite your heart to pray for your own needs. One day, a part of the Lord's Prayer will bring about a heartfelt prayer, which tomorrow might be completely different. This is actually a sign that the Holy Spirit is at work in your prayers. This is the way I pray the Lord's Prayer, like a small child, I suckle at it and get out of it all the nourishment it has to offer. The Lord's Prayer is the best prayer, because the Master himself has composed it and taught it.

Your Friend,
Martin Luther

I constantly pray to God for food and safety...what do you pray for the most?

Write & Share with a Partner...

What do you think about Martin Luther's explanation to his barber?

....

....

> The Lord's Prayer is my favorite...
> must be all that 'daily bread'!

The A.B.C.'s of Praying

It is not complicated or difficult to use each of the nine parts of the Lord's Prayer as a *spring-board* for our own spontaneous prayers to our heavenly Father:

A. **Memorize** the nine parts of the Lord's Prayer and each of their meanings.

B. **Take time** to pray one of the nine parts of the Lord's Prayer, repeatedly.

C. **Meditatively pray** one of the nine parts of the Lord's Prayer until your heart spontaneously creates a sentence prayer to God.

What is your experience in praying the Lord's Prayer?

The Lord's Prayer: Nine Parts

The following format of the Lord's Prayer has been divided into nine parts. Each part contains several elements: The **bold** type is the traditional Lord's Prayer; a contemporary version of the Lord's Prayer is provided [in brackets]; and the *italicized* sentences describe how that part of the Lord's Prayer encourages us to pray for specific concerns in our daily lives.

Part One
Our Father, who art in heaven,
   [Our Father in heaven]

In this part, Jesus teaches us that we have a very intimate union with God (Rom 8:15-17). It is the same type of intimate union that children have with their parents. *This first part of the Lord's Prayer encourages us to share our concerns and needs with God in the same way we would share our concerns and needs with loving parents.*

*Our...*encourages us to ask for help in accepting all of God's children as brothers and sisters in God's family.

Father... encourages us to depend upon God for help in our daily lives just as loving parents help their children.

Heaven... encourages us to ask for God's help as the creator and sustainer of all life.

Explanation: When we pray *Our* we are encouraged to love others as God loves all those he has given life.

My Spontaneous Prayer:

Sample: *Help me to accept Jim as a brother in your eternal family.*

Your Sample:

Part Two

Hallowed be thy name
[Holy be your name]

In this part, Jesus teaches us that God's name and being, is love (1 John 4:8) so that we stand in awe of him. We are asking God to help us live a life of love, which reflects the nature of his being. *This second part of the Lord's Prayer encourages us to share our concerns and needs for God's help in living a life of love for God, for others, and for the creation.*

Hallowed... encourages us to make God's name (love) a special part of our lives.

Name... encourages us to pray that God's *name*, which is *love*, may be experienced in our daily lives.

Explanation: When we pray *Name* we are asking to be empowered by God's love in every area of our lives.

My Spontaneous Prayer:

Sample: *Help me to be more patient and loving with Stephanie, and when it is possible, to help her.*

Your Sample: ....

....

....

....

Part Three
Thy kingdom come
[Your kingdom come]

In this part, Jesus invites us to recognize God's presence and rule within our daily lives (Luke 12:32). *This third part of the Lord's Prayer encourages us to experience his presence* in the mundane areas of life.

Kingdom... encourages us to pray that we might be aware of the Lord's influence with the people and in the experiences of our daily lives.

Come... encourages us to ask for the assurance we need to have hope in our eternal inheritance, especially in difficult times.

Explanation: When we pray *kingdom* God is challenging us to recognize his power and presence in the world.

My Spontaneous Prayer:

Sample: May I recognize the love, peace and joy of

your kingdom through my friends at work.

Your Sample:

· ·

· ·

· ·

Part Four

Thy will be done, on earth as it is in heaven.

[Your will be done, on earth as in heaven.]

In this part, Jesus teaches us that God's will (accomplished desire) for our world is the expansion of his kingdom on earth as it is in heaven (Rom 12:1-2). *This fourth part of the Lord's Prayer encourages us to share our concerns and needs with God to be faithful workers in his kingdom.*

Thy will... encourages us to pray that the plans we make for our lives will not keep us from recognizing the plans God has for us.

Be done... encourages us to ask for help in determining if our plans are also God's plans.

Explanation: When we pray for God's *will* we are praying that his love might increase our capacity to join with his will.

My Spontaneous Prayer:

Sample: Help me to care for my sister Mary in a way that reflects your will for her.

Your Sample:

Part Five

Give us this day our daily bread;
   [Give us today our daily bread.]

   In this part, Jesus teaches us that when we ask God to provide us with daily bread, we are recognizing that all we have in life comes from God (Matt 6:25-34). *This fifth part of the Lord's prayer encourages us to share our praise to God for all that he has given us.*

Give us... encourages us to frequently ask and to thank God for our life and all that he does to sustain our living.

Daily bread... encourages us to ask God to move us to be content with the belongings we have received.

Explanation: When we pray for daily bread we are recognizing that God is the giver of every good gift, which grows our gratitude.

My Spontaneous Prayer:

Sample: *Make me more appreciative for all the*
....

        material and spiritual gifts you have given me.
....

Your Sample: ....

....

....

....

Part Six

and forgive us our trespasses, as we forgive those who trespass against us;

[Forgive our sins as we forgive those who sin against us.]

In this part, Jesus teaches us that forgiveness is at the center of our relationship to God, and at the center of our relationships with each other (Luke 15:11-32). *This sixth part of the Lord's Prayer encourages us to desire to forgive others as God forgives us.*

Forgive us... encourages us to recognize that for the sake of Christ, God forgives all, even when many don't ask for forgiveness. God freely forgives us so that we might repent, trust in him, and freely forgive others.

Our trespasses... encourages us to pray for God's help in breaking our pride and keeping us humble, so we might repent and be able to *forgive others*.

Explanation: When we pray for God's forgiveness we are asking God to cleanse us from anger and lust, and give us his own ability to forgive one another.

My Spontaneous Prayer:

Sample: *Reveal how you forgive me, and why it is best for me to forgive John.*

Your Sample:

Part Seven
and lead us not into temptation,
   [Save us from the time of trial]

In this part, Jesus teaches us that God never tempts anyone to evil and that we are praying for protection from satan and his temptations (Matt 4:1-11). *This seventh part of the Lord's Prayer encourages us to share our concerns and needs with God for daily deliverance from the evil and the destructive forces of satan in our world.*

Lead us not... encourages us to pray for God's guidance in our daily lives, so that we do not live overly self-centered lives which are little or no life at all, but rather fight temptation.

 Temptation... encourages us to ask God to enlighten us to the devil's temptations, which are all directed to destroy our heartfelt relationship with Christ.

Explanation: When we pray for God's protection from satan's temptations we are asking for God's help to resist satan's plan to draw us away from our relationship with Christ our Savior.

My Spontaneous Prayer:

Sample: *Make me aware of how the devil tempts me to live my life in a self-centered and Godless way.*

Your Sample:

. . . .

. . . .

. . . .

. . . .

Part Eight

but deliver us from evil.

[and deliver us from evil.]

In this part, Jesus teaches us that evil is not an abstract idea, but originates out of satan, the evil one (1 Cor 10:6-13). Each and every day we are invited to celebrate Christ's victory over the *prince of evil. This eighth part of the Lord's Prayer encourages us to share our concerns and needs with God so that nothing in all of life, especially evil, would be able to separate us from the love of God in Christ Jesus, our Lord.*

Deliver us... encourages us to turn to God for help when our lives have taken a spiritual turn for the worse.

From evil... encourages us to ask God to keep us, and our loved ones, safe from the evil one's plan to destroy our relationships with God and others by avoiding kindness and tolerating evil.

Explanation: When we pray for God to deliver us from evil, we are asking God to protect our relationship with Christ that Satan wants to destroy.

My Spontaneous Prayer:

Sample: *Help me to resist satan's evil plan to make me more self-centered and less connected to Christ.*

Your Sample:

....

....

....

Part Nine

For thine is the kingdom, and the power, and the glory, forever and ever. Amen

> [For the kingdom, the power, and the glory are yours, now and forever. Amen.]

In this part, the Lord's Prayer teaches us that our God is all powerful and should always be recognized and given our highest praise (Rom 8:28-39). This ninth part of the Lord's Prayer encourages us to share our concerns and needs with God because he is the only one who can and will listen to our prayers and will respond to them as a loving parent.

Kingdom, power, glory... encourages us to praise God for his majesty, help in the past, and the promise of his help in the future.

Amen... The word *Amen* can be best translated, *Yes, I hope it happens! Yes, I am confident in God's response because my prayer request to him was based on his Son!*

Explanation: When we praise God in prayer, we are asking him to increase our trust in him as the Creator and Sustainer of the universe.

My Spontaneous Prayer:

Sample: *Help me recognize Christ's Lordship in every area of life, especially with family and at work.*

Your Sample:

....

....

....

....

I Cannot Pray...

I cannot pray OUR, if my daily life has no room for others.

I cannot pray FATHER, without a living relationship to him.

I cannot pray WHO ART IN HEAVEN, if I am earthly-minded.

I cannot pray HOLY BE YOUR NAME, and not desire to be holy.

I cannot pray THY KINGDOM COME, without Christ's Lordship.

I cannot pray THY WILL BE DONE, and reject it in my daily life.

I cannot pray AS IN HEAVEN, and ignore heaven on earth.

I cannot pray GIVE US DAILY BREAD, and not feed the hungry.

I cannot pray FORGIVE US, if I'm unforgiving and hold grudges.

I cannot pray NOT INTO TEMPTATION, and remain tempted.

I cannot pray DELIVER US FROM EVIL, without resisting evil.

I cannot pray THINE IS THE KINGDOM, and not obey the King.

I cannot pray THINE IS THE POWER, and be seeking power.

I cannot pray AND GLORY, without praising God for eternity.

I cannot pray FOREVER AND EVER, if I am too anxious.

I cannot pray AMEN, unless this prayer becomes my life.

– Anonymous

There is perhaps no better way to learn the state of our soul than to note how we pray the Lord's Prayer. If the words come too easily, half thoughtlessly, from our lips, it testifies to great immaturity, to sloth and indifference, for they are such weighty and powerful words, so rich in content!...When we thank God for all his blessings, we must reckon the Lord's Prayer as one of the greatest, for it is wonderfully adapted to all. They are the same words, repeated again and again, yet how they can change their shape...How flexibly it fits itself to our needs while remaining always the same, ever embraced and borne up by the words, "Our Father"! We desire no higher wisdom than to be able to pray our Lord's Prayer with ever greater sincerity and inwardness, and we do not wish to die with any other prayer on our lips. Therefore we thank thee, our God, for Our Lord's Prayer.

Ditlev Monrad (1811-1887)

Write & Share with a Partner...

What are some of the most important insights you discovered in this chapter on Praying?

....

....

....

....

♫♫♫♫♫♫♫♫♫♫♫♫♫♫♫♫♫♫♫♫♫♫♫♫♫♫♫♫

What a Friend We Have in Jesus

What a friend we have in Jesus,
All our sins and griefs to bear!
What a privilege to carry,
Everything to God in prayer!
Oh, what peace we often forfeit,
Oh, what needless pain we bear.
All because we do not carry,
Everything to God in prayer!

Have we trials and temptations,
Is there trouble anywhere?
We should never be discouraged,
Take it to the Lord in prayer.
Can we find a friend so faithful?
Who will all our sorrows share?
Jesus knows our every weakness,
Take it to the Lord in prayer.

Joseph Scriven (1820-1886)

 We end our session by joining hands in a circle to pray together the Lord's Prayer.

Insights for developing my Praying HABIT:

*How will adding the habit of praying to God **help** me live a more Christ-centered life?*

....

....

....

....

....

....

....

....

*How often will I **attempt** to do the habit of praying to God?*

....

....

....

....

....

....

....

....

....

....

*How will the habit of praying to God **become** part of my life?*

....
....
....
....
....
....
....

*How is praying to God **important** to my maturity as a disciple of Christ?*

....
....
....
....
....
....
....

*What is my **timeframe** to make praying to God a habit?*

....
....
....
....
....

THE SEVEN HABITS OF JESUS

1. **REMEMBERING**......our baptismal adoption into God's family

2. **LISTENING**..............to God's law & gospel voice in Scripture

3. **PRAYING**................for God's help with all of our daily needs

4. **PREPARING**.............to hear God's forgiving voice in worship

5. **RETURNING**........... a percentage of what God has given us

6. **INVITING**..................others to baptism and Christ's mission

7. **CARING**................. for others and creation with Christ's love

3b. PRAYING

Praying to God for Help With Our Needs

pray·ing (vb)
1. to earnestly request help for our needs
2. to address God with our thanks and praise
3. to ask for forgiveness with humility

Opening Prayer

Lord, make plain to me that no circumstance nor time of life can occur but I may find something either spoken by our Lord himself or by his Spirit in the prophets or apostles that will direct my conduct, if I am but faithful to you and my own soul. Amen.

Susanna Wesley (1670-1742)

Praying Goal

The goal of praying is to develop an ongoing conversation in Christ's name with our heavenly Father, through which we share the needs of our daily lives. To assist us with our daily conversational prayer, Jesus has given his disciples the *Lord's Prayer,* which encourages spontaneous prayers to God for each of our needs. Our conversations and spontaneous prayer are referred to in the Bible as *unceasing prayer.*

Write & Share with the Group...

Why is prayer often described as a conversation with God?

....

....

Anticipation

Expectation and answered prayer go together. Our anticipation of an answer to our prayers helps us to hear God's answer. It is important that we always expect that God will answer all of our prayers. If we pray, but do not expect an answer, we most likely will not hear what God has to say because we are not listening with anticipation and expectation. When we pray and expect God to answer our prayers, we can anticipate an answer. Just as God expects to hear from us throughout each day, we can also expect an answer to all of our prayers.

How is expectation related to anticipation for you?

Prayers are not always granted. This is not because prayer is a weaker kind of causality, but because it is a stronger kind. When it works at all it works unlimited by space and time. That is why God has retained a discretionary power of granting or refusing it; except on that condition prayer would destroy us.

C.S. Lewis (1898-1963)

God Answers Prayer

Simply because God listens compassionately to all of our requests and fully understands what we want, does not mean he will give us whatever we ask for. However, **God will always answer each and every one of our prayers with one of four answers**:

1.) **Yes**, as evidenced by the way in which what was requested has been received
2.) **No**, as evidenced by an absence of what was requested
3.) **Yes, but later**, as evidenced by what was requested has been received according to God's timing
4.) **Yes, but in another way**, which may not, at first, be recognized as a *yes* answer until the Spirit reveals God's way of saying *yes*

Who first talked to you about God's answers to prayer?

Every day I pray for food, and God gives me food...And then I thank him with a short prayer.

God's Answers

Jesus taught his disciples that through prayer we encounter God's answers to prayer.

Scripture

Through a word, phrase, or text of Scripture, God's voice speaks to us an answer to our prayer.

Conscience

Through our inner voice of conscience, God speaks to us with his voice of morality.

Inner Peace

Through inner peace God's presence is felt.

People

Through those we know well, and even those we do not know, God's voice can speak to us an answer to our prayer.

God-Incidents

Through the many God-incidents of our daily lives, God answers our prayers.

Opportunity

Through an opportunity that is good for us and for others, God's voice speaks to us an answer to our prayers.

Remember: Unless we keep a list of God's answers to our prayers, we will not be able to keep track of how God has, or has not, answered our prayers.

How important do you think is it to know God's answer to a prayer?

I asked God for strength, that I might achieve...
I was made weak that I might learn humbly to obey.

I asked for health, that I might do great things...
I was given infirmity, that I might do better things.

I asked for riches, that I might be happy...
I was given poverty, that I might be wise.

I asked for power, that I might have others' praise...
I was given weakness, that I might feel the need of God.

I asked for all things, that I might enjoy life...
I was given life, that I might enjoy all things.

I got nothing that I asked for...
But everything that I hoped for.

Almost despite myself, my prayers were answered...
I am among all men most richly blessed. Amen.

Found in the clothing of an unknown
Civil War soldier

God Dwells Within

Prayer always begins with recognizing that our heavenly Father is intimately and completely present in our lives. Prayer begins with the confidence that through faith in Christ, God *abides* within the depths of our souls. Some people have been taught that God lives *in the sky* or in outer space. But, the Prophet Isaiah reminds us that God's presence is always near to us. Even, *before you call, I am with you, before you speak, I know your prayer* (Isa 65:24). In the fifteenth chapter of John's Gospel, Jesus describes our new relationship with God, *If you abide in me, I abide in you, ask for whatever you wish, and it will be done for you.*

How do you sense God's presence within your soul?

Then Jesus told them a parable about their need to pray always and not lose heart.

Luke 18:1

Do you not know that you are God's temple and that God's Spirit dwells in you?

1 Cor 3:16

Write & Share with a Partner...
What would encourage you to pray more often?

....

....

Meditative Prayer

Meditative prayer dates back to the early roots of our Judeo-Christian faith tradition. Christian meditative prayer is not the type of mind-emptying meditation found in Eastern religions. Instead, Christian meditation is a way for the Word of God to engage our hearts and fill our souls. The unique aspect of Christian meditation is that the Holy Spirit creates within us an inner sanctuary to receive the living voice of God when it is in conformity with Scripture. Through meditative prayer we grow in our dependency upon God's Word and our inner friendship with the Lord Jesus.

What do you think keeps you dependant upon God's Word?

It is not necessary that we should discover new ideas in our meditation. Often this only diverts us and feeds our vanity. It is sufficient if the Word, as we read and understand it, penetrates and dwells within us. As Mary "pondered in her heart" the things that were told by the shepherds, so it is in meditation: God's Word seeks to enter in and remain with us. It strives to stir us, to work and operate in us, so that we shall not get away from it the whole day long. Above all, it is not necessary that we should expect to have any extraordinary experiences in meditation. This can happen, but if it does not, it is not a sign that the meditation period has been useless.

Dietrich Bonhoeffer (1906-1945)

Meditative Prayer Explained

Meditative prayer complements our daily praying of the Lord's Prayer and invites the Lord Jesus to enter our inner sanctuary with a Gospel message that speaks to our souls. Meditation trains our ability to be attentive to the Lord's presence within and around us. There are three basic steps to meditative prayer: **Quieting, Dwelling,** and **Listening**.

STEP 1: QUIETING

We allow the Lord Jesus to silence the noise that rages within us **(1 Pet 5:7). In a comfortable place, free of interruptions, we quiet our inner sanctuary by focusing on relaxed breathing, which is experienced by bringing our attention to our inhaling and exhaling.** We may inhale to the count of **five** while silently saying **J-E-S-U-S** in our minds...We then may hold that breath to the count of **six** by silently saying: **C-H-R-I-S-T** then we can exhale to the count of **seven** while spelling: **O-U-R L-O-R-D**. We do this for approximately five to ten minutes. An alternative to counting our breathing is to observe the temperature of our inhaling and exhaling breath. We can quiet ourselves by observing that the breath we inhale is slightly cooler than the warmer air we exhale. As we become attentive to our inhaling and our exhaling, we become more relaxed, which allows us to enter into our inner sanctuary. There are also other ways to meditate which allow us to be open to hearing the Lord speak to us.

STEP 2: DWELLING

God has constructed an inner sanctuary within each of us where the Lord Jesus speaks to us (1 Cor 3:16). Our inner sanctuary is a peaceful place within us where we can be with the Lord Jesus and hear his voice. Using our favorite sights, sounds, smells and feelings, our *mind's eye* is able to visualize our inner sanctuary as a place to encounter Jesus. For some, an inner sanctuary will be located within a rain forest, for another it will be located in a desert. For all, it will be a place of peace and beauty within God's creation, which allows us to be with the Lord Jesus. Once we have rested within our inner sanctuary we may begin to sense Jesus approaching us. As Jesus draws closer to us, we focus all our attention on his peaceful and loving presence.

STEP 3: LISTENING

The most important aspect of meditative prayer is to be open to the loving presence of the Lord Jesus. Prior to meditation, it is helpful for us to prepare ourselves to hear God's voice. As Dietrich Bonhoeffer explains, *God's Word seeks to enter our souls and remain with us.* God does all the work of speaking to our souls. Our singular, and yet daunting task, is to be attentive to the Word of God as it is spoken to us through Jesus. We are confronted by the fact that the Holy Spirit opens our hearts and minds to the voice of the Lord. Through meditative prayer, we are given the opportunity to listen to a message that the Lord desires to share with us. Jesus said, *my sheep can hear and know my voice* (John 10:11). It is the voice of Jesus that nourishes and refreshes our souls. It is always in conformity with Scripture.

Must you always expect to encounter the Lord in meditation?

Listening to God's Voice

God's voice is...

+Recognized by the way it impacts our heart, soul, and innermost being with divine authority.

+The Spirit of God, which is a Spirit of peace, confidence, joy, and goodwill.

+Pure, gentle, full of mercy, and without any trace of partiality.

+Consistent with the truths about God's nature and kingdom as they are described in the Bible.

We can learn from George Washington Carver's trials at listening to God: *One night I prayed and asked God when he made the universe. He listened and then I heard him say that question was too big for me and to try again! So again, I prayed and asked God why he created people. He listened and again I heard him say that question was too big for me and to try again! So again I prayed and asked God why he made the peanut. He listened and I heard him tell me that the question was just my size and that he would explain why he made the peanut!* George Washington Carver went on to invent more than three hundred ways to use the peanut...all by listening to God.

In meditative prayer we are growing into what Thomas a Kempis called, a familiar friendship with Jesus. Through meditation we are learning to experience the perpetual presence of the Lord within our souls. In meditative prayer we are opening up a space within us that allows God to construct an inner sanctuary in our hearts. The wonderful verse: Behold, I stand at the door and knock (Rev. 3:20), is intended for the baptized not unbelievers. Jesus is knocking at the door of our heart – daily, hourly, moment by moment. Jesus is knocking; meditative prayer opens the door!

Richard Foster

For most mice,
silence is "golden."

Place your mind before the mirror of eternity! Place your soul in the brilliance of glory! Place your heart in the figure of the divine substance! And transform your whole being into the image of the Godhead Itself through meditation!

Clare (1193-1253)

Through meditation, God's Word seeks to enter our souls and remains with us. Then the Word will do its work in us, often without our being conscious of it. Above all, it is not necessary that we have any extraordinary experiences in meditation. It is enough for us to ponder God's Word as Mary did. There may be times when we will experience spiritual dryness and apathy, even an inability to meditate. Above all, we must not allow these difficulties to turn us away from our meditation upon God's Word, but allow us to adhere to our times of meditation with greater patience and fidelity.

Dietrich Bonhoeffer (1906-1945)

Be still and know that I am God.

Psalm 46:10

Nothing calms my troubled soul better than letting the Lord fill it with his peace.

When you pray and involve your body you give power to your prayer. This is particularly needed at the times when you feel unable to pray, when your mind is distracted, your heart has turned to stone, and your soul seems dead. Then try to stand in the presence of the Lord in a very devout way, hands devoutly joined in front of you with your eyes looking at him supplicatingly... Some of this devotion you are expressing through your body is likely to seep through into your spirit, and after a while you may find it much easier to pray. People sometimes run into difficulty in meditation because they fail to attend to their bodies in prayer; they fail to take their bodies along with them into the holy temple of God. You may think you are standing or sitting in the presence of the Risen Lord, but you are carelessly slouched in your chair or you are standing in a very slovenly fashion...You are obviously still not gripped by the living presence of the Lord.

Anthony DeMello (1931-1987)

Solitude and Prayer

By his example, our Lord Jesus invites us to often leave the noise and chaos of our lives to be with him in the solitude of our hearts. Throughout his three years of preaching, teaching, and healing, Jesus took times of solitude to cultivate an inner space with God. Jesus taught his disciples the act of solitude, the art of inward attentiveness. Jesus made it clear that his sheep are able to hear and know his voice (John 10:11-15). But, how exactly do we hear the voice of God? The answer is more obvious than we would think. We learn to hear God's voice by experience. Sheep know the voice of the shepherd by experience. Our family pets know our voices by experience. Babies quickly recognize their parents' voices by experience. Certain factors help us to experience the Lord's voice within us:

A. The Lord's voice makes an impact on our soul, our innermost being. The Lord's voice does not dispute or convince. It simply speaks the truth with authority.
B. The Lord's voice is a pure, gentle, peace-filled, confident, and joyful voice.
C. The Lord's voice is always the same as his voice in the Bible. What God tells us about the law and the gospel in the Bible is the norm for how he speaks to us in the silence of our inner sanctuary.

Meditative prayer helps us create a place of solitude in our hearts. This is a peaceful place of solitude through which our Lord might speak to us, not just when we pray, but at other times throughout the day.

How does solitude and prayer make a difference for you?

Fasting and Prayer

On several occasions when Jesus taught his disciples to pray, he also encouraged them to fast. Jesus said, *When you fast and pray.* He united fasting and prayer as two sides of the same coin. Fasting can have a very positive influence on our praying because it sharpens our concentration on *what* to pray for, and helps us to more clearly *hear* God's answer to our prayers. Fasting, or taking away food, helps to expose our deep-seated negative feelings of anger, anxiety, fear, depression, etc. Food, and frequently too much food, can be used to cover up our deep seated negative feelings. When we fast, these negative, troublesome feelings will automatically surface. Although this can be very distressing, it reveals those negative feelings within us that are keeping us from the prayer partnership our Lord desires to have with us. Fasting usually involves abstaining from all food, except water, for a designated period of time, as an accompaniment to prayer. For Christians, fasting is not done for its physical health benefits, but for spiritual strength, a renewed focus on what to pray for, and how to listen and respond to God's answers to our prayers. Often, Christians fast for one day at a time, usually within the course of a week when they want a more clear focus on God's will for their life. It is essential to drink more water during a fast than we usually do; approximately one gallon per day would be an average. It can be helpful if the last meal before starting a fast consists of fresh fruits and vegetables. Fruit juice is also a good first meal when going off a fast. **Diabetics, pregnant mothers, children, and those with health/heart problems should not fast. To be on the safe side, it is best that all those preparing to fast first seek medical advice.**

Would you be willing to fast and pray?

Praying with Others

There are regular times that families and friends pray together, often associated with gathering together at meal times and other special occasions. The two most common ways families pray together are by using: (1) prayers written by others, and (2) spontaneous prayers.

I cannot tell why there should come to me
  A thought of someone miles and years away,
In swift insistence on the memory,
Unless there has to be a need that I should pray.
        Marianne Farningham (1834-1909)

Prayers Written by Others
Luther's Morning Prayer:

I thank you, my Heavenly Father, through Jesus Christ, your dear Son, that you have kept me this night from all harm and danger; and I pray that you would keep me this day from sin and every evil, that all my doings and life may please you. Into your hands I commend myself, my body and soul, and all things. Let your holy angel be with me, that the evil foe may have no power over me. Amen.

Luther's Evening Prayer:

I thank you, my Heavenly Father, through Jesus Christ, your dear Son, that you have graciously kept me this day; and, I pray that you would forgive me all my sins where I have done wrong, and graciously keep me this night. Into your hands I commend myself, my body and soul, and all things. Let your holy angel be with me, that the evil foe may have no power over me. Amen.

Luther's Mealtime Prayers:

Heavenly Father, bless us and these your gifts which we are about to receive from your bountiful goodness, through Christ Jesus our Lord. Amen.

Come Lord Jesus be our guest, our morning joy our evening rest; and with this daily bread impart, your love and peace to all our hearts. Amen.

God is great, God is good! Let us thank him for our food. By his hands we must be fed, give us Lord our daily bread. Amen.

Do you regularly pray before mealtimes?

Spontaneous Prayers

A vital aspect of growth in our prayer life is to pray spontaneous prayers alone, with others, and as a family or in a fellowship group setting. Praying out loud with others improves our ability to pray openly in a spontaneous way. Praying with others can, at first, be difficult. However, a helpful way for us to learn how to

comfortably pray with others is to use a style of spontaneous prayer referred to as sentence prayer. First, the leader shares a prayer concern with the whole group. Then, each person in the group is given the opportunity to pray a single sentence prayer. Some may choose to *pass*, which they can do by simply saying, *Amen*. After each person shares their sentence prayer, it is helpful to pause for a short time of reflection before the next person shares their sentence prayer.

Why regularly pray with others?

Praying in Jesus' Name

To pray in Jesus' name is to ask God to answer our prayers in accordance with his desire for our lives to become more like Christ Jesus. To pray in the name of Jesus generally means two things: 1.) The awareness that without Jesus' sacrificial death and reconciliation for us with God, we would not be able to pray confidently to God. 2.) Becoming like Jesus is God's ultimate desire for our lives.

What hope do you have for becoming more like Christ Jesus?

Close Your Eyes

It is customary at dinner, bedtime, and in worship for many to close their eyes when they pray. This practice is particularly useful for meditation. Research has discovered that when one of the five senses receives less information, it allows the other four senses to operate more efficiently. An example of this is how those who do not have sight exhibit an improvement in one of their other senses. Even more fascinating is what happens when we close our eyes in silence. When we limit two of our senses at the same time we enhance the function of the remaining three. This may be the lesson of 1 Kings 19:9-13. Elijah could not hear the Lord in the *wind, fire, or an earthquake*. However, in sheer silence, Elijah heard the Lord. We benefit from opportunities to listen for God in sheer silence.

What does it mean to you that God speaks even in silence?

Amen!

The word **Amen** is best translated, **Yes, I hope it happens!** Christians received the practice of putting the word *Amen* at the end of their prayers from the Jews. Amen emphasizes the strong hope that what is being said in prayer will actually happen. The meaning behind *Amen* took on added significance for Christians because Christ became the true *Amen* in being the world's Savior. For Christians, the word *Amen* has taken on more than just a simple *Yes*. Now, Christians conclude their prayers with *Amen*, meaning **Yes, Christ is our Savior.**

Did you hear that there's a big potluck dinner coming up?

Amen! That's an answer to my prayer!

God, listen! Listen to my prayer, listen to the pain in my cries. Don't turn your back on me just when I need you so desperately. Pay attention! This is a cry for help! And hurry – this can't wait!

Psalm 102:1-2

I love God because he listened to me, listened as I begged for mercy. He listened intently as I laid out my case before him. Death stared me in the face, hell was hard on my heels. Up against it, I didn't know which way to turn; then I called out to God for help: Please God! I cried out. Save my life! God is gracious! God is gracious – it is he who makes all things right, our most compassionate God.

Psalm 116:1-7

Write & Share with a Partner...

What are some of the most important insights you have discovered about prayer and meditation?

....

....

....

....

♫♫♫♫♫♫♫♫♫♫♫♫♫♫♫♫♫♫♫♫♫♫♫♫♫♫

What a Friend We Have in Jesus

What a friend we have in Jesus,
　　All our sins and griefs to bear!
What a privilege to carry,
　　Everything to God in prayer!
Oh, what peace we often forfeit,
　　Oh, what needless pain we bear.
All because we do not carry,
　　Everything to God in prayer!

Are we weak and heavy laden?
　　Cumbered with a load of care?
Precious Savior still our refuge,
　　Take it to the Lord in prayer.
Do your friends despise, forsake you?
　　Take it to the Lord in prayer.
In his arms he'll take and shield you,
　　You will find a solace there.

Joseph Scriven (1820-1886)

 We end our session by joining hands in a
circle to pray together the Lord's Prayer.

Insights for developing my Praying HABIT:

*How will adding the habit of praying to God **help** me live a more Christ-centered life?*

. . . .

. . . .

. . . .

. . . .

. . . .

. . . .

. . . .

. . . .

*How often will I **attempt** to do the habit of praying to God?*

. . . .

. . . .

. . . .

. . . .

. . . .

. . . .

. . . .

. . . .

. . . .

. . . .

*How will the habit of praying to God **become** part of my life?*

....

....

....

....

....

....

....

*How is praying to God **important** to my maturity as a disciple of Christ?*

....

....

....

....

....

....

....

*What is my **timeframe** to make praying to God a habit?*

....

....

....

....

....

Self-Study for Praying
Prayer (3a)

*They devoted themselves to the Apostles'
teaching and fellowship, to the breaking of bread
and prayer (Acts 2:42).*

Prayer can be an unending conversation with God. Our prayer conversations are about what we and God are doing together. Prayer is an ongoing conversation with God as we live out our daily lives. Any yet, prayer is more than just conversation; it is a way for us to share with God the needs that we and our loved ones are experiencing. **One of the most amazing aspects about prayer is that God answers each and every one of our prayer requests with one of four answers: Yes; No; Yes, but later; Yes, but in another way.** The key to noting God's answer to our prayer request is to always expect an answer and to keep a list of answered prayers.

Exploring Scripture:
Luke 18:1-8; Rom 8:26; 1 Peter 4:7; Gen 18:23-33

How would you describe your prayer life with God?
....
....
....
....

Self-Study for Praying
Meditation (3b)

In the morning, while it was still very dark,
he got up and went out to a deserted place, and
there he prayed (Mark 1:35).

The **place** for meditation:
> A place of quiet with few interruptions

The **posture** of meditation:
> A posture that reduces tension

The **breathing** of meditation:
> Inhaling and exhaling slowly

The **sanctuary** within meditation:
> Your favorite place in God's Creation

Exploring Scripture:
Psalms 1:2; 119:148; 63:6

How would you describe your
experiences with meditation?

....
....
....
....

Use your answers from the Insights questions in parts A and B to help make **PRAYING** *a*

Help

Attempt

Become

Important

Timeframe

---

*How will adding the habit of praying to God **help** me live a more Christ-centered life?*

....

....

....

....

---

*How often will I **attempt** to do the habit of praying to God?*

....

....

....

....

How will the habit of praying to God **become** part of my life?

....

....

....

....

How is praying to God **important** to my maturity as a disciple of Christ?

....

....

....

....

What is my **timeframe** to make praying to God a habit?

....

....

....

....

THE SEVEN HABITS OF JESUS

1. **REMEMBERING**......our baptismal adoption into God's family

2. **LISTENING**..............to God's law & gospel voice in Scripture

3. **PRAYING**.................for God's help with all of our daily needs

4. **PREPARING**.............to hear God's forgiving voice in worship

5. **RETURNING**............ a percentage of what God has given us

6. **INVITING**...................others to baptism and Christ's mission

7. **CARING**................... for others and creation with Christ's love

4a. PREPARING

Preparing To Hear God's Forgiveness in Worship

pre·par·ing (vb)
1. to make or to get ready
2. to put in the proper condition
3. to arrange or plan beforehand

Opening Prayer

May God the Father, and the ever-living high priest Jesus Christ, strengthen us in faith, truth, and love; and give to us our portion among the saints with all those who trust in our Lord Jesus Christ. We pray that our fruit may abound and that we might be made complete in Christ Jesus our Lord. Amen.

Polycarp (69-155)

Preparing Goal

Each week, prior to joining our faith community in worship, we prepare to bring the sins we have committed in the past week in order to receive God's gracious forgiveness through: Baptismal renewal; God's Word; and Holy Communion.

<u>Baptismal Renewal</u> is an act of confessing our sins and through Christ receiving God's renewing forgiveness.

<u>God's Word</u> through its law voice condemns our sinful nature. Through God's gospel voice, we are forgiven and Christ within us is strengthened.

<u>Holy Communion</u> invites us to bring our broken relationships with God and others for forgiveness and healing through Christ.

Write & Share with the Group...
What comes into your mind when
you think about worship?

....

....

> *O come, let us worship and bow down, let us kneel before the Lord, our Maker! For he is our God, and we are the people of his pasture, and the sheep of his hand.*
>
> Psalm 95:6-7

Worship Expectations

Most of us who grew up in the church were not expected to prepare for worship. The emphasis was merely on being in worship every week, not getting ready for worship. One of the most important aspects of weekly worship, as experienced by Jesus' disciples throughout the ages, is our need to prepare for worship. Throughout the ages Christians have brought to worship two expectations. First, we can expect to hear from Scripture a proclamation of God's love for us, as evidenced by the Savior. Second, we expect to hear through the sacraments of baptism and holy Communion that God will forgive us our sins and freely offer us a renewed capacity to experience wholeness in our relationships with God and one another. Being prepared for worship is not an option for a disciple of Jesus; it is a necessity.

How does Word and sacrament worship make a difference to you?

Worship is an art form of the Holy Spirit.
M.L. King, Jr. (1929-1968)

Preparing for Worship

At no other time or place in our daily lives is the Holy Spirit more active than when we are gathered in a faith community and engaged in worship. Through worship, God's voice of forgiveness is most clearly and powerfully heard within the depths of our souls. Because of the critical importance of worship, it is important for us to be prepared to hear God's voice. Through worship, God's transforming power breaks into our lives to shatter our me-centered lives with his condemning law, so that our Christ-centered lives might be restored by his comforting gospel. Sadly, too many attend worship without adequately preparing to hear God's transforming voice. Many, unfortunately, turn their attention to things within worship which are not essential.

Why do you think the Holy Spirit is so active in worship?

Worship is God-centered

Worship is to be God-centered. Worship is not only about what we do, it is about what God is doing to change our lives! Worship is about what God is saying and doing, to us and for us! The word *worship* has been defined by the church throughout the ages as *reverence*, a *profound sense of awe*, for God's free gift of grace. True worship is about having *reverence* **for** the transforming power of God's grace. Martin Luther described our sinful tendency to approach *worship in a me-centered way*, which focuses on our own personal experience in worship. When we approach worship as a *God-centered* activity, we focus on God's power alone to transform our lives.

Why is worship me-centered for so many people?

> *Cheap grace means forgiveness of sins proclaimed as a general truth, the love of God taught as the Christian conception of God. An intellectual assent to that idea is held to be of itself sufficient to secure remission of sins. Cheap grace therefore amounts to a denial of the living Word of God, in fact, a denial of the incarnation of the Word of God...Costly grace is the treasure hidden in the field; for the sake of it a man will gladly go and sell all that he has. Costly grace is the gospel which must be sought again and again, the gift which must be asked for, the door at which a man must knock. It is costly because it costs a man his life, and it is grace because it gives a man the only true life. Above all, it is costly because it cost God the life of his Son: and what has cost God much cannot be cheap for us.*
>
> Dietrich Bonhoeffer (1906-1945)

Three Means of Grace

The transforming power of God's forgiveness is experienced through his three *means of grace*—BAPTISM, BIBLE, and COMMUNION. Through these three means of grace, God transcends time and space to connect us to the saving power of Christ's death and resurrection. Through these means of grace:

Christ's death brings death to our self-centered sin.
Christ's resurrection brings forgiveness and new life.

God's three *means of grace*, describe how he changes us through worship. Worship must never be limited to the thanks and praise we offer to God. Most importantly, worship emphasizes God's gift of love and forgiveness, which claims us as his children. If we are to be truly open to receiving God's grace, we need to:

1. Prepare before worship to receive God's forgiveness.
2. Be attentive in worship to receiving God's forgiveness.

When a worship service is *shaped* around God's three *means of grace*, it is said to be a *liturgical service of Word and Sacrament*. This format of worship has been the church's principle style of worship throughout the ages, and the style of worship for nearly eighty percent of Christians in the world today.

How would you describe God's grace in your own words?

Imitate Christ at all times, signing your forehead with sincerity. This is the sign of his passion, shown and proven against the devil, if you make it with faith, not in order to be seen by others, but knowingly setting it forward as a shield. For, when the adversary sees that its power comes from the heart, because it shows forth publicly the image of baptism, he is put to flight.

Hippolytus (170-235)

Word & Sacrament Worship

Each week baptized believers gather together for Word and Sacrament worship to receive God's grace through: BAPTISM, BIBLE, and COMMUNION. Word and sacrament worship allows baptized believers to:

+ **BE RENEWED IN THE COVENANT OF BAPTISM.**

+ Offer thanks and praise to God through music.

+ **LISTEN TO GOD'S GOSPEL VOICE IN THE BIBLE.**

+ Respond with a creed, prayers, and a tithe.

+ **RECEIVE FORGIVENESS THROUGH COMMUNION.**

 + Leave worship to serve God by serving others.

What is your experience of receiving God's grace in worship?

What is a Sacrament?

The Lutheran church defines and uses two sacraments: Baptism and Holy Communion. There are three parts to a sacrament:

1. Commanded by Jesus
2. Connected to a physical item (water, bread, wine)
3. Promises God's unconditional forgiveness

Who first talked to you about the Sacraments?

Worship liberates the soul by giving us God's own perspective on life.
Roswell Long (1807-1869)

Why is it a Sacrament?

Luther defined a sacrament as *that which exists because God commanded it,* **and because it expresses the fullness of God's will to offer forgiveness of sins, life, and salvation.** The best way to be renewed in our baptism, or receive the forgiveness of Holy Communion within a worship service, is by recognizing that these are God's own acts of love. The best way for us to participate in a sacrament as a recipient is to be clear that we bring nothing and have nothing to offer for grace. We merely receive the sacraments and the forgiveness God freely offers us. God is the one, who once again, is offering us his amazing grace.

Why do you think God has given us Sacraments?

Mysticism keeps us sane. As long as we have mystery we have health: when we destroy mystery we create morbidity. The ordinary person has always been sane because the ordinary person has always been a mystic. We have always had one foot in earth and the other in fairyland. We have always cared more for truth than for consistency. Our spiritual sight is stereoscopic, like our physical sight: We see two different pictures at once and yet we see all the better for that. We admire youth because it is young and age because it is not. It is exactly this balance of apparent contradictions that has been the buoyancy of the spiritually healthy person. The whole secret of mysticism is this: that we can only understand life by the help of what we do not understand.

G.K. Chesterton (1874-1936)

How do you experience the sacraments as a mystery?

Write & Share with a Partner...
What does God's grace mean to you?

....

....

....

....

We mice iove the bread of Communion! And, the obvious presence of the Holy Spirit!

One of God's Three Means of Grace

Listening to God's Voice through Baptismal Renewal

At the beginning of each worship service, usually near the baptismal font, we participate in the *renewal of baptism*. The sacrament of baptism is not something that happened to us in the past, but instead is a *truly splendid on-going act of God*, said Luther. Even though the act of baptism is a once-and-for-all paramount act of God, it takes a lifetime to

fully complete. **When we were baptized, a lifelong process of transformation was set into motion to move us away from our sinful identity, toward a new life with God. Martin Luther was fond of saying...*I am baptized* (using the present passive verb) rather than, *I was baptized* (the past perfect tense verb). By this Luther was emphasizing that baptism affects our ongoing identity and relationship to God.** Luther said, b*aptism defines both who we are and what we will become, because the drowning of sin lasts throughout our whole life. Therefore, the life of a Christian, from our beginning in baptism to the grave, is nothing else than a series of deaths and risings to prepare us for our final day when God will make us altogether new.* Just as we daily benefit from putting on clothes, we daily benefit from putting on our baptismal identity. To *put on our baptism* is to allow the Holy Spirit to bring the transforming power of Christ's death and resurrection into our daily lives. As the apostle Paul described in the sixth chapter of Romans, *We know that our old sinful nature is in the process of being put to death* *just as Christ was put to death on the cross.* To *put on baptism* is to recognize that God daily wraps his arms around us to keep us in his eternal family. We are renewed in this baptismal embrace and can daily thank God for our baptismal adoption into his eternal family.

How has baptism given you a new way to look at yourself?

Chosen in Baptism

Each day we need to be reminded that baptism is God's work, not ours. The salvation we have received through baptism is God's gift, not our achievement. Our baptism is undeserved because God's grace is always a gift, not something we earn. Through baptism God adopts us into his family; he makes us his own. But, our initial baptismal washing is not the end. When God baptizes us (washing us of our sin) it is only the beginning of a lifelong journey with God. Baptism is a lifelong process of conversion which begins when we are baptized and does not end until God takes us into the eternal *communion of saints.* Until then, we are invited to live out our baptism every day. With Christ's own Spirit in our hearts, we never know where he will lead us, or what gifts will emerge out of us for the work of his kingdom. However our lives may *play out*, we can be sure that Christ within us will draw us into his mission of reconciliation to restore (**redeem**) and heal (**make new**) our relationship with God and one another. Some weeks, Christ is obviously at work within us. Some weeks his work is less obvious. And yet, the transforming power of Christ's death and resurrection (Rom 6) is always at work within us, and will never leave us. That's God's baptismal promise to us!

How do you respond to God's promise to us through baptism?

Our Response

Even though God's baptismal work in us cannot be limited by what we *do*, *believe*, or *decide*, God's work in us will not benefit us without our acceptance of his work. A gift that is offered and rejected may still be a gift. However, if God's gift in baptism is rejected, it is a most profound tragedy. For Martin Luther, our rebirth was not so much an *experience* as it is a *fact*, which has happened to us. For those who were unnecessarily worried about the salvation they received in baptism, Luther said, *This new life with God is often not experienced because it is so foreign to our hearts.*

What is your reaction to Luther's statement?

Daily Renewal

Daily we turn to the One who turned to us in our baptism. Daily we do well to recite the promises God planted in our hearts when we were baptized. Most of the time our turning to God is quiet and reasoned. Sometimes it may be a conscious turn, but often it will be an unconscious and mysterious turn of our hearts to the eternal promises of God within us. We must never lose sight of the fact that our baptism is the majestic and miraculous work of God.

What can keep you focused on God's baptismal promise to you?

Baptismal Renewal

When the renewal of baptism occurs at the beginning of the worship service it functions primarily as an act of confession and forgiveness. It is the forgiveness of our sins that restores us to our true identity as a baptized child of God. When we begin worship by restoring our identity as a baptized child of God, it encourages us to daily be renewed in our baptism. A useful part of our baptismal renewal is to make the sign of the cross upon our forehead, or chest. This act of *signing* reminds us that in baptism we were immersed (drowned) into the death of Christ (Rom 6:4), and marked with his cross forever. Christ's cross now brings death to our sinful self and claims us as God's own child.

How is baptismal renewal present in confession?

Before Worship

Receive God's grace through the renewal of baptism.
+ Practice the renewal of baptism each day.
+ Recall times in the last week when you *died* to self.
+ Recall times when you experienced new life in Christ.

During Worship

Receive God's grace through the renewal of baptism.
+ Silently confess a specific sin during the renewal.
+ Silently thank God for his renewing forgiveness.
+ Thank Christ in your heart for the promises of a new life.

Why do pastors have to use so much water when they baptize? I don't like getting too wet!

One of God's Three Means of Grace

Listening to God's Voice through Scripture Readings & the Sermon

The powerful and transforming voice of God comes to us through the reading and preaching of Scripture. If we are to hear God's voice clearly in worship, we do well to prepare to hear his voice by familiarizing ourselves before worship with each of the four assigned Bible readings for that week. These four weekly Bible readings are a part of the church's three year *lectionary*. The word *lectionary* means a *list of readings* which Christians throughout the ages have identified as those passages in the Bible which best express both God's *law voice* about sin, and God's *Gospel voice* about the Savior. (A lectionary is available in the appendix). The lectionary is often referred to as the *Bible within the Bible* as a way of describing those Gospel-centered passages in the Bible that have been most valued by the faithful throughout the ages. It is very helpful to do a law and gospel study of the four assigned Bible readings (see the chapter on *Listening*). However, if all four readings are not studied, it is most important to study the assigned gospel reading of the week before each worship service, since the sermon is normally based upon the gospel text for the week.

Why do you think most Christians follow a lectionary?

The most basic law & gospel Bible study asks:
+ How does this passage describe my SIN? (law)
+ How does this passage describe my SAVIOR? (gospel)

Listening to the Sermon

God's gospel voice strongly speaks to our hearts and minds through the sermon, referred to as the Gospel proclamation. If we are to be open to God's Gospel voice, we need to be alert and involved listeners in two important ways:

1. Listen for both God's law voice and God's gospel voice as the sermon is being preached. The law content of every sermon should challenge us to personally identify how we are currently violating the first commandment: *You shall have no other gods.* What might some of those other gods be? In our society, some common *gods* are: health, wealth, leisure, and a variety of self-indulging behaviors. **The gospel content of every sermon should comfort us with the Good News that through the death and resurrection of Christ we receive God's unconditional grace; his forgiveness for our worship of other gods, and the power of Christ to live our lives for God alone.** The gospel content of the sermon reveals God's presence in our daily lives and gives us the power we need to resist evil and the temptations of satan. The gospel content of the sermon renews God's promise that we are his adopted children and will live with him for eternity. The best news about the gospel is that through Christ we can turn away from all other *gods* so that the true God remains our Father.

2. **Taking notes on the sermon. Note-taking is one of the best ways to listen to the sermon and remember its content.** Note-taking promotes active listening and helps us to get the most out of the sermon. Note-taking also allows us to jot down those parts of the sermon that are God's law voice, and those parts of the sermon that are God's gospel voice, because without this distinction it is too difficult for us to be readily open to God's Good News message. Also, writing out what we hear allows us to better process some of the more complicated parts of the gospel text and sermon. Some preachers provide a written outline and/or a space for note-taking in a worship booklet or bulletin. After worship, it can be very helpful for us to read through the sermon notes we have taken. Sharing this review with our family or a friend will allow God's gospel voice to penetrate our daily lives in a meaningful way.

Why is it important that sermons present both the law and gospel?

Before Worship
Receive God's grace through a Bible study.
+ Identify the current week's Bible readings.
+ Identify a possible theme of the assigned Bible readings.
+ Do a law & gospel study of the gospel reading.

During Worship
Be attentive to receiving God's grace through the Bible readings and the sermon.
+ Identify the law in the sermon as it relates to you.
+ Identify the gospel in the sermon as it relates to you.
+ Take notes on the sermon for further reflection.

I take sermon notes to share with my friends who couldn't be in worship.

One of God's Three Means of Grace

Listening to God's Voice through Holy Communion

When God offers us forgiveness through Holy Communion, he is purifying, cleansing, and removing the sins that separate us from a healthy relationship with him and one another. The forgiveness we receive in Holy Communion:

+ Reconciles our broken relationship with God.
+ Reconciles our broken relationships with others.

Before we come to worship we prepare to hear God's voice of forgiveness, which he offers us through Holy Communion. Through Holy Communion, God's law voice is quite silent, although his gospel voice becomes a loud proclamation of forgiveness and reconciliation. When God forgives us, he is reconciling our broken relationships with himself and others. And yet, only when we prepare to receive God's gift of forgiveness will we be able to properly identify the forgiveness and reconciliation he offers us. *If we confess our sins, God who is faithful and just will forgive us our sins and cleanse us from all unrighteousness (1 John 1:9).*

Unfortunately, some liken Holy Communion to taking medicine, which works even if we don't know how it works. And yet, the forgiveness that we each receive through Holy Communion is meant to be specific to a broken relationship we bring to the altar to be reconciled by God. Because the forgiveness of receiving Holy Communion is primarily for our broken relationships with

God and others, it is essential for us to be intentional about bringing those broken relationships to the altar for forgiveness. For many, this will mean carrying the person's name to the altar. **Through Christ, God is reconciling all people to himself, not counting their sins against them, but entrusting to them his message of reconciliation (2 Cor 6:19).** As we come forward to the altar to receive the body and blood of Christ, we are receiving the power of Christ's reconciling love.

How do you normally prepare to receive Holy Communion?

Worship is about being open to God's gift of forgiveness, which heals our broken relationships with God and one another.

Before Worship
Prepare to receive God's grace through Holy Communion.
+ How does my relationship with God need to be restored?
+ How does my relationship with others need reconciliation?
+ Is there anger in my heart that needs healing?

During Worship
Be attentive to receive God's grace through Holy Communion.
+ Bring a broken relationship with God to the altar.
+ Bring a broken relationship with another to the altar.
+ Bring the hurt and anger in my heart to the altar for healing.

The Lord's Supper is an occasion of joy for the Christian community. Reconciled in their hearts with God and with each other, the congregation receives the gift of the Body and Blood of Jesus Christ, and receiving that, it receives forgiveness, new life, and salvation. Through the Sacraments, our communities are given new fellowship with God and humankind.
Dietrich Bonhoeffer (1906-1945)

Mice don't like wafers as much as they like the tasty loaves of bread that Jesus used.

And forgive us our debts, as we forgive our debtors. As bread is the first need of the body, so forgiveness for the soul. And the provision for the one is as sure as for the other. We are children, but sinners too; our right of access to the Father's presence we owe to the precious blood and the forgiveness it has won for us. Let us beware of the prayer for forgiveness becoming a formality. Let us in faith accept the forgiveness as promised; as a spiritual reality, an actual transaction between God and us, it is the entrance into all the Father's love and all the privileges of his children.
Andrew Murray (1828-1917)

Write & Share with a Partner...

What are some of the most important insights you discovered about God's Means of Grace?

....

....

....

....

List your Favorite Hymns...

....

....

....

....

....

....

....

....

♫♫♫♫♫♫♫♫♫♫♫♫♫♫♫♫♫♫♫♫♫♫♫♫♫♫♫

All are Welcome

Let us build a house where love can dwell,
  And all can safely live.
A place where saints and children tell
  How hearts learn to forgive.
Built of hopes and dreams and visions,
  Rock of faith and vault of grace;
Here the love of Christ shall end division:
    All are welcome, all are welcome, all are
    welcome in this place.

Let us build a house where love is found,
  In water, wine and wheat.
A banquet hall on holy ground where
  Peace and justice meet.
Here the love of God, through Jesus,
  Is revealed in time and space;
As we share in Christ the feast that frees us:
    All are welcome, all are welcome, all are
    welcome in this place.

Marty Haugen (b.1950)

We end our session by joining hands in a circle to pray together the Lord's Prayer.

Insights for developing my Preparing HABIT:

*How will adding the habit of preparing for worship **help** me live a more Christ-centered life?*

....

....

....

....

....

....

....

....

*How often will I **attempt** to do the habit of preparing for worship?*

....

....

....

....

....

....

....

....

....

....

*How will the habit of preparing for worship **become** part of my life?*

. . . .

. . . .

. . . .

. . . .

. . . .

. . . .

. . . .

*How is preparing for worship **important** to my maturity as a disciple of Christ?*

. . . .

. . . .

. . . .

. . . .

. . . .

. . . .

. . . .

*What is my **timeframe** to make preparing for worship a habit?*

. . . .

. . . .

. . . .

. . . .

. . . .

. . . .

THE SEVEN HABITS OF JESUS

1. **REMEMBERING**......our baptismal adoption into God's family

2. **LISTENING**..............to God's law & gospel voice in Scripture

3. **PRAYING**.................for God's help with all of our daily needs

4. **PREPARING**............to hear God's forgiving voice in worship

5. **RETURNING**........... a percentage of what God has given us

6. **INVITING**....................others to baptism and Christ's mission

7. **CARING**................. for others and creation with Christ's love

4b. PREPARING

Preparing To Hear God's Forgiveness in Worship

pre·par·ing (vb)
1. to make or to get ready
2. to put in the proper condition
3. to arrange or plan beforehand

Opening Prayer

O Lord, give us we beseech thee in the Name of Jesus Christ thy Son our Lord, that love which can never cease, that will kindle our lamps but not extinguish them that they may burn in us and enlighten others. Do thou, O Christ, our dearest Savior, enlighten our darkness and lessen the darkness of the world. Amen.

Columba of Iona (521-597)

Preparing Goal

Each week, prior to joining our faith community in worship, we prepare to bring the sins we have committed in the past week in order to receive God's gracious forgiveness through: Baptismal renewal; God's Word; and Holy Communion.

<u>Baptismal Renewal</u> is an act of confessing our sins through which we receive God's renewing forgiveness.

<u>God's Word</u> through its law voice condemns our sinful nature. Through God's Gospel voice we are forgiven and Christ within us is strengthened.

<u>Holy Communion</u> invites us to bring our broken relationships with God and others for forgiveness and healing.

Write & Share with the Group...
How do you experience God's grace through baptismal renewal, God's Word, and Communion?

....

....

....

....

Worldly Forgiveness

The forgiveness that we receive through our reception of Holy Communion is God's own forgiveness, which empowers us to forgive others with whom we have broken relationships. The world's understanding of forgiveness is that forgiveness is about forgetting. However, the forgiveness we receive as a gift from God through Holy Communion is not about forgetting. The forgiveness which God gives empowers us to relate to the person who has hurt or wounded us, even without forgetting what they did or did not do. When we receive Holy Communion, we are receiving Christ's own capacity to relate to others who have hurt us, with his own love. When we receive Holy Communion we are receiving the *real presence of Christ*, which empowers us to relate to others, in a way that Christ Jesus himself would relate to them.

How is the meaning of forgiveness different in the Bible?

Forgiveness is <u>not</u>...

- -Making up excuses for another's bad behavior
- -Trying to forget the wrong another has done to us
- -Glossing over our feelings of hurt and revenge
- -A one-time decision
- -Continuing our relationship with someone who has hurt us as though nothing is wrong

Forgiveness <u>is</u>...

- +Perceiving the person who has hurt us from God's perspective, as both a sinner and perhaps a saint at the same time (like us!)
- +Accepting that through the forgiving power we receive in Holy Communion, we are given the real presence of Christ, which gives us his capacity to see the one who has hurt us from his own perspective
- +A process that involves a series of decisions to forgive
- +Receiving Holy Communion as a means of God's grace, which removes our *fight* and *flight* instincts
- +Looking beyond the act and seeing the person that hurt us as a child of God

Do you need a better understanding of forgiveness?

I will have to study what forgiveness is and is not... I think I've been doing it wrong!

A Process of Forgiveness

The Bible contains more than 130 references to forgiveness. Christ's universal mission of reconciliation instructs us to make forgiveness a part of our regular relationships. However, forgiveness is not easy for any of us. Even Jesus' disciples could not understand the basics of how forgiveness works; they asked, *how many times does one need to forgive?* (Matt 18:22) Forgiving another is not a one-time event, but instead an unfolding process of five steps toward healing.

DENIAL: Our first response to any hurt is to deny that we have been hurt. We need time to understand how we have been hurt before we can be forgiving.

ANGER: It is essential to connect our anger to our hurt, instead of to the one who hurt us. To move through our anger, we need to accept that we may be both sinners and saints at the same time.

BARGAINING: In this step, we identify the terms and conditions we demand in order to forgive. We must accept that nothing can change what has happened.

DEPRESSION: When we are hurt and get angry, we often end up feeling depressed and will benefit from a list of rational reasons why we are *not* a helpless victim.

ACCEPTANCE: In this step, the goal is to stop perceiving ourselves as victims and to no longer see those who have hurt us as really *bad* people.

Forgiveness is rarely the result of a neat, step by step process. Instead, we hop, skip, and jump from one step to another. It is not a process we can rush; for most it is a process that will take much longer to work through than anticipated. Because Christ lives in our hearts, he gives us his own ability to forgive others in ways we could not forgive without him.

We need to....

+ Pray often for Christ's help in being more forgiving.
+ Ask for Christ's help in working through the five steps.
+ Pray for the *other* person and the broken relationship.
+ Meditate and see Jesus giving our relationship forgiveness and healing.
+ Bring our broken relationships to Holy Communion for forgiveness & healing.

How does it make sense to you that forgiveness is a process?

Forgiveness isn't easy, but Christ promises to help us!

If anyone is in Christ, there is a new creation, the old has passed away; everything has become new! All this is from God, who reconciled us to himself through Christ, and has given us the ministry of reconciliation.

2 Cor 5:17-18

The deacon then says in a loud voice: "Welcome one another and embrace one another!" This signifies the union of souls with one another, and the forgetfulness of all wrongs done. This is why Christ said: "If you are presenting your gift at the altar, and there you remember that your brother has a grievance against you, leave your offering there before the altar, and go first to be reconciled to your brother; then return and present your offering" (Matt 5:23-24). This then, is an act of reconciliation. That is why it is holy, as blessed Paul proclaims it to be when he says: "Greet one another with a holy kiss" (1 Cor 16:20); Peter also says: "Greet one another with a kiss of love" (1 Peter 5:14).

Cyril of Jerusalem (315-386)

Stories of Forgiveness
The Lost Son (Luke 15:11-32)

The parable of The Lost Son is a story about God's deep desire to forgive us. God's unconditional love for us is so radically different from our own. We tend to love what we like. God loves what is in the other person's best interest. We are inclined to forgive when we think it is in our best interest to do so. God wants us to forgive when it is in the best interest of someone else to do so. To love as God loves requires that we be willing to forgive others because it is in their own best interest. This ability to love and forgive can happen when we have first been forgiven by God. In the parable of The Lost Son, the father's response is contrasted with the older brother's. The Heavenly Father's love, God's grace, is given freely to those who seek it. The older brother's resentment and his inability to forgive robbed him of the joy of living, and in the end, he became the *lost son*.

My father was very forgiving, but not as forgiving as the father in the *Lost Son*

The Hiding Place

In the closing passages of *The Hiding Place*, evangelist Corrie Ten Boom tells a story that helps us understand how we are able to forgive. After World War II and her release from a Nazi concentration camp (where her sister Betsie died), Corrie ten Boom lectured and preached on the need to forgive our enemies. The struggle to forgive was brought home with stunning force when, after one of her guest preachings, Corrie greeted a man whom she recognized as the Nazi guard in the shower room at her concentration camp. *How grateful I am for your message*, he said. *To think that, as you say, the Lord has washed all my sins away!* Corrie then recalls, *Suddenly, his hand thrust out to shake mine. And I, who had preached so often the need to forgive, kept my hand at my side. As the angry and vengeful thoughts boiled through me, I saw my sin. Lord Jesus, I prayed, forgive me and help me to forgive him. I felt nothing, not the slightest spark of charity. And so again I breathed a silent prayer. Jesus I cannot forgive him; give me your forgiveness. As I took his hand, a most incredible thing happened. From my shoulder along my arm and through my hand a current seemed to pass from me to him, while into my heart sprang a love for this stranger that almost overwhelmed me.* **And so I discovered that it is not on our forgiveness any more than on our goodness that the world's healing hinges, but on his. When Jesus tells us to forgive our enemies, he gives to each of us along with the command, the love we need to forgive!**

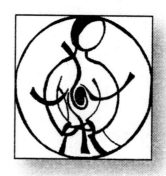

How do you expect the Lord to help you forgive others?

Natural Moral Law

From the very beginning, God has placed within every person he creates a moral standard by which to live (Rom 2). This moral standard is referred to as God's natural moral law. Throughout the ages, within diverse cultural settings, God's natural moral law has been imprinted upon every heart, for the sake of order in society and to serve as the moral standard for all human societies. Jesus did not eliminate or change the natural moral law of God. Even though it is true that Paul teaches us that, the Moral Law of God cannot put us *right* with God (Romans 6:14-15), God still expects all people, especially Christians, to live by his moral law. **Even though there is only one natural moral law of God, the Lutheran Confessions distinguish between two *uses* of God's moral law.**

The *first use* of God's moral law functions as a *curb* for all people (1Tim 1:9). As a *curb*, the moral law of God provides a limit, a civil restraint, and the threat of punishment for all who violate the law. This *first use* of God's moral law is to restrain our impulsive self-centered desires in order to maintain a level of peace in society.

The *second use* of God's moral law functions as a *mirror* for Christians (Rom 3:20). As a *mirror*, the natural moral law of God, like the Ten Commandments, makes us aware of how we *break* God's moral laws, and how we are in need of God's forgiveness. This second use of God's moral law reveals our sins and should drive us to the Savior. The natural moral law of God is made plain in the Ten Commandments, which God gave to Moses on Mount Sinai.

What do you know about both uses of God's moral law?

Write & Share with a Partner...

*How might the Ten Commandments help
us identify our need for forgiveness?*

....
....

*How might God's Grace be visualized breaking
into the lives of worshipers?*

....
....

Mice often get falsely accused of stealing.

Seven Sinful Habits

The church of the Middle Ages in Europe developed a list of seven sinful habits that create a pattern (habit) of sinning that produces other sins. For example, the sin of greed can lead to lying, cheating, and stealing.

1. PRIDE **is the first sinful habit because it is a root sin which is behind many other sins.** This is the sin of Adam and Eve; doing what we want and disregarding what God tells us to do or not to do. Christians cannot, in any way, become more like Christ unless they regularly recognize and confess their sin of pride.

2. ENVY **is the sinful habit of being jealous of others, which leads to hatred of them.** The result of envy is withdrawal from others into a bitter life.

3. ANGER **is the sinful habit of attacking others with either hurtful words or actions.** Anger secretly comes from deep within us and sometimes needs to be released through Christian counseling.

4. SLOTH **is the sinful habit of apathy or laziness.** It is the sin which keeps us from seeking God or caring about our neighbors.

5. GREED **is the sinful habit of manipulating other people or circumstances to acquire power or possessions.** Greedy persons place all their faith in themselves instead of in God's providential care.

6. GLUTTONY **is the sinful habit of having all the pleasures we crave** as opposed to what we realistically need as a child of God.

7. LUST **is the sinful habit of sexual gratification that is against God's moral Law.** (adultery, pornography and other sexual sins commonly portrayed in the media.)

Ten Commandments

1. **You shall have no other gods before me.**

The most important part of a healthy life is a loving relationship with God. The triune family of God is our future home.

What other god (health, wealth, leisure, etc...) has become overly important to you?

2. **You shall not misuse the name of the Lord your God.**

The name of God, the character and essence of God is love. God lovingly pays attention to our needs and desires to help us.

What has recently disconnected you from God's love? Do you use God's name carelessly as an expression of feeling?

3. **Observe the Sabbath day by keeping it Holy.**

Sunday is the day of worship and relaxation with our family and friends. We are most productive when we totally relax at least once each week.

What has recently kept you from preparing for or attending worship? How can we keep a sacred day holy?

+ The first three commandments are about our relationship with God.
+ The last seven commandments are about our relationships with others.

4. **Honor your father and your mother.**

God brings into our lives those we admire, respect, and desire to imitate. Children with parents, and adults with mentors, are stronger people.

How well do you accept the mentors God gives you?

5. You shall not kill.

Killing is always rooted in anger and resentment. Few emotions can kill our bodies and our quality of life more than anger.

How much anger and frustration is in your heart?

6. You shall not commit adultery.

For love to grow, and forgiveness to be practiced, a committed relationship is required.

How have you been tempted by immoral thoughts and opportunities?

7. You shall not steal.

If we are not to steal money and possessions from others, then we will need to return a tithe (10% of our income) back to God.

What is keeping you from being more generous? Do you protect and help others?

8. You shall not be a false witness against your neighbor.

If you cannot say something good about another person, then don't say anything at all.

How much do you talk about others behind their backs? Are you truthful?

9. You shall not desire your neighbor's property.

We need to refrain from purchasing stuff we don't need and can't pay for without a credit card.

When did you last buy something you didn't need? When does wanting become greed?

10. You shall not desire your neighbor's lifestyle.

Christians are called to live a modest, simple, and environmentally friendly lifestyle.

How are you fascinated by the lifestyles of others?

The Ten Commandments help us to prepare for worship by assisting us to identify how we are in need of God's forgiveness.

What is your experience of using the Ten Commandments?

Write & Share with a Partner...

What are some of the most important insights you discovered in this chapter on Preparing?

....

....

....

....

What did you learn about the 10 Commandments?

....

....

....

....

♫♫♫♫♫♫♫♫♫♫♫♫♫♫♫♫♫♫♫♫♫♫♫♫♫

All are Welcome

Let us build a house where hands will reach
  Beyond the wood and stone.
To heal and strengthen, serve and teach,
  And live the Word they've known.
Here the outcast and the stranger,
  Bear the image of God's face;
Let us bring an end to fear and danger:
  All are welcome, all are welcome, all are
  welcome in this place.

Let us build a house where all are named,
  Their songs and vision heard.
And loved and treasured, taught and claimed
  As words within the Word.
Built of tears and cries and laughter,
  Prayers of faith and songs of grace;
Let this house proclaim from floor to rafter:
  All are welcome, all are welcome, all are
  welcome in this place.

Marty Haugen (b.1950)

 We end our session by joining hands in a circle to pray together the Lord's Prayer.

Insights for developing my Preparing HABIT:

*How will adding the habit of preparing for worship **help** me live a more Christ-centered life?*

....

....

....

....

....

....

....

....

*How often will I **attempt** to do the habit of preparing for worship?*

....

....

....

....

....

....

....

....

....

....

*How will the habit of preparing for worship **become** part of my life?*

....

....

....

....

....

....

....

*How is preparing for worship **important** to my maturity as a disciple of Christ?*

....

....

....

....

....

....

....

*What is my **timeframe** to make preparing for worship a habit?*

....

....

....

....

....

....

Self-Study for Preparing
Worship (4a)

*O come, let us worship and bow down, let us
kneel before the Lord, our Maker* (Psalm 95:6).

Worship is the heart and soul, the very center, of a
Christian's life with God. On Sundays, the day of Jesus'
resurrection, we come together with other Christians to offer
God thanks and praise, confess our sins and receive
forgiveness, listen to God's Word, offer prayers to God, and
celebrate the gift of the sacraments of holy baptism and holy
Communion. Our worship of God continues as we are sent
out of the weekly gathered community to be scattered out into
the world to serve God by serving our neighbors. Although
we bring our own thoughts and faults to worship, the focus of
worship is not us; it is instead a focus upon God and his
gracious forgiveness!

Explore Scripture:
Psalm 95:7; Matt 28:16-20; John 4:23; Col 3:16-17

---

*When are you most aware of God's
presence during worship?*

....

....

....

....

Self-Study for Preparing
Sacraments (4b)

But we have this treasure in clay jars, so that it may be made clear that this extraordinary power belongs to God and does not come from us
                                                    (2 Cor 4:7).

The sacraments are another form of God's Word, through which his voice is heard. Baptism and Holy Communion are another way God speaks his loving words to our hearts. A sacrament is a sacred act that: 1.) Imparts God's grace, 2.) Uses visible means such as water, bread, and wine, 3.) Is connected with God's Word of promise, and 4.) Was commanded by Christ. People are made members of God's family through the sacrament of Holy Baptism, and Christians are sustained for their life of faith through the sacrament of Holy Communion.

Explore Scripture:
Matt 26:26-28; Mark 16:16; 1 Cor 11:26; Gal 3:26-27

What is most important about your baptism?
What is most meaningful about your
participation in Holy Communion?

....

....

....

....

Use your answers from the Insights questions in parts A and B to help make **PREPARING** *a*

Help

Attempt

Become

Important

Timeframe

How will adding the habit of preparing for worship **help** me live a more Christ-centered life?

....

....

....

....

How often will I **attempt** to do the habit of preparing for worship?

....

....

....

....

How will the habit of preparing for worship **become** part of my life?

....

....

....

....

How is preparing for worship **important** to my maturity as a disciple of Christ?

....

....

....

....

What is my **timeframe** to make preparing for worship a habit?

....

....

....

....

THE SEVEN HABITS OF JESUS

1. **REMEMBERING**......our baptismal adoption into God's family

2. **LISTENING**..............to God's law & gospel voice in Scripture

3. **PRAYING**.................for God's help with all of our daily needs

4. **PREPARING**.............to hear God's forgiving voice in worship

5. **RETURNING**............ a percentage of what God has given us

6. **INVITING**...................others to baptism and Christ's mission

7. **CARING**.................. for others and creation with Christ's love

5a. RETURNING

Returning Our Tithe Offering to God

re·turn·ing (vb)
1. sending back to an origin
2. giving back to an earlier owner
3. an act of going back to a former place

Opening Prayer

Father, we pray Thee not that Thou shouldest take us out of the world, but we pray Thee to keep us from evil. Give us neither poverty nor riches, feed us with bread convenient for us. And let Thy songs be our delight in the houses of our pilgrimage. Entreat us not to leave Thee or refrain from following Thee. Thy people shall be our people, Thou shalt be our God. Amen.

Vincent Van Gogh (1853-1890)

Returning Goal

Within our Judeo-Christian tradition, wealth has been identified as one of the most potentially destructive forces in a person's life. In order that the faithful not become possessed by their possessions, a tithe offering was established by God. After thousands of years of *field testing*, both Jews and Christians have determined that a tithe offering gives us the capacity to appreciate that all our material blessings have been given to us by God alone.

Returning

Jesus taught that money is more than a medium of exchange. For Jesus, our money has the potential for us to do what is right or to do what is wrong. Arthur Simon, founder of *Bread for the World* said, *our real problem with money is that we are addicted.* Few would disagree; we are certainly addicted. The author Rudyard Kipling once told a graduating class of medical students: *You'll go out from here and very likely make a lot of money. One day you'll meet someone for whom money means very little. Then you will know how poor you are.* This sounds very much like Jesus' teaching about money.

Why do you think Jesus taught so much about wealth and money?

Returning our Offering to God

When we give a weekly offering in worship, we are returning a small portion of all that God has first given us. An important aspect of our offering is to help us recognize that everything we have has been directly, or indirectly, given to us by God. We ought not give our offering out of obligation, but instead out of gratitude for all that God has first given us. A renewed sense of appreciation toward God as the giver of all good gifts helps us to realize that we came into this life with nothing, and we will leave this life with nothing. When we present our offering before God's altar, we accompany it with a prayer like this: *Father, we return to you a portion of all that you have first given us—ourselves, our time, and our possessions—signs of your gracious love.* Being grateful to God for all the material and spiritual blessings in life was one of the most important subjects Jesus shared with his followers. **Apart from Jesus' teachings about God's kingdom, he taught more about how we are to manage the material gifts God has given us than any other subject!** What does this tell us about God's expectations for how we use or misuse what he has given us?

Do you agree or disagree that our giving is out of gratitude?

MERCIFUL
FATHER,
WE OFFER
WITH JOY
AND THANKSGIVING, WHAT YOU HAVE
FIRST GIVEN US: OURSELVES, OUR TIME
AND OUR POSSESSIONS, SIGNS OF YOUR
LOVE.
RECEIVE
OUR TITHE
FOR THE
ONE WHO
OFFERED
HIMSELF
FOR US,
JESUS CHRIST
OUR LORD, AMEN.

Jesus teaches us how to live a grateful life. I love Jesus very much!

The Rich Fool

Someone in the crowd said to him, "Teacher, tell my brother to divide the family inheritance with me." But he said to him, "Friend, who set me to be a judge or arbitrator over you?" And, "Take care! Be on your guard against all kinds of greed; for one's life does not consist in the abundance of possessions." Then he told them a parable: "The land of a rich man produced abundantly. And he thought to himself, 'What should I do, for I have no place to store my crops?' Then he said, 'I will do this: I will pull down my barns and build larger ones, and there I will store all my grain and my goods. And I will say to my soul, Soul, you have ample goods laid up for many years; relax, eat, drink, be merry.' But God said to him, 'You fool! This very night your life is being demanded of you. And the things you have prepared, whose will they be?' So it is with those who store up treasures for themselves, but are not rich toward God (Luke 12:13-21).

The man in this parable is called the *Rich Fool* because he put his security in the wrong area of life - possessions. We are taught through this parable that in the end our lives will not be measured by our possessions, but by our relationship with God and people. In the end, only Christ Jesus can save, not our money, or our possessions. Jesus said, *It is easier for a camel to walk through the eye of a sewing needle than for someone who puts their security in riches to enter eternal life* (Luke 18:25). Jesus is the only security that lasts forever. The *Rich Fool* in this parable hoarded all of his wealth for himself. He didn't accept that riches were given to him by God so he could share some of it with others.

WEALTH
Christ Transforms our Wealth

Wealth is a Gift from God
When we realize that our wealth is a gift from God, we are then able to appreciate that all of life is a gift from God.

Wealth is a Short-Term Trust
When we realize that our wealth is a short-term trust from God, then we are empowered to be more prudent managers of God's trust fund.

Wealth is Less Important than People
When we realize that our material wealth is limited to our earthly journey, we begin to truly value our chance to share as God does.

Wealth can Destroy Our Faith
When we realize how possessions can possess us and become the *root of all evil*, we become more content with our limited material wealth.

Wealth can Strengthen Our Faith
There are times when we must think our way into new ways of acting. When it comes to managing wealth, it can often be more helpful to act than to plan and over think.

Wealth is Best Managed by 10-10-80
When we realize how poor stewardship of wealth can destroy marriages and families, we are motivated to practice the 10-10-80 model of Judeo-Christian wealth management:

10% of weekly income is _returned_ as a tithe offering
10% of weekly income is _invested_ in long-term savings
80% of weekly income is _used_ for daily living expenses

How do you feel about 10-10-80 money management?

The world lets itself be deceived that wealth is an unfailing indication of God's favor. We think it natural that if we have good fortune, wealth, and health that we have been blessed by God. This sort of deduction is utter nonsense. God does not bestow riches on us so we may draw conclusions about his graciousness. God has given us a greater blessing from which we may draw a more proper conclusion—he gives us faith as a free gift of his grace. Faith is the best indicator that we have been blessed by God!

-Martin Luther (1483-1546)

Write & Share with a Partner...

Why is it often easier to identify wealth, instead of faith, as an indicator of God's blessings?

....

....

Ten Principles

Our weekly offering is about returning back to God a portion of what he has first given us. The apostle Paul provides ten principles for understanding how we can grow in our appreciation of all that God has given us.

Principle One
Give with the generosity of God.

> *He wants us to know how the generosity of God has been at work in the hearts of those in the Macedonian churches* (2 Cor 8:1).

✓ We are able to be generous givers when God, who is generous, is at work in our hearts.

Principle Two
The Holy Spirit helps us to excel in giving.

> *It is the gift of the Holy Spirit that allows you to excel in your giving* (2 Cor 8:7).

✓ The Holy Spirit gives us the capacity to excel in our giving beyond what we are able to accomplish by our own efforts.

Principle Three
Christ's sacrifice inspires sacrificial giving.
> *Though he was rich (in heaven), for our sake he became poor (on the cross), so that we might become rich (in heaven)* (2 Cor 8:8).

✓ Christ's sacrificial death on the cross inspires us to give God sacrificial offerings, in addition to a tithe.

Principle Four
Our offering is to be a proportionate offering.
> *Our gift is acceptable to God according to what we have, not according to what we do not have* (2 Cor 8:12).

✓ Within the Judeo-Christian tradition a tithe has been the only numerical standard in determining the actual amount of our offering. This Old Testament practice of returning to God ten percent (10%) of our weekly income (usually adjusted, not gross) is one of the three key parts of God's money management plan:

10% of weekly income is _returned_ as a tithe offering
10% of weekly income is _invested_ in long-term savings
80% of weekly income is _used_ for daily living expenses

Principle Five

We financially assist those in our family, and church family, who are experiencing hardship.

The one who gathered much did not have too much, and the one who gathered little did not have too little (2 Cor 8:15).

✓ When we share our financial resources, the person with greater financial resources will have enough left over. However, for the person with less financial resources, nothing will be lacking. There is an unspoken desire among those within families, and sometimes church families, for there to be equality among those of different income levels.

Principle Six

Managers of a congregation's offerings must be honest.

Those sought to manage the collection and accounting of offerings must have a good reputation (2 Cor 8:20).

✓ Those assigned to count and manage a congregation's offerings and income must be prudent, frugal, transparent, and above all else, must be honest and trustworthy. Their money management must have several overseers and an annual audit.

Principle Seven

An occasional sacrificial offering is encouraged in addition to a regular tithe.

I have urged them to visit you so they might receive the sacrificial offering you had promised them (2 Cor 9:4).

✓ We are to give both a weekly tithe offering and an occasional sacrificial (extra) offering. A sacrificial offering is usually designated for a specific mission or ministry need.

Principle Eight

God provides for all our *needs* and many of our *wants*.

Remember, whoever sows sparingly will also reap sparingly, and whoever sows generously will also reap generously (2 Cor 9:6).

✓ When we give a tithe offering as a *cheerful giver* we have more left over for our *wants* than we would anticipate.

If you see a brother or sister in need and have the means to do something about it but turn a cold shoulder and do nothing, what happens to God's love within you? It disappears!

(1 John 3:17)

Principle Nine

Our desire to give a tithe offering reveals our heartfelt relationship with Christ.

Our giving is an outward manifestation of our inner life with Christ (2 Cor 9:13).

✓ Our regular weekly tithe and occasional sacrificial gifts are visible manifestations of our inner union with Christ.

Principle Ten

Within the heart of a grateful person is a great faith.

When you give with a grateful heart it is the same as thanking and praising God (2 Cor 9:11). A generous offering is a confession of the gospel of Christ (2 Cor 9:13).

✓ Giving generously allows us to thank and praise God for all he has first given us.

Truly I tell you, this poor widow has put in more than all others.

(Mark 12:43)

To what dangers and sufferings people will submit themselves on land and sea to acquire great wealth. Yet, they neither try nor care to acquire the virtues or to suffer the least bit of pain to have them, though these are the riches of the soul. In the holy Gospel it is more impossible for a rich person to enter eternal life than for a camel to pass through the eye of a needle. Such are those who possess or desire wealth with miserably disordered affection. They cannot pass through the gate because it is narrow and low. Only if they throw their load to the ground, restrain their affection for the world, and bow their head in humility, will they be able to pass through. And there is no other gate but this that leads to eternal life. The gate is broad that leads to eternal damnation, and blind as they are it seems they do not see their own destruction, for even in this life they have a foretaste of hell.

Catherin of Sienna (1347-1380)

Write & Share with a Partner...

What are some of the most important insights you discovered in this chapter on Returning?

....

....

....

....

♫♫♫♫♫♫♫♫♫♫♫♫♫♫♫♫♫♫♫♫♫♫♫♫♫♫

We Give Thee But Thine Own

We give thee but thine own,
Whatever the gift may be;
All that we have is thine alone,
A trust, O Lord from thee.

May we thy bounties thus,
As stewards true receive;
And gladly as thou blessest us,
To thee our first fruits give.

The captive to release,
To God the lost to bring;
To teach the way of life and peace,
It is a Christ-like thing.

And we believe thy word,
Though dim our faith may be;
Whatever we do for thine,
O Lord, we do it unto thee.

William W. Howe (1864-1897)

 We end our session by joining hands in a circle to pray together the Lord's Prayer.

Insights for developing my Returning HABIT:

*How will adding the habit of returning a tithe offering **help** me live a more Christ-centered life?*

....

....

....

....

....

....

....

....

*How often will I **attempt** to do the habit of returning a tithe offering to God?*

....

....

....

....

....

....

....

....

....

....

*How will the habit of returning a tithe offering **become** part of my life?*

....

....

....

....

....

....

....

*How is returning a tithe offering **important** to my maturity as a disciple of Christ?*

....

....

....

....

....

....

....

*What is my **timeframe** to make returning a tithe offering to God a habit?*

....

....

....

....

....

THE SEVEN HABITS OF JESUS

1. **REMEMBERING**......our baptismal adoption into God's family

2. **LISTENING**..............to God's law & gospel voice in Scripture

3. **PRAYING**.................for God's help with all of our daily needs

4. **PREPARING**.............to hear God's forgiving voice in worship

5. **RETURNING**........... a percentage of what God has given us

6. **INVITING**..................others to baptism and Christ's mission

7. **CARING**................. for others and creation with Christ's love

5b. RETURNING

Returning Our Offering to God

re·turn·ing (vb)
1. sending back to an origin
2. giving back to an earlier owner
3. an act of going back to a former place

Opening Prayer

Lord Jesus, make me willing to be changed, even though it requires surgery of the soul, and the therapy of discipline. Make my heart warm and soft, that I may receive and accept now the blessings of Thy forgiveness, the benediction of Thy "Depart in peace....and sin no more." In Jesus' name. Amen.

Peter Marshall (1902-1949)

Returning Goal

Within our Judeo-Christian tradition, wealth has been identified as one of the most potentially destructive forces in a person's life. In order that the faithful not become possessed by their possessions, a tithe offering was established by God. After thousands of years of *field testing*, both Jews and Christians have determined that a tithe offering gives us the capacity to appreciate that all our material blessings have been given to us by God alone.

> # *Write & Share with the Group...*
> *Why do you think so few people in the Church today give a tithe offering?*
>
> ....
>
> ....

The A.B.C.'s of Tithing

Setting aside 10% of our take-home adjusted income as a way to support God's Kingdom is a practice that keeps us focused on a number of spiritual truths:

A. <u>Tithing reminds us that God has given us all that we have in life</u>

The practice of tithing reminds us of our total dependence upon God for everything. It keeps us focused on being generous and makes us co-givers with God as our gifts are used to support Christ's mission in the world.

B. <u>Tithing has the capacity to put the things of this world into perspective</u>

There is nothing wrong with wealth or possessions. As Paul teaches in 1 Timothy, it is not money, but the *love of money that is the root of all evil* (6:10). Tithing is an ongoing reminder of our true loyalties. Jesus teaches us that: *where your treasure is, your heart will be there also* (Matt 6:19-21). Tithing can help our hearts remain close to God.

C. <u>Tithing can lead and draw us into a deeper trust in the goodness of God in our lives</u>

Tithing creates a change in our hearts. Although tithing is practiced by some legalistic believers, it is not legalism. We are not able to earn God's favor by giving a tithe. Over time, tithing encourages the Holy Spirit to penetrate our hearts. Tithing can open us up to the wonder and mystery of God's presence in our daily lives. Tithing has a marvelous way of helping us to recognize God's kingdom in our lives.

Do you budget 10% of your income for a tithe? Why or why not?

> *Begin by being honest. Do honest people rob God? But you rob me day after day. You ask, 'How have we robbed you?' The tithe and the offering - that's how! And now you're under a curse - the whole lot of you - because you're robbing me. Bring your full tithe to the Temple treasury so there will be ample provisions in my Temple. Test me in this and see if I don't open up heaven itself to you and pour out blessings beyond your wildest dreams.*
>
> (Malachi 3:8-10)

It makes me so sad to think that there are some who are robbing God.

Tithing Helps Us

Tithing has little to do with the congregation's budget or expenses, but has much to do with our hearts. God is the giver of everything we have in all of life, and he simply asks us to give one-tenth of our income to reveal the heartfelt trust we have in him. Our tithe does not benefit God. After all, God owns it all! The command to give is for our own benefit and for the benefit of Christ's mission in our world. Tithing helps us to keep our priorities from being displaced, and protects our souls. The promise of God in Malachi 3:8-10, is that God will *open the windows of heaven for you and pour down for you an overflowing blessing.* **The promise is straightforward: You cannot out-give God! Giving a tithe offering is a necessity for a disciple of Christ. When a disciple of Christ turns away from tithing, they are turning away from an opportunity to grow in faith. Because we have been created in the *image of God*, we have a need to give. Scripture teaches us that when we refuse to share we are rejecting the way we have been created.**

Of all the many personal advantages there are to being a tither, there are two that stand out: First, tithers are among the best financial managers because tithing forces them to live by a budget, which does not allow for the overwhelming interest and fees associated with credit card debt. Second, it **is understood that tithing allows us to accept that God is in control of life, which increases our trust in God and causes us to be filled with unspeakable joy.**

What do you think about these two benefits of tithing?

Money Management

Because a tithe offering is not a set amount, but a percentage, it requires us to manage our money. It is surprising how few Christians today have a working plan to help them manage the money God has entrusted to them. Without a working money management plan in place, it is all but impossible to tithe. Sadly, too many Christians

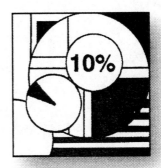

today are unable to give a tithe offering because of the debilitating amount of credit card debt they have incurred. In many respects, the inappropriate use of credit cards is the opposite of tithing. Tithing enables us to recognize that all of life is a gift from God. Credit cards seem to reinforce the false idea that our money comes from our own efforts and we can use it, and abuse it, in any way that we desire.

The general intention of a faith-based personal money management plan is to provide for a 10% tithe offering, a long term savings of 10%, and a living expense account of 80%. For ages, this has been the standard 10-10-80 money management plan that has served the Judeo-Christian faith communities for thousands of years!

How can you develop a faith-based money management plan?

All we ever have is what we give away.
Louis Ginsburg (1903-1990)

10-10-80 Money Mgmt. Plan

Monthly or bi-weekly take-home total income $_____
1.   RETURN 10% of income as a tithe offering $_____
2.   INVEST 10% of income in long-term savings $_____
3.   USE 80% of income for living expenses $_____

Living expenses include: Housing Mortgage or Rent, Maintenance/Repairs, Electric, Gas, Water, Phones, Trash, TV, Internet, Food, Beverages, Medicine, Transportation, Car Payments, Insurances, Clothing, Leisure, Family Expenses, Entertainment, Vacations, Emergency Fund, Misc.....

What is your experience of making and using a working budget?

Write & Share with a Partner...

Why do you think the 10-10-80 money management plan has been the standard for more than 4,000 years?

....

....

More Blessed to Give

When we are able to cheerfully and generously give away money, it may be a clear indicator that Christ dwells richly within our hearts. This is why it is more blessed to give than it is to receive. Tithing and sacrificial giving are visible signs of Christ's inner presence. It is not possible to cheerfully and generously give away money without Christ's inner presence and empowerment. We are always more blessed when we give than receive!

How have you been blessed by giving (returning)?

> *One of the dangers of having a lot of money is that you may be quite satisfied with the kinds of happiness money can give and so fail to realize your need for God. If everything seems to come simply by signing checks, you may forget that you are at every moment totally dependent on God. Natural gifts carry with them a similar danger. If you have intelligence and health and popularity and even a good upbringing, you are likely to be quite satisfied with your character as it is.*
>
> C.S. Lewis (1898-1963)

> *Blessed are those who can give without remembering and take without forgetting.*
> Elizabeth Bibesco (1897-1945)

Giving from Love

The only things we will experience in eternity will be the love we have given to others. Only what we have been able to *give away* **will remain with us in our heavenly home.** The Apostle Paul writes, *And now faith, hope, and love abide, these three; and the greatest of these is love* (1 Cor 13:13). Paul is not referring to romantic love, but rather the love of Christ that we were able to share and give away. Our giving and caring are the only aspects of our lives that will last the test of time into eternity. Sharing is essential for a disciple of Christ because when we are able to give of ourselves and the money we have received from God, it is then that we experience heaven on earth. If we cling to our money and the things of this world, we cannot long for heaven. **Disciples of Christ invest their treasures where their hearts already are—in Christ and his mission.** There can be no such thing as a *stingy* disciple. We will never be the disciples God intends us to be if we are unable to generously return a goodly share of what we receive. God did not give his Son's life as a sacrifice for us to devote ourselves to a self-indulgent lifestyle. **Deep within the soul of every disciple of Christ lies the truth, that more** *creature comforts* **will only further disconnect us from Christ's eternal kingdom.**

How important to you is returning a tithe offering to God?

I don't have much but I am willing to share because I know everything comes from God!

Take Care

Giving less than a tithe offering is often rationalized. Some people become defensive about not returning a tithe offering, and consider the time and talents they voluntarily share within their congregation to be a way of compensating for giving less than a tithe offering. This is to misunderstand the purpose of a tithe offering. We are not giving a tithe offering to primarily benefit the church. When we give a tithe offering we benefit by recognizing that all we have comes from God. **By substituting our gifts of time and talents in place of a tithe offering, we mistakenly identify ourselves as the giver, instead of God!**

What is your reaction to time and talents not being part of a tithe?

Discipleship

If we are to become a disciple of Christ we must resolve the matter of money in our lives. Jesus taught, *No one can serve both God and money* (Luke 16:13). **Jesus did not say, You should not, but instead, You cannot.** More people are sidetracked from becoming a disciple by their inability to tithe than by anything else. Money, wealth, and financial security are not bad or sinful things in and of themselves. However, when our money becomes more important than being a disciple, it becomes a destructive force within our lives that disconnects us from God's presence, power, and promises. The Bible teaches that money tests our faith more than anything else in all of life! When we are able to *pass* this test of money, with the Spirit's help, it is then that our faith grows exponentially.

How do you think tithing would keep you from 'serving' money?

A.B.C.'s of Sacrificial Giving

A. <u>The Spirit will allow a certain ministry or mission project to touch our hearts.</u>

For many, it will be caring for *at risk* children. It is important that our sacrificial gifts support a project which is transparent and can be trusted.

B. <u>A sacrificial gift is usually a monetary gift which has been generated by giving up an expense we can do without.</u>

For example, the money saved by abstaining from sugary sodas for one year is enough to help an entire family in the developing world start a sustainable farm with livestock, tools, and training (<u>www.elca.org/goodgifts</u>).

C. <u>Each day we pray for those who benefit from our sacrificial gift.</u>

We continue to pray for the Lord's help to live a more simple lifestyle, in order that we might grow in our financial ability to share a sacrificial gift with those who need it.

> *Don't hoard treasure down here where it gets eaten by moths and corroded by rust or - worse!-stolen by burglars. Stockpile treasure in heaven, where it's safe from moths and rust and burglars. It's obvious, isn't it? The place where your treasure is, is the place you will most want to be, and end up being.* (Matt 6:19-21)

<u>Our tithe offering is never to be given:</u>
-With a negative spirit or a sense of being forced (Mal 1).
-With the intent of being recognized by others (Matt 6).
-With the idea that God will bless us in return (2 Cor 9).

Seven Offering Myths

1. Members will automatically, over the years, increase the amount of their offerings.

WRONG! Increased giving is the result of Christian discipleship, not of being a long time church member.

2. If the attendance increases in worship, the members will give more.

WRONG! Usually new members do not tithe and have not developed a commitment to giving.

3. Our members are giving all they can.

WRONG! The average member, in any denomination, gives around 1% of their income, instead of a 10% tithe.

4. Telling members the Church needs support will increase giving in a Congregation.

WRONG! As Christian disciples, we are not motivated by giving *to* the church, but *from* our hearts.

5. Members usually increase their giving by a little each year.

WRONG! Unless a Christian becomes more mature in Christ, they probably give the same amount every year.

6. The church should use methods that other charitable groups use, like fundraisers.

WRONG! Christians are to give based upon the biblical principles of stewardship and tithing, not fundraising gimmicks.

7. Most members will increase their giving as they get older.

WRONG! Increased giving and tithing only happen when a Christian is properly educated about the meaning behind their offering.

Which of the offering myths is most interesting to you?

Jesus reminds us that it is not money, but rather the *love of money* (deep desire) that is the problem. How much is *enough*? For most people it seems that their idea of enough is often ten percent more than their current income. What we *need* and what we *want* are two competing desires within all of us. One of the many benefits of tithing is that it helps us control our *wants*. Once our *wants* are under control we are more satisfied with living within our means, and our desire for ten percent more income is no longer a factor.

Write & Share with a Partner...

What are some of the most important insights you discovered about Returning?

....

....

....

....

It is ok to ask God for help in working toward a tithe!

I don't think I will ever be able to give more than 5%...

♪♫♪♫♪♫♪♫♪♫♪♫♪♫♪♫♪♫♪♫♪♫♪♫♪♫♪♫

We Give Thee But Thine Own

We give thee but thine own,
    Whatever the gift may be;
All that we have is thine alone,
    A trust, O Lord from thee.

May we thy bounties thus,
    As stewards true receive;
And gladly as thou blessest us,
    To thee our first fruits give.

The captive to release,
    To God the lost to bring;
To teach the way of life and peace,
    It is a Christ-like thing.

And we believe thy word,
    Though dim our faith may be;
Whatever we do for thine,
    O Lord, we do it unto thee.

William W. Howe (1864-1897)

 We end our session by joining hands in a circle to pray together the Lord's Prayer.

Insights for developing my Returning HABIT:

*How will adding the habit of returning a tithe offering **help** me live a more Christ-centered life?*

....

....

....

....

....

....

....

....

*How often will I **attempt** to do the habit of returning a tithe offering to God?*

....

....

....

....

....

....

....

....

....

....

*How will the habit of returning a tithe offering **become** part of my life?*

....
....
....
....
....
....
....

*How is returning a tithe offering **important** to my maturity as a disciple of Christ?*

....
....
....
....
....
....
....

*What is my **timeframe** to make returning a tithe offering to God a habit?*

....
....
....
....
....

Self-Study for Returning
Amazing Grace (5a)

For by grace you have been saved through faith, and this is not your own doing; it is the gift of God — not the results of your own efforts, so that no one may boast (Eph 2:8-9).

Grace is, above all else, God's unconditional love for us, love we do not deserve. The gospel, the Good News, tells us that we cannot earn God's love; we can only receive it. Despite humanity's sinful rebellion against God, and our propensity to place ourselves first, God has taken the initiative through his Son's life, death, and resurrection to restore our relationship with him. God's grace, his love, is his gift of a renewed relationship with him. In every way, God is for us...this is God's grace. This grace, more than anything else, should affect our desire and ability to return a tithe offering.

Explore Scripture:
Rom 5:1-2; 6:1-2; 2 Cor 5:17-19; 2 Thes 2:16-17; 2 Tim 4:8

How does God's grace affect your feelings about yourself, other people, and a tithe offering?

....

....

....

....

Self-Study for Returning
Jesus our Savior (5b)

He's given us life from his life, from his very own Spirit. Also, we've seen for ourselves and continue to state openly that the Father sent his Son as Savior of the world (1 John 4:14).

God so passionately desired a relationship with all people that he did the unimaginable: God became one of us! Jesus is God's Son, both fully human and fully God. Through Jesus' suffering, death, and resurrection we experience God's total love for us. Through Jesus, God overcame the power of sin and death, so that all creation might be reconciled with the creator God. Our relationship with God has been restored by God alone; we were not able to contribute anything. We are saved from an eternal separation from God by the work of his Son; we were able to contribute nothing! Jesus, our Savior, stands in our place, for our sins, to exchange our broken relationships with God for his own.

Explore Scripture:
Luke 1:47; Eph 5:23; 1 Tim 4:10; 2 Peter 2:20

How does God's gift of his Son affect your ability to return a tithe offering?

....
....
....
....

Use your answers from the Insights questions in parts A and B to help make **RETURNING** *a*

Help

Attempt

Become

Important

Timeframe

---

*How will adding the habit of returning a tithe offering **help** me live a more Christ-centered life?*

....

....

....

....

---

*How often will I **attempt** to do the habit of returning a tithe offering to God?*

....

....

....

....

How will the habit of returning a tithe offering **become** part of my life?

....

....

....

....

How is returning a tithe offering **important** to my maturity as a disciple of Christ?

....

....

....

....

What is my **timeframe** to make returning a tithe offering to God a habit?

....

....

....

....

THE SEVEN HABITS OF JESUS

1. **REMEMBERING**......our baptismal adoption into God's family

2. **LISTENING**..............to God's law & gospel voice in Scripture

3. **PRAYING**.................for God's help with all of our daily needs

4. **PREPARING**...........to hear God's forgiving voice in worship

5. **RETURNING**........... a percentage of what God has given us

6. **INVITING**...................others to baptism and Christ's mission

7. **CARING**................... for others and creation with Christ's love

6a. INVITING

Inviting Others to Christ Through Baptism

in·vit·ing (vb)
1. to request one's participation
2. to ask another to be present
3. to welcome one's involvement

Opening Prayer

Teach us, good Lord, to serve Thee as Thou desires; to give and not to count the cost; to fight and not to heed the wounds; to toil and not to ask for rest; to labor and not to ask for any reward, save that of knowing that we do Thy will. Through Jesus Christ our Lord, Amen.

Ignatius Loyola (1491-1556)

Inviting Goal

Christ has given each of us, as disciples, a mission assignment to invite *all people of every nation* to be baptized in the Triune name of God the Father, Son, and Holy Spirit (Matt 28:18). The followers of Jesus have always understood this as Christ's *great commission* to baptize and make disciples. As Christians we are instructed to invite our family, friends, neighbors, colleagues, and casual acquaintances to become children in God's eternal family through baptism.

Write & Share with the Group...

Why do you think Jesus identifies inviting others to be baptized as his great commission?

....

....

Lifesaving Station Parable

On a dangerous seacoast where shipwrecks often occur there was once a crude little lifesaving station. The building was just a hut, and there was only one boat, but the few devoted members kept a constant watch over the sea, and with no thought for themselves went out day and night tirelessly searching for the lost. Many lives were saved by this wonderful little station, and it soon became famous. Some of those who were saved, and various others in the surrounding area, wanted to become associated with the station and give of their time and money and effort for the support of its work. New boats were bought and new crews trained. The little lifesaving station quickly grew. Some of the members of the lifesaving station were unhappy because their building was so crude and poorly equipped. They felt that a more comfortable place should be provided as the first refuge of those saved from the sea. So, they replaced the emergency cots with beds and put better furniture in the enlarged building. Now the lifesaving station became a popular gathering place for its members, and they decorated it beautifully and furnished it exquisitely, because they used it as a sort of club. Fewer members were now interested in

going to sea on lifesaving missions, so they hired lifeboat crews to do this work. The lifesaving motif still prevailed in this club's decoration and there was a model lifeboat in the room where the club initiations were held. About this time, a large ship was wrecked off the coast, and the hired crews brought in boatloads of cold, wet, and half-drowned people. They were dirty and sick and most looked like foreigners. The newly decorated club was in chaos. So the property committee immediately had a shower house built outside the club where victims of a shipwreck would be cleaned up before coming inside. At the next meeting, there was a split in the club membership. Most of the members wanted to stop the club's lifesaving activities as being disruptive and a hindrance to the normal social life of the club. Some members insisted upon lifesaving as their primary purpose and pointed out that they were still called a lifesaving station. But they were finally voted down and told that if they wanted to save the lives of all the various kinds of people who were shipwrecked in those waters, they could begin their own lifesaving station down the coast, and so they did. However, as the years went by, that new station down the  coast experienced the same changes that had occurred in the old one. It evolved into a club and some left to build another lifesaving station. History continued to repeat itself, and if you visit that seacoast today, you will find a number of exclusive clubs along that shore. Shipwrecks are still frequent in those waters, but now most of the people tragically drown!
-Anonymous

How are lifesaving stations like today's congregations?

Lifesaving Parable

The parable of the *lifesaving station* challenges us to participate in Christ's *Great Commission* to save lives by inviting others to be baptized. The *lifesaving station* reminds us that an important part of our lives must be the Lord's Great Commission. It is a Commission to reach out to others and invite them to be disciples of Christ by encouraging them to be baptized into God's Triune name: Father, Son, and Holy Spirit. As baptized disciples of Christ we have been commissioned by our Lord to invite our family, friends, neighbors, colleagues, and even those we only know as casual acquaintances to become adopted children in God's eternal family through baptism.

Christianity has always been and will be a missionary organization that expects each Christian to invite others to receive salvation from God through baptism. As Christians, as Christ followers, we are expected to tell others how God has adopted us into his eternal family through baptism. We are expected to use every opportunity to invite people to be baptized, so that they may be *born from above* by God (John 3:3). The New Testament challenges us by asking, *How can your friends be a part of God's family unless they have heard the gospel from you* (Romans 10:14)?

Inviting our friends and family is always easier when we remind ourselves that inviting others to be baptized does not imply that we have the ability to convince someone to be baptized. Only the Holy Spirit can work the miracle of faith and conversion in a person's soul. And yet, the Holy Spirit does request our cooperation!

How do you feel about being tools of the Holy Spirit?

These two things I know about the ocean and God: this portion which touches me is real; beyond it is far, far more than I can ever know. The creeds and dogmas of the church, then, are no pat formulas which provide all the neat answers man can ever find as to the nature of God. Nor are they barriers bearing the legend, "Thus far; no farther." Rather are they invitations to adventure, a kind of spiritual road map offering you the experience of others who have found a rich and exciting experience of God.

Edmund A. Steimle (1907-1988)

Becoming a Christian

There is widespread misunderstanding in our society about what it means to be a Christian, and how someone becomes a Christian. What does it mean for us to invite a friend to become a Christian? Let's begin with what Christianity is not:

First, being a Christian is not the same as simply attending worship services. Church membership and attending worship are very essential parts of a Christian life, but we are not necessarily Christians because we are members or attendees.

Second, being a Christian is not the same as having a compelling testimony or confessing one of the creeds. Many people think that if they confess the Apostles' Creed without any mental reservations, it will make them a Christian. This is not true. Some believe that if they are able to stand before a Christian congregation and confess that Jesus Christ is their personal Savior, they will be a Christian. But this, also, does not in itself make anyone a Christian.

Third, being a Christian is not mainly about subscribing to a moral code of conduct. There are an unfortunate number of Christians who can so easily, and yet heretically, share with everyone they meet that, *It really doesn't matter what you believe as long as your lead a decent life.* So they go through the whole of their life highlighting those *commandments* that they *keep*, but never mentioning the other commandments for which they need regular forgiveness. Christianity has the highest ethic the world has ever known. However, the essence of being a Christian is not about following an ethical code of conduct.

If being a Christian is **not** primarily about membership and attending worship, **not** primarily about confessing a creed or a personal testimony, and **not** about subscribing to a moral code of conduct, then how does one become a Christian? **The essence of Christianity is Christ! We are Christians because Christ has entered our lives through baptism. A Christian is someone who by *water and the Word* has begun to live the death and resurrection of Jesus Christ in his or her soul.** It is that simple and yet, it is that profound.

How does Christ enter our souls? The New Testament teaches us that through baptism we are filled with the power of Christ's death, which brings death to the evil forces of sin, death, and the devil within us. Through baptism we are also filled with the power of Christ's life, to exercise faith, hope, and reconciling love into a new relationship with God and one another.

What is your experience of inviting a friend to be baptized?

How could anyone not invite a friend to be a part of something so powerful and important!

Being a Christian

When Martin Luther was asked how someone could be certain they were a Christian, the great reformer replied, *You know you are baptized, and that's all you will ever need to know.* A Christian is one who has been given the Spirit of Christ through their baptism. This indwelling presence of Christ is the Spirit of his death, and the Spirit of his resurrection. **Paul teaches us in the sixth chapter of Romans that when we are baptized we are given the power of Christ's death and resurrection.** It is as simple as that, and yet, as profound and mysterious as that!

What do you think of baptism defining the Christian life?

Christ's Death

Through our baptism, we are given Christ's own power, his own capacity, to bring death to our sin, our dying, and our inner relationship to the devil. Christ brings death to the destructive nature of our inward self-centeredness. Our sin (inner and instinctive rebellion against God) is so profoundly destructive that it cannot be corrected by our own efforts. To make matters worse, our problem is not just the sins that we commit. Our greatest problem is with our sinful nature. Our sinful nature, says Scripture, is inclined to approach every area of our lives with self-centeredness, irresponsible choices, and the failure to love.

The intensity of self-centeredness shatters our relationship with God and one another. Our sinful nature's most insidious characteristic is that we may genuinely believe we are acting out of justifiable motives, when in truth, we are acting out of selfishness and self-centeredness. As St. Paul lamented, *I do not do the good I want, but the evil I do not want to do...this is because there is a sinful nature within me* (Rom 7:20). It has been said, our biggest problem in life is believing that we have no problem. Our sinful nature cannot be limited or controlled by our own efforts. Our problem is that we blindly live out our lives believing that we are acting with selflessness. And yet, in truth the average life is a life that rejects not only a relationship with God, but also relationships with others. Our problem is not that we have a few minor flaws. Our problem is that we are predisposed, by our sinful nature, to be totally absorbed in ourselves and our needs.

It's only human to assume that we are *basically nice people who try to help others*. And yet, the truth about us suggests otherwise. When we were baptized, we were baptized into Christ's death, which brings death to our self-centeredness. This is the only chance we have of ever truly experiencing the life God desires for us. St. Paul teaches us that when we are baptized we receive the power of Christ's death and resurrection to shape us into a child in God's own family.

How has baptism already brought death to your self-centeredness?

Christ's Resurrection

Within St. Paul's teaching on baptism, he not only describes the power of Christ's death, he also describes how the power of Christ's resurrection is given to us through baptism. The power of Christ's resurrection within us is his power of love and forgiveness. It is Christ's love that establishes our relationship with God and one another. The power of Christ's resurrection lives within us to give us Christ's own capacity, his own ability, to be loving and forgiving. Through Christ's resurrection we are made a *new creation* in which the old sinful body is replaced with obedience, servanthood, and community. Of course, our conversion and the power of Christ's resurrection may not produce immediate changes. Day by day we ask Christ to do for us, through the power of his resurrection, what we could never do for ourselves. The power of Christ's resurrection that we receive in baptism takes a lifetime to change us. The power of Christ's resurrection brings triumph over the sin, the death, and the devil within our souls. The power of Christ's resurrected Spirit preeminently gifts us with faith. In our society we have some very strange ideas about faith. Scripture teaches that faith happens, it is not achieved. Faith comes into our hearts, not when we *will* it into being. Faith is a gift of God that allows us to accept the indwelling of Christ, given in baptism. In other words, **faith is given to us in the same way our physical life has come to us—as a gift of God. We did nothing to earn our physical life; we did nothing to receive faith.** When parents adopt a baby, the baby has no idea of the act taking place. We have received faith as a gift of the resurrected Christ. It is a faith that enables us to trust in the Savior for eternal salvation.

How is the power of Christ's death different from his resurrection?

Christ's Great Commission

God authorized and commanded me to commission you: Go out and make disciples of everyone, far and near, baptizing them in God's name: Father, Son, and Holy Spirit. Then instruct them in the practices of all that I have instructed you (Matthew 28:18-20).

As baptized disciples of Christ, we have been commissioned to baptize and instruct all people everywhere. Christ expects us to invite as many people as is possible in the course of our earthly journey to become baptized and adopted children in God's eternal family.

Who first talked to you about Christ's Great Commission?

Being an Evangelist

An evangelist is someone who verbally shares the Christian faith with another person. The Christian faith is a proclamation of Christ's death and resurrection, the benefits of which are given to us through baptism. Being an evangelist may seem easy enough, but it is not very easy for most Christians. The average Christian finds it very awkward to talk about Christ or their faith. This awkwardness is made worse because talking about religion makes most people feel uncomfortable and inadequate. If we are to be the evangelists our Lord expects us to be, we need to practice talking about Christ. Through conversation in small groups, Christians can be encouraged to share their faith in Christ. **When a Christian is able to casually share with another Christian the name *Jesus Christ,* and when they no longer feel strange when talking about *Jesus Christ,* they are ready to be an evangelist with their friends and acquaintances.** The basic requirement for being a Christian evangelist does not lie in special techniques; it rests upon one's ability to verbalize a message about Jesus Christ.

Sharing Christ

The traditional way of talking about Christ is to explain to others their need for eternal salvation by focusing on the damning effects of their sin. However, **we might find it helpful to first share our understanding of the life, death, and resurrection of Jesus. We might want to ask what the name Jesus (God's Savior) means to someone.** It is important to not equate evangelism with conversion. Too often Christians feel obligated to convince others to believe in Jesus with a high-pressured intensity. Our job is only to be faithful evangelists. Only God, by the power of the Holy Spirit at work in our friend's life, can effect a conversion. The evangelistic message is a joy-filled telling of what Jesus did for us and now does.

Two Stories

The evangelistic message is two stories: *God's story* and *my story*. Both are necessary. The best way to get to feel comfortable about sharing these two stories with a friend is to participate in *role playing*. Role playing is experience-based learning that utilizes a representation of a real life situation in a nonthreatening setting. Role playing consists of the unrehearsed, verbal, and nonverbal interactions between two people who agree to play the *part* of another person that represents the friend or family member to be evangelized. By taking roles, and afterwards discussing what took place, individuals are able to develop the skills and insights needed for being an evangelist for Christ.

How important is proclaiming Christ's offer of salvation?

Write & Share with a Partner...

Role play your God Story and My Story with your partner and share your experience below:

....

....

....

....

....

....

....

....

....

....

....

Baptism: God's Action

Just as we are unable to create our own bodies, or sustain them, we are unable to create a relationship with God or sustain it. Baptism is often referred to as the *Sacrament of Faith* because through baptism God gives us faith to experience a relationship with him. As the great teacher Tertullian (A.D. 211) said, *Christians are not born, they are made by God through baptism.* No one becomes a Christian because they were born to Christian parents. Baptism is all God's work.

What is your reaction to baptism being all God's work?

-*You were washed, you were sanctified, you were justified in the name of the Lord Jesus Christ and in the Spirit of God.* (1 Cor 6:11)

-*Our relationship with God is established by God through baptism.* (John 3:3)

-*Only God is able to initiate a relationship with us.* (1 Cor 2:14)

-*We have been introduced to Jesus the Savior by the Holy Spirit.* (Romans 1:16)

> I don't know much about it, but I do know that God is the one who saves us!

Baptism as Adoption

A common misunderstanding about being baptized is that baptism merely signifies that we have become members of a congregation. St. Peter describes baptism as our adoption into God's eternal family, which is much bigger than a congregation. *You have been chosen by God to be a member in his own family. Once you were without a family, but now you are a part of God's family; once you had not received love, but now you have received God's own love* (1 Peter 2:9-10).

We read in the New Testament that when people were baptized they were promised a new identity. The emphasis of baptism in Scripture is about God choosing us. Baptism is a miraculous act of God. Our baptism is the most important *act of God* which will ever occur in our lives. St. John describes baptism as being chosen by God, *You did not choose me, but instead I chose you* (John 15:16). When we invite friends to be baptized, we are inviting them, as God's representative, to become adopted children in his own family. Luther said, *What is our greatest comfort in both life and death? It can only be that I belong—body and soul, life and death—not to myself, but to my faithful Savior, Jesus Christ.*

When a person is baptized an oil cross is *marked* upon their forehead. Anointing with oil is rooted in the Old Testament and signifies our adoption into God's royal family. This oil cross, is seen as an indelible mark that connects our baptismal adoption to the crucified One. This oil cross is a *branding mark,* that identifies the family which now owns us; the family of our Savior.

Do you expect that you will always be in God's family?

Baptismal Salvation

Jesus was baptized by John, not because he needed to be baptized, but to identify with God's ways for righteousness. Jesus reveals in his baptism how God longs for us to come to him. Christian baptism is a means of salvation, in the same way God used circumcision to give his chosen people salvation. Out of gratitude for God's free gift of salvation, we *Go out to all people of every nation*. Through baptism we become God's chosen people. **Our salvation is not about what we think, feel, do or don't do. Nor is it about our decisions or doubts. Through baptism God promises to be our Father, to never leave us, and to bring us to his eternal home!**

How would you describe baptism as salvation?

Family of God

The great heresy of American popular Christianity is the assertion that religion is a private and personal decision. However, the Christian faith is unarguably a way of life together with others. Few Christians have described this more authentically than Dietrich Bonhoeffer in his classic work, *Life Together: Jesus preached, taught, healed, and acted in community. As Paul said to the faction-ridden church in Corinth, The church is Christ's body. Paul's point was that one cannot be in Christ without being baptized into the body.* Baptism reminds us that from beginning to end, our salvation and identity, is living within the *body of Christ.* There is no Christianity apart from the baptizing community of Christ.

Baptism teaches us that Christianity is not a do-it-yourself religion. Our salvation is always a gift, something which is received from God though his own people. We hear people say that religion is simply a matter of *trying to get to heaven.* However, for those who have been baptized, the truth is that by God's grace, we have already reached our goal. God has already paid the price for us and bought us. As baptized people of God we can live our lives in quiet confidence. Luther said, *We need not fear, in baptism God owns me!* As the Heidelberg Catechism (1563) asked, *What is our only comfort in life and in death? We belong, body and soul, in life and in death, not to ourselves but to our faithful Savior, Jesus Christ.* **Why not trace the sign of the cross on your forehead now? From now on, never let a day go by that you forget it!**

What assurance do you have of being in God's eternal family?

Baptizing Infants

For the first sixteen-hundred years of Christianity whole families, including infants, were baptized. Then in the late 17th Century two movements, the Enlightenment (emphasizing personal reason), and Pietism (emphasizing personal emotions) rejected baptism as a sacrament, eliminating the baptism of children. When inviting people to become baptized into God's eternal family, our invitation must be for people of every age, including infants.

The true essence of baptism is revealed through the baptism of infants and young children. When salvation is understood as an individual decision, or worse yet an achievement, then infant baptism will appear simply as a sign of a decision. However, **when salvation is correctly understood as a free gift from God, then baptism makes sense for all ages.** The only way to receive a gift is to be receptive. The only way to be helped is to be helpless. We begin life dependent upon God, we live our lives dependent upon God, and we end our life dependent upon God. Whatever our age might be, we are dependent upon God to adopt us into his eternal family, and in the end to bring us to our eternal home in his family. As Paul said to those who thought of salvation as a result of their own righteousness,

While we were yet helpless, at the right time Christ died for the ungodly (Rom 5:6). In Scripture, God seeks and saves the weak and helpless. Because the strong and self-sufficient have no perceived need for a Savior, they reject the Savior.

There are those churches that do not baptize infants until they think the child knows what baptism means or until the child can make a decision for Christ. And yet, the Bible does not establish insight or knowledge as a precondition to be saved. However, the Bible does ensure us that our entire life is under the promise and sign of the cross. The baptism of a person, at any age, is a means of God's grace; to restore our broken relationship with him. Every time a baby is baptized we give witness to the truth that God's grace is free and sufficient for salvation.

What does it mean that you are promised eternal life as a gift?

Have you ever read the book, *All God's Creatures Go to Heaven?*

Unconditional Birth & Rebirth

God's saving work in baptism is not dependent upon our cooperation. Scripture teaches us that both our lives and our salvation are gifts given to us by God alone. There is no more beautiful or powerful statement of salvation than God's saving action in baptism. Baptism is the Church's proclamation that we are who we are, **not** because we decided to believe in God, but because God has chosen us to be in his eternal Kingdom. Christianity is not, and can never be, a do-it-yourself activity. In the same way we are unable to give birth to ourselves, we are also unable to be *born from above as a child of God* (John 3:3).

How does your baptism as a gift define your life?

Ten Blessings of Baptism

+ Our original sinful nature is washed clean (1Cor 6; Acts 2)
+ The seed of faith is planted in us by the Holy Spirit (Titus 3)
+ We are given power to turn from a sinful nature   (1Cor 10)
+ The Holy Spirit becomes involved in our daily lives   (Col 2)
+ The real presence of Christ begins to live within us   (Gal 2)
+ We are given the *love, joy, and peace* of the Trinity   (Gal 5)
+ Spiritual gifts are given for church growth & unity (Rom 12)
+ The Lord gives power to resist satan's temptations (Matt 4)
+ The righteousness of Christ is imprinted upon us   (Rom 6)
+ God gives eternal life to us as an unearned gift   (Mark 16)

How can you best describe baptism as a sacrament?

Through your Baptism

+You are now a part of Christ's body, the church
+You are now adopted into God's eternal family
+You are now saved and reborn by the Trinity
+You are now given Christ's capacity to love and forgive
+You are now filled with the Holy Spirit
+You are now a child of your Heavenly Father
+You are now forgiven all of your sins

Because of these unconditional promises God made to us through baptism, our relationship with God will never be affected by....
X How we feel
X Having doubts
X Rebelling against God

Baptismal Descriptions

In the New Testament we find a variety of explanations to describe God's promise of salvation through baptism:

+**God drowns** our sin (Rom 6, Col 2:12)
+**God restores** our life from heaven (John 3:3)
+**God washes** away our sin (Acts 22:16, Titus 3:4)
+**God adopts** us as his own children (2 Cor 1:21, Eph 1:13)
+**God clothes** us with Christ's forgiveness (Gal 3:27, Col 3:9)
+**God enlightens** us by the Holy Spirit's indwelling (Eph 5:14)
+**God grafts** us to Christ's body and life (John 15, Rom 11:19)

Through baptism, God delivers us from sin, death, and the devil, and gives us all the benefits of his kingdom.

Martin Luther (1483-1546)

Mission of Reconciliation

When we were baptized we were *baptized in the name of the Father, Son, and Holy Spirit*; the name of the Triune God. The Triune God is best understood through their *mission of reconciliation*. All three persons of the Trinity were involved with the creation of the world. Now, each person of the Trinity is involved with an aspect of the mission of reconciliation, to bring wholeness to all those broken areas of the creation. The Trinity is making all things new, so that in the end there will be an all new eternal heaven and earth.

The Father planned for the creation of the world. The Father's greatest priority is for all people in the world to experience harmony with creation and one another.

The Son was sent by the Father into the world to reconcile (reunite) God to the world and all people to God. *God has reconciled us to himself through Christ and has now given us his own mission of reconciliation* (2 Cor 5:18).

The Spirit continues to work within creation to animate reconciliation in every area of life through the life of the baptized. The Spirit calls us through our baptism, gathers us in community, enlightens us with God's mission, and gives us the ability to discern and participate in God's reconciling work in our world.

The Spirit uses the *habits of Jesus* to draw us into God's mission of reconciliation. Congregations exist to encourage disciples to participate in God's mission of reconciliation in the community in which they exist. Congregations are agents of healing and reconciliation in a broken world and share God's love to reveal Jesus Christ to all people. Each congregation will do this differently depending upon their local context. However, God's grand design is to bless the world through Christ's mission of reconciliation.

Even though most congregations have a mission statement, too few have a mission statement which connects them to God's mission of reconciliation in their neighborhood. Congregations have been planted to become active participants in God's mission in the world and are critical in spreading God's reconciling love throughout the world, beginning with the neighborhoods in which they are located. Each congregation is responsible for discovering where and how God's reconciling mission is already present, and needs to discern how they might become more active participants in God's mission of reconciliation for all people. Only when a congregation is engaged with God's mission of reconciliation in the world will they be able to sincerely invite all people to be baptized into God's mission

How does your congregation relate to their neighbors?

 Christianity is the largest and fastest growing religion in the world today!

Write & Share with a Partner...

What are some of the most important insights you discovered in this chapter on Inviting?

....

....

....

....

♪♪♪♪♪♪♪♪♪♪♪♪♪♪♪♪♪♪♪♪♪♪♪♪

I Love to Tell the Story

*I love to tell the story of unseen
things above,
Of Jesus and his glory, of Jesus
and his love.
I love to tell the story because I
know it's true:
It satisfies my longings as nothing
else would do.*

*I love to tell the story, twill be my
theme in glory.
To tell the old, old story or Jesus
and his love.*

Katherine Hankey (1834-1911)

 **We end our session by joining hands in a
circle to pray together the Lord's Prayer.**

284 | Seven Habits of Jesus

Insights for developing my Inviting HABIT:

*How will adding the habit of inviting others to a new life in Christ **help** me live a more Christ-centered life?*

....
....
....
....
....
....
....
....

*How often will I **attempt** to do the habit of inviting others?*

....
....
....
....
....
....
....
....
....
....

How will the habit inviting others to a new life in Christ **become** *part of my life?*

. . . .

. . . .

. . . .

. . . .

. . . .

. . . .

. . . .

How is inviting others **important** *to my maturity as a disciple of Christ?*

. . . .

. . . .

. . . .

. . . .

. . . .

. . . .

. . . .

What is my **timeframe** *to make inviting others to a new life in Christ a habit?*

. . . .

. . . .

. . . .

. . . .

. . . .

THE SEVEN HABITS OF JESUS

1. **REMEMBERING**......our baptismal adoption into God's family

2. **LISTENING**..............to God's law & gospel voice in Scripture

3. **PRAYING**.................for God's help with all of our daily needs

4. **PREPARING**.............to hear God's forgiving voice in worship

5. **RETURNING**........... a percentage of what God has given us

6. **INVITING**....................others to baptism and Christ's mission

7. **CARING**.................. for others and creation with Christ's love

6b. INVITING

Inviting Others to Christ Through Baptism

in·vit·ing (vb)
1. to request one's participation
2. to ask another to be present
3. to welcome one's involvement

Opening Prayer

Lord God, whose strength is sufficient for all who lay hold on it, grant us in you to comfort our hearts and be strong. Humility, meekness, temperance, purity, large-heartedness, sympathy, zeal — grant us these evidences of faith, servants of hope, fruits of love; for the sake of Jesus Christ, our strength, our righteousness, and our hope of glory. Amen.

Christina Georgina Rossetti (1830-1894)

Inviting Goal

Christ has given us, as his disciples, a mission assignment to invite *all people of every nation* to be baptized in the Triune name of God the Father, Son, and Holy Spirit (Matt 28:18). The followers of Jesus have always understood this as Christ's *great commission* to baptize and make disciples. As Christians we are instructed to invite our family, friends, neighbors, colleagues, and casual acquaintances to become children in God's eternal family through baptism.

Write & Share with the Group...
What makes it difficult to invite another
person to be baptized?

....
....

Baptismal Salvation

The Old and New Testaments of the Bible describe salvation as God's work, not ours. Israel was *no people*, a wandering tribe of desert nomads. However, God chose to make Israel his own people. Israel did nothing to earn or deserve God's favor and love. Instead, Israel repeatedly rejected God. Nevertheless, God still loved Israel and repeated his loyalty to her. In the New Testament God expands his favor to all people. God expands his favor to all people through his Son. Through Christ Jesus, all people—including the marginalized—were chosen by God. The Bible does not tell of people who deserve God, but a God who offers himself to undeserving people. **There is no more powerful statement of God's salvation than his free gift of salvation through baptism. No one can do their own baptism. Neither can a person bring anything to their baptism. Baptism is entirely God's work of salvation.** We are who we are because God first *chose* us and *loved* us and *called* us into his eternal family. **The challenge of the church in our time is to take seriously our role of baptizing and making disciples.** When we reflect upon how much effort a congregation can devote to worship, learning, fellowship, and their property in lieu of baptizing all people, it is more than sobering. Truly, baptism is the church's experience and proclamation that we are who we are, solely because God has first chosen us. Our salvation is always a free gift, something that is received from God, working through God's chosen people. Baptism is a public declaration of the promise of God to be our God, to never let us go, and to bring us to our eternal home. After we were baptized, many of us received an oil cross on our foreheads, which can be likened to a *branding* to show that we are owned by God. Luther reflected upon baptism as a sign of God's ownership. God has paid a price for us, marked us, and bought us. Therefore, said Luther, *We can live our lives in quiet confidence because our body and soul no longer belong to us, but to our Savior, Jesus Christ.*

Baptismal Invitation

When someone asked Martin Luther how they might be confident that they are a Christian, Luther replied, *All you need to know is that you are baptized!* A Christian is someone who by *water and the Word* has been given a new life in God's eternal family through the indwelling power of Christ's death and resurrection.

As Tertullian said, *Christians are made, not born.* Christ told his disciples that the way to become a Christian is through baptism (Matt 28:19). Tragically, we have often limited the good news of the gospel of Jesus Christ with our *oughts* and our *ought nots.* Baptism says nothing about what we ought or ought not do. Instead, baptism asserts that we are adopted children in God's family. We are a holy nation. Baptism does not assert, *You can be God's own, if you do this or believe that.* Baptism says, *You are God's own with no doubts about it.* **The saving work of God is not made possible by our feelings, our understanding, our actions, or anything that we do or don't do! Baptism is first and foremost a miraculous act of God!** The story of Pentecost ends with Peter's sermon about what we must do to be saved. He says, *Repent and be baptized every one of you in the name of Jesus Christ for the forgiveness of your sins.*

Peter further explains that the gift of the Holy Spirit, given through baptism, *is for you and your children.*

Baptism is God's work, not ours. Salvation is God's gift, not ours. Grace is a gift, not ours. In baptism, God adopts us, claims us as his chosen heirs; members of his royal family. All this is to say—baptism begins a lifelong relationship with the Triune God. Baptism is an act of God that takes a lifetime to complete. Every day we are invited to live out our baptism. Every day we need to respond to the spiritual power of Christ's death and resurrection within us, which fashions us into *Little Christs*, says Luther.

How does God's gift of salvation make a difference to you?

The Unbaptized

→ Less than 10% of the unbaptized are anti-church or anti-Christian.

→ Less than 10% of the unbaptized have been personally invited by a friend to be baptized.

→ Over 80% of the unbaptized would be likely to discuss being baptized if requested by a good friend.

→ Less than 11% of all Christians have ever invited a friend (non-family member) to be baptized.

→ Over half of the unbaptized have a family connection to the church.

→ Less than 10% of the unbaptized have someone in their circle of friends or relatives who can provide a helpful explanation of the benefits to being baptized.

→ More than 50% of the unchurched and unbaptized are more concerned about having their children baptized, than being baptized themselves.

These percentages are based on research conducted by the Barna Group in the last decade in North America.

All must receive baptism from Christians already baptized, and they in their turn must have received the sacrament from former Christians, themselves already incorporated in a body then previously existing. And thus we trace back a visible body or society even to the very time of the Apostles themselves; So that the very sacrament of baptism, as prescribed by our Lord and his Apostles, implies the existence of one visible association of Christians, and only one; and that permanent, carried on by the succession of Christians from the time of the Apostles to the very end of the world.

John Henry Newman (1801-1890)

Nothing is colder than a Christian who does not care for the salvation of others. Do not say, "It is impossible for me to invite others to the faith," for if you were really a Christian, it would be impossible for you not to do so. As all of nature acts in accordance with its own properties, so in this case too; this is part of the very nature of being a Christian.

John Chrysostom (344-407)

Help for Inviting *(check-mark your responses)*

→ Christians are caring people and often find it difficult to invite someone to be baptized for fear that they might offend them. Before inviting someone, it may be helpful to have a friend evaluate your invitation to determine if it is in any way offensive.

☐ **Very Helpful**   ☐ **Helpful**   ☐ **Not Helpful**

→ Inviting another person to be baptized is a Spirit-led and learned behavior. It is usually necessary for congregations to provide training (usually role playing) on the *how to* aspects of inviting a friend to be baptized.

☐ **Very Helpful**   ☐ **Helpful**   ☐ **Not Helpful**

→ People need practice in talking about their faith in general, and the blessings of baptism in particular. When the name, *Jesus Christ* no longer makes us uncomfortable, it becomes easier to invite a friend to be baptized.

☐ **Very Helpful**   ☐ **Helpful**   ☐ **Not Helpful**

→ An essential factor for inviting another to be baptized is to feel comfortable talking about one's relationship with Christ in their daily life.

☐ **Very Helpful**   ☐ **Helpful**   ☐ **Not Helpful**

→ Role-playing or describing our relationship with Christ to a good friend can be very useful.

☐ **Very Helpful**   ☐ **Helpful**   ☐ **Not Helpful**

→ Our invitation to be baptized is better received when we share our own blessings of living with Christ. It's not necessary for another to understand all the teachings or theology of baptism.

☐ **Very Helpful**   ☐ **Helpful**   ☐ **Not Helpful**

→ We must never understand our invitation as *converting* or even *convincing* the other person to our perspective on Christianity. Our only task is to share the blessings of being baptized and adopted into God's eternal family.

☐ Very Helpful   ☐ Helpful   ☐ Not Helpful

→ We want to avoid trying to explain theological terms like justification. We do not want to associate being baptized into a congregation's membership but rather into God's eternal family. While membership is only temporal, baptism is both temporal and eternal.

☐ Very Helpful   ☐ Helpful   ☐ Not Helpful

→ Evaluating whether someone, in your opinion, has *accepted Christ* or experienced a *conversion* has little to do with inviting a friend to be baptized. Baptism is for all the unbaptized.

☐ Very Helpful   ☐ Helpful   ☐ Not Helpful

→ The New Testament recognizes an *evangelist* as one of the many gifts of the Spirit (Eph 4:11). If inviting another to be baptized is extremely difficult, it may be helpful to have another person with us who is more comfortable with extending an invitation to baptism.

☐ Very Helpful   ☐ Helpful   ☐ Not Helpful

→ Be patient in extending an invitation to baptism with another person until you both feel relaxed around each other.

☐ Very Helpful   ☐ Helpful   ☐ Not Helpful

Believing

Belief is not about believing in something (like Jesus' resurrection) which cannot be proven by facts. Belief is not about my decision, my receiving, my accepting, or anything that I do.

Belief is the inner trust given to us by the Holy Spirit from the testimony of God's Word that enables us to recognize our need for God and enables us to accept a relationship with Jesus as our Savior. Belief is the promise the Holy Spirit plants into our hearts through the proclamation of the Gospel.

Why do you think some Christians view belief as a decision?

Faith Alone

Faith is the inner belief given to us as a gift of the Holy Spirit. *God gives us the gift of faith in order that we might have the ability to believe in Christ Jesus* (Eph 2:8). *No one can say, Jesus Christ is the Lord except by the Spirit's gift of faith* (1 Cor 12:3).

Faith is given through our baptism. *Baptism is referred to as the sacrament of faith* (Mark 16:16), because it reveals to our soul the need for a Savior.

Faith gives us the capacity to cling to God's gift of grace in Christ our Savior. *Faith alone saves because only faith can cling to Christ as our Savior*, said Martin Luther. *We have been made God's children through our faith in Christ Jesus* (Gal 3:26).

How would most people define faith?

Scripture on Believing

I cannot by my own reason or strength believe in Jesus

+*We are born spiritually blind* (1 Cor 2:14)

+*We are born to be enemies of God* (Rom 8:7)

Nor can I come to Him on my own

+*No one can say, 'Jesus is Lord,' except by the Holy Spirit* (1 Cor 12:3)

+*We are unable to initiate a spiritual relationship with God* (1 Cor 2:14)

The Holy Spirit calls me to Jesus

+*We have been introduced to Jesus as our Savior by the Holy Spirit* (Rom 1:16)

+*The Holy Spirit called me to the good news of the Gospel message* (2 Thes 2:14)

The Holy Spirit enlightens me

+*We have been given the saving knowledge of Jesus the Savior* (1 Peter 1:8)

+*God's light shines in our hearts to give us the knowledge of Christ* (2 Cor 4:6)

The Holy Spirit sanctifies me

+*We have entered God's eternal family through the water and Spirit of baptism* (John 3:5)

+*Faith is born in us by the word of God, which is the word of Christ* (Rom 10:17)

The Holy Spirit keeps me in the faith

+*God who gave you salvation can keep you in his family forever* (Phil 1:6)

+*The faith you have received will be protected by God's power until the end* (1 Peter 1:5)

What is your definition of believing?

Write & Share with a Partner...

Review the material for sessions 6a and 6b on *Inviting* and list the *strengths* and *weaknesses* you have when inviting a friend or family member to be baptized.

Describe why baptism is important to you in your daily life:

. . . .

. . . .

. . . .

. . . .

My Inviting Weaknesses:

. . . .

. . . .

. . . .

. . . .

My Inviting Strengths:

. . . .

. . . .

. . . .

. . . .

My plan for inviting that only involves my strengths:

. . . .

. . . .

. . . .

. . . .

Create three multi-faceted questions that could be used to invite a friend to be baptized. Example: *Has anyone ever invited you to be baptized, have you ever thought about being baptized, or how baptism might benefit you?* In general, people find multi-faceted questions less threatening than one direct question. Write down three multi-faceted questions you could use to invite a friend to be baptized:

1)...

....

....

....

....

....

2)...

....

....

....

....

....

3)...

....

....

....

....

....

Baptismal Invitation

Talking about Jesus, even with a best friend, can be difficult. The idea of inviting a friend to be baptized can be even more difficult. The most challenging factor associated with inviting a friend to be baptized, is our common fear of being misunderstood or being rejected. Rejection is our most dreaded fear. We must remember that our friend's decision to accept or reject our invitation is not dependent solely upon us or our friend. Scripture teaches us that we are all baptized as passive recipients. Baptism is an *act of God*; the New Testament makes this clear (2 Cor 5:17, Gal 6:15, Col 2:12, Titus 3:5). Baptism can be compared to being physically born; we have nothing to do with making our birth happen. It is the same with being spiritually born; we have nothing to do with making our spiritual birth happen. There is no need to get stressed out about inviting a friend to be baptized. Either they are going to be baptized or they're not. It's that simple. Most reassuring, if a friend's baptism is meant to be within God's great design, it will happen. If not now, then later.

We are called by God to be faithful to Christ's Great Commission to invite *all people of all nations* **to receive the gift of baptism. We are not called to be effective, since we do not have the ability to persuade anyone to be baptized.** Only God's Spirit, the Holy Spirit, is effective in baptizing those for whom God has *elected to be baptized*. All we need to do is invite others to be baptized and our part is done! That means we have no part in another person's salvation. That's God's job! Remember, God has always used ordinary people.

Do you agree that inviting does not involve rejection?

Roadblocks and Responses

Often a person will initially refuse an invitation to be baptized with a negative *roadblock*. It is always best to respond to a negative roadblock with a positive and constructive response. Most often a roadblock is not intended to be a final *no*. Instead, a roadblock is intended to slow down the process of coming to baptism too quickly. We want to consider how each roadblock is important in helping our friend be baptized. It is important that we consider how each roadblock most likely has a positive meaning.

Common Roadblocks
X I can be a Christian without being baptized
X All churches do is ask for money
X Why are there so many hypocrites in the church?
X Why do bad things happen to good people?
X Where is God when all these bad things happen?
X Going to church never really helped my parents
X Sunday is my only time off; I can't give it up

Constructive Responses
✓ I honestly don't know how to answer that question
✓ Being baptized is about our relationship to God
✓ For me, a real benefit of baptism is that Christ fills our hearts with concern for others
✓ When we are baptized we are given Christ's own capacity to forgive and live in peace with others
✓ Baptism is bigger than the organized church. Baptism adopts into God's eternal family
✓ When Christ lives in our hearts through baptism we are given a new sense of control over our negative and destructive desires
✓ Being a baptized child of God helps us understand the true meaning and purpose of our lives

It might be helpful to put some of these phrases in your own words, and then commit them to memory. You might also want to talk about the benefits of *Remembering* your baptism, and the benefits of the daily renewal of baptism in your own life.

Are you passionate about the benefits of remembering baptism?

Reasons others Consider Baptism

1. Influence of Christian people who witness to:

   Poise in times of stress; being a silent/verbal witness; living with Christ-like values; being a good friend, neighbor, or co-worker.

2. Family relationships and the responsibility of:

   A new parent; a newly married partner; a parent with strong faith; a parent with Christ-like values; a loving and caring family member; a compassionate friend.

3. A relative or close friend in times of crisis:

   In response to loneliness, failure, or rejection; after a marital breakup or the loss of a job; in order to cope with one of life's many transitions.

I wish that everyone would get baptized.

> *But how are they to call on one in whom they have not believed? And how are they to hear without someone to proclaim him? And how are they to proclaim him unless they are sent?*
>   Romans 10:14-15

Listening

It may seem counter-intuitive; however, inviting another person to baptism will involve more listening than inviting. Being able to listen attentively is tremendously important to our invitation. Effective and attentive listening includes responding to *what* is being said and *how* it is being said. Dietrich Bonhoeffer was right in saying that, *listening stands at the center of a Christian's ministry of caring for others.*

Attentive listening involves:
- ✓ Suspending quick criticism of what is being said
- ✓ Never interrupt, rather pause before responding
- ✓ Offering feedback by repeating what was said verbatim, or rephrasing their message in their own words, or sharing with them the actual words or phrase that seemed to be most important to them.

We want to remember that listening attentively will be perceived as one of the most caring and loving acts we can share with another person. Listening attentively brings to life how good it would be for the unbaptized to have Christ's love live within their hearts through baptism.

Why is listening better than telling when we are inviting?

The Four P's

When all is said and done we need to be prayerful, perceptive, patient, and positive when inviting another person to be baptized.

Prayerful: Because God's Holy Spirit brings us to faith and gathers us into Christ's community, we need to regularly pray for the Spirit's work in drawing our friend to the life giving waters of baptism.

Perceptive: Through our listening we want to develop our perception of what is most important to our friend and be able to relate that to baptism.

Patient: Paul teaches us that one of the *fruits* (results) of the Spirit is patience (Gal 5:22). We must be patient with another's strong criticisms of Christianity or of God himself. It is not unrealistic to anticipate that your invitation to baptism might take a year, or longer, to show fruit.

Positive: We must always keep invitations positive. We need to be cautious not to seem overly serious. We must never respond with a negative attack toward any faith traditions. We need to be able to keep our focus on the positive aspects of baptism and a new life with Christ.

Which "P" is your strength and which is your weakness?

Christian Conversion

When a person, for the first time in their life, responds to God's grace as revealed in Christ, there is often a considerable change from a former life-style. We can call this change a *conversion*. How God effects these changes varies. That which was formerly at the edge of awareness and personal concern for one newly baptized, has moved to the center. More and more the new way of life becomes dominant and decisive. This important and life-changing commitment to a new way—a new life-style—is more apt to occur when certain conditions are present. These are:

- Attachment to the central element of a new life-style; **for Christians, that is Christ**
- Participation in a group which illustrates and proclaims the new style as essential for a better way of life; **for the baptized, this new life is being a disciple, a follower of Jesus**
- Engagement in selected activities which will reinforce one's choice of the new way, with sufficient rewards for faithfulness so that the rightness of the new way diminishes the appeal of the former; **this involves one's involvement in Christian community**

Does it make sense to you that conversion can be an adjustment?

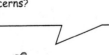

I can tell you about being baptized, but what are your concerns?

Why do people have so many problems with inviting their friends to be baptized, but no problem inviting them out to a favorite restaurant?

Write & Share with a Partner...

What are some of the most important insights you discovered in this chapter on Inviting?

....

....

....

....

♫♫♫♫♫♫♫♫♫♫♫♫♫♫♫♫♫♫♫♫♫♫♫♫♫

I Love to Tell the Story

I love to tell the story
  how pleasant to repeat
What seems, each time I tell it,
  more wonderfully sweet!
I love to tell the story for some
  have never heard
The message of salvation, from
  God's own holy Word.

I love to tell the story, twill be my
  theme in glory.
To tell the old, old story or Jesus
  and his love.

Katherine Hankey (1834-1911)

 We end our session by joining hands in a circle to pray together the Lord's Prayer.

Insights for developing my Inviting HABIT:

*How will adding the habit of inviting others to a new life in Christ **help** me live a more Christ-centered life?*

....

....

....

....

....

....

....

....

*How often will I **attempt** to do the habit of inviting others?*

....

....

....

....

....

....

....

....

....

....

How will the habit inviting others to a new life in Christ **become** *part of my life?*

....

....

....

....

....

....

....

How is inviting others **important** *to my maturity as a disciple of Christ?*

....

....

....

....

....

....

....

What is my **timeframe** *to make inviting others to a new life in Christ a habit?*

....

....

....

....

....

Self-Study for Inviting
Witnessing (6a)

Then Philip began to speak, and starting with Scripture, he proclaimed to him the good news about Jesus (Acts 8:35).

Philip, one of the seven deacons appointed by the first Christian community (Acts 6), provided a model for all faith teachers when he responded to the leading of the Holy Spirit. When Philip encountered the Ethiopian he explained the Scriptures to him. At some point all believers must respond to the promptings of the Spirit to share with a friend the message of salvation from Scripture. With our own faith experiences and knowledge, we will be given many opportunities to share Christ with others.

Explore Scripture:
Acts 1:8; 3:15; 1-:41; 1 Tim 5:19; 6:12; Matt 18:16

What is the most difficult aspect of being a witness of Christ Jesus as the world's Savior?

....

....

....

....

Self-Study for Inviting
Holy Spirit's Invitation (6b)

Come! say the Spirit and the Bride. Whoever hears, echo, Come! Is anyone thirsty? Come! All who will, come and drink, Drink freely of the Water of Life! (Revelation 22:17).

Martin Luther, in his explanation of the third part of the Apostle's Creed, confesses, *I believe that by my own understanding or strength I cannot believe in Jesus Christ my Lord or come to him.* Instead, it is God's own Spirit that *enlightens us, makes us holy, and keeps us in faith.* Luther's full job description of the Holy Spirit is...*The Spirit does it all! The Spirit calls, gathers, enlightens, and makes us holy within the whole Christian Church on earth* (Small Catechism). We can see in our own lives, in our own relationships with God, that from the beginning to the end it is God's love, God's action at work in us!

Explore Scripture:
Acts 1:8; 1 Cor 2:14; 2 Tim 1:9; 1 Peter 2:9

When have you been most aware of the work of the Holy Spirit in your life?

....

....

....

....

Use your answers from the Insights questions in parts A and B to help make **INVITING** *a*

Help

Attempt

Become

Important

Timeframe

How will adding the habit of inviting others to a new life in Christ **help** *me live a more Christ-centered life?*

....

....

....

....

How often will I **attempt** *to do the habit of inviting others?*

....

....

....

....

How will the habit inviting others to a new life in Christ **become** part of my life?

....

....

....

....

How is inviting others **important** to my maturity as a disciple of Christ?

....

....

....

....

What is my **timeframe** to make inviting others to a new life in Christ a habit?

....

....

....

....

THE SEVEN HABITS OF JESUS

1. **REMEMBERING**......our baptismal adoption into God's family
2. **LISTENING**..............to God's law & gospel voice in Scripture
3. **PRAYING**.................for God's help with all of our daily needs
4. **PREPARING**.............to hear God's forgiving voice in worship
5. **RETURNING**........... a percentage of what God has given us
6. **INVITING**...................others to baptism and Christ's mission
7. **CARING**................. for others and creation with Christ's love

7a. CARING

Caring for Family

car·ing (vb)
1. Unselfish concern for others
2. Christ-like love for those in need
3. Paying attention to another's needs

Opening Prayer

Help me to spread your fragrance everywhere I go — let me preach you without preaching, not by words but by my example — by the catching force, sympathetic influence of what I do, the evident fullness of the love my heart bears to you. Amen.

John Henry Newman (1801-1890)

Caring Goal

The true meaning and purpose of our lives is to recognize that God has put us on earth to *love one another as God loves us. Because God is love, the most important lesson he wants us to learn is how to love.* Mother Theresa often said, *It's not so much what we do for others, but how much love is in all that we do.* Why is it so important that Christians lovingly care for one another? Because Christ tells us it is not possible to love God without loving one another. Our love of God is revealed in our capacity to love others, especially those in need of our help.

> ## *Write & Share with the Group...*
>
> *What do you think it means to care for another person?*
>
> ....
>
> ....

*God's love slays what we have been that
we might be what we were not.*

Augustine (354-430)

Caring for Others

Too often when we try to care for another in need we rely upon our own will and determination to be caring. And yet, the New Testament tells us that loving one another, caring for another in need, is not something we can make happen on our own. Our ability to love and care for others is dependent upon the indwelling presence of Christ in our hearts. The apostle Paul is very specific about our ability to care for others.

Our capacity to share loving care comes not from us, but from Christ within us. *Christ's love compels us to love others* (2 Cor 5:14). Jesus and his disciples model for us what it looks like when we are motivated by God's love in

our hearts. Jesus fed the hungry, healed the sick, comforted the sad, befriended the lonely, forgave others, and defended the poor. Jesus even modeled how to love our enemies and do good to those who want to harm us. The love of Christ Jesus in our hearts notices, listens, and cares about the needs of others. As Dietrich Bonhoeffer said in *Life Together*, *Christ's love is something completely strange, new, and quite incomprehensible to those who do not know him.*

Why do you think Jesus made caring a major part of his ministry?

I give you a new commandment, that you love one another. (John 13:38)

All the beautiful sentiments in the world weigh less than a single act of loving care.
James R. Lowell (1819-1891)

God loves the world through you and me.
Mother Teresa (1910-1997)

Whoever wishes to become great among you must be your servant. (Mark 10:43)

The Spirit of the Lord is upon me, to bring good news to the poor. (Luke 4:18)

The Way to Love

In his book, *The Way to Love,* Fr. Anthony DeMello describes the four characteristics of God's love in our souls.

The first quality of love is its inclusiveness

Just as a shade tree gives shade to all in need of shade, even to the one that cuts it down (!), so it is with God's love that lives within our souls.

The second quality of love is its graciousness

Like a flower, or a mother's love for her children, love gives and asks for nothing in return. So it is with God's love that lives within our souls.

The third quality of love is its selflessness

Love enjoys the act of loving and is blissfully unaware of itself. Love is like a rose that gives out its fragrance to others, whether or not it is enjoyed. So it is with God's love that lives within our souls.

The fourth quality of love is its freedom

Love does not allow us to force itself on others. The moment the element of control is attached to love it ceases to be love. Just as a tree cannot force us into its shade, we cannot force God's love upon another. So it is with God's love in our souls.

Why do you agree or disagree with the four characteristics of love?

I think most mice have all four characteristics of God's love in their souls!

Christ's Love Compels Us

Many have recognized Paul's description of love in the thirteenth chapter of 1 Corinthians as one of the most helpful descriptions of how we are to lovingly care for one another. We would be wrong to conclude that Paul is suggesting that we are able, on our own, to love one another in this way. For Paul, it is only when Christ is in our hearts that we are able to genuinely love and care for others in this way. It can be a helpful exercise to insert the words *Christ in me* into Paul's pre-eminent chapter on love.

How do you feel about genuine love requiring Christ's presence?

Christ in me never gives up.
Christ in me cares more for others than myself.
Christ in me doesn't want what it doesn't have.
Christ in me doesn't brag,
  Doesn't have a swelled head,
  Doesn't force himself on others,
  Isn't always me first.
Christ in me doesn't fly off the handle,
  Doesn't keep score of the sins of others,
  Doesn't revel when others grovel.
Christ in me takes pleasure in truth,
Christ in me puts up with anything,
Christ in me trusts God always,
  Always looks for the best,
  Never looks back,
Christ in me keeps going to the end.
(1 Cor 13:1-13)

Called to Care

Jesus extends his ministry of loving care for others through his disciples. The distinctive Christian way of caring for others lies not in *what* we do, but in *why* we do it. Christ-like caregiving recognizes that *we love and care because Christ Jesus first loved and cared for us* (1 John 4:19). Christ Jesus' love for us is the reason we care for others. As a Christ-like caregiver:

> +We realize that we are an extension of Jesus' ministry of loving care for others.
> +We are given Christ's own attitude of humility instead of a sense of superiority.
> +We are able to care for others in difficult situations, confident that Christ's presence is with us.
> +We trust in Christ's presence and power to directly help those in need.

Do most Christians realize that Christ motivates their caring?

I think we Christians are very loving & kind.

Christ compels us to love and care for others.

Christian Caregiving Principles

GOD GIFTS US WITH AN ABILITY
God gifts us with an ability to care for others. Throughout our lives the Lord presents us with opportunities to help others in ways that match our ability to help.

Your Example:.......................................

...

CARING FOR OTHERS IS RARELY EASY
Often those with the greatest need of our help are not able to accept our help. Those who accept our help may not be pleased with the way in which we have helped them.

Your Example:.......................................

...

HELPING OTHERS IS PRIVATE
Christ-like loving care does not call attention to itself. Most often, important acts of caring and kindness remain a private matter. Overt recognition is not a part of Christian caregiving.

Your Example:.......................................

...

CHRIST'S LOVE EMPOWERS OUR CARE
Christ's love, which he has planted in our hearts, reaches out to touch the hearts of those we are helping. The transforming power of Christ's love flows through our Christ-like caring and kindness.

Your Example:.......................................

...

Jesus' Habit of Caring

Jesus' habits of remembering, listening, praying, preparing, returning, and inviting all culminate in Jesus' habit of caring. The habit of caring is dependent upon the other six habits, because collectively those six habits give us the capacity of Christ to participate in Jesus' habit of caring. Jesus modeled for us how to live a God-pleasing life of humble caregiving through our families, daily work, and within the world. The loving care we are able to share with others reveals that it is Christ's own love which animates our love for others. The love of Christ is the right motivation for all caring, as described in 1 John 4:19: *We love because he first loved us.* The unique distinction of Christian caregiving lies not in what we do, but in why we do it. The loving care we share with others, does more than we could ever imagine, because Christ has made us a channel of his own love. The habit of caring invites us to become an active participant in Christ's mission of love and reconciliation in the world. **The seven habits of Jesus do not turn us inward, but outward to the world; to the whole of God's creation.** Christ's mission can be summed up in the Great Command: *Love the Lord with all your heart, soul, and mind. Just as you love your neighbor as yourself* (Matt 22:36-40).

Pastor Dietrich Bonhoeffer, who died in a Nazi concentration camp in April 1945, has this to say in his book *The Cost of Discipleship: When Christ calls us, he first invites us to share in his death on the cross. Christ's call is to die to ourselves.* Jesus taught his disciples that only when we deny our own self-centered desires can we die to ourselves. **Too often, Christians falsely believe that being a disciple of Christ Jesus means being a little more religious. However, to be a disciple means dying to our old nature of self-centeredness, and rising with Christ to live a life of loving care of others.**

How do you picture the need to die and rise with Christ?

Three Spheres of Caring

<u>First Sphere</u>: Caring for Family
Means of caring: Listening & forgiving through forgiving love

<u>Second Sphere</u>: Caring for Society
Means of caring: Using God-given talents through service

<u>Third Sphere</u>: Caring for Creation
Means of caring: Christ's reconciliation through stewardship

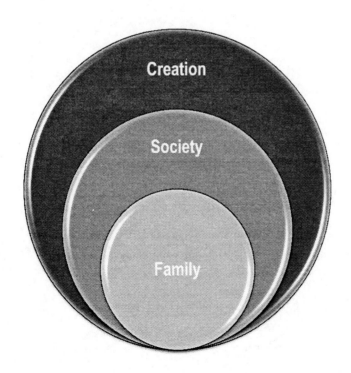

First Sphere of Caring: Family
Means: Listening & Forgiving

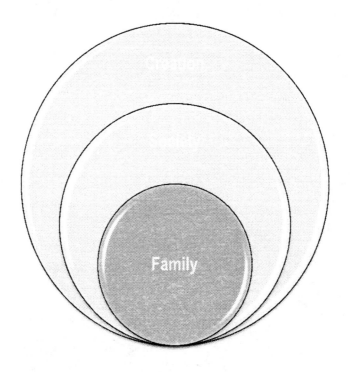

The teachings of Jesus stressed the heart and inner motivation rather than outward behavior. The life of love is hidden, and although it is known by its fruits, there is no act of love about which we might unconditionally dare to say: He who does this proves without a doubt that he loves.

Soren Kierkegaard (1813-1855)

Family & Friends

According to the Bible, the first institution God established was the family. A primary function of the family is to teach us how to give love, receive love, and be forgiving. The old saying is true: *Charity begins at home.* Within our families we learn how to love one another by listening, helping, and forgiving. Our Christian claim is that only Jesus Christ can give us the capacity to love one another as we learn how to listen and forgive each other when it is needed.

We live in a time of social disintegration. Too many people are discovering that their closest relationships with family and friends lack true love and genuine caring. Today, people in our society find it increasingly difficult to relate to one another, or even experience forgiveness within the intimacy of marriage. Mother Theresa, who devoted her life to caring for the poorest of the poor in India, shares this perspective on the lack of love and caring in our society. She said, *People today are hungry for love. There are too many who are lonely and live in despair. Too few have ever learned how to love and forgive in their families of origin.*

What is your experience of learning to give and receive love?

Listening

One of the most important and yet much neglected qualities of Christ-like caregiving is to become good listeners. The apostle James is clear about the importance of being a good listener: *Dear friends, lead with your ears, not your tongue, always be slow to speak. This is the righteous life God desires of us* (James 1:19). Poor listening skills often show that we are unable to listen to God as he speaks to us through Scripture. When we listen to one another, our goal is to listen to what is being said and what is behind what is being said.

In his classic book, *Life Together*, Dietrich Bonhoeffer explains the great importance of listening to one another: **The first way to help one in Christian fellowship is to simply listen to them. Just as our love of God begins with listening to his Word, so the beginning of love for**

another begins by listening to them. Christians too often think that they must contribute advice or encouragement while downplaying and minimalizing the importance of listening.

How is giving advice to someone different from listening?

Listening Basics

- **Be yourself. Be sure to suspend judgment and try to be aware of another's point of view.**
- Use a relaxed but attentive posture.
- Convey a sense of understanding by maintaining good eye contact and speaking in a comforting tone of voice.
- Accept that listening is not about giving advice, analyzing, or correcting, even when it may be needed.
- A variety of federal statutes and the *Volunteer Protection Act* keep all volunteer listeners safe from legal liability.

Which is most helpful for you?

Most mice are quiet, and very good listeners.

Listening with Love

- Be aware of non-verbal content of what a person is sharing: such as their tone of voice, posture, facial expression, and their eyes.
- Try to suspend your own immediate thoughts and feelings about how another ought to think, feel, or act.
- Resist jumping to your own conclusions about what needs to happen for another to be healthy. Take time.
- Remember that *silence can be golden* and it is not necessary to respond to everything that is said.
- Do not interrupt or change the subject. When a person takes a short pause it does not mean they have finished talking. Always be patient. Remain calm.
- It is not desirable, to respond to everything that is shared. There is no need to always share our thoughts.
- Caring communication is 95% listening and 5% talking.
- Encourage others to talk by asking for more information.
- Most often asking for a *yes* or *no* stifles the further expression of feelings. Also, avoid the *why* questions because they are often taken as criticisms.
- For those with a preference for extroversion, there is no other way to say it, just keep your mouth closed!
- Listen with curiosity and fascination, even when you hear ideas with which you may not personally agree.
- Listen for how certain words are connected to their strongest beliefs.

Which is most helpful for you?

Listening Feedback

- Periodically it can be helpful to paraphrase or offer a brief summary of what has been shared.
- It's helpful to ask questions in clarifying what is or is not being said, but it must be done tactfully.
- Help divide problems into small achievable steps when the person is ready to engage in problem-solving.
- Do not interrupt, lecture, or tell of your own experiences. Never suggest a quick fix for another's problems.
- Use open-ended *who, what, when, where,* and *how* type questions to encourage sharing in greater detail.
- Do not offer unrealistic assurances or avoid problems.
- As the listener, ask yourself: *How does he feel about himself? What defense mechanisms is she using? Are her values being expressed?*
- Also ask: *Do you want to solve the problem or do you want to learn how to live with it?*

Which is most helpful for you?

In general, I think mice are better at listening than people.

Our love ought to follow the love of God in always seeking to produce reconciliation. It was to this end that God sent his Son. Has anybody offended you? Seek reconciliation. "Oh, but I am the offended party." So was God, and he went and sought reconciliation. "Oh, but I have been insulted." Just so: so was God; all the wrong was towards him, yet he sent. "Oh, but the party is so unworthy." So are you; but "God loved you and sent His Son." I do not mean that this love is to come out of your own heart, but that it is to flow out of your heart because God has made it to flow into it. Make reconciliation, not only between yourself and your friend, but between everyone and God. Let that be your object. Christ has become our reconciliation, and we are to allow this reconciliation near to every person in need that comes our way. Your work and mine is reconciliation, and everything that tends that way.

Charles Spurgeon (1834-1892)

Forgiving

Within the first sphere of the family, we learn how to provide ongoing care by forgiving one another. Forgiveness makes it possible to strengthen our relationships. Forgiveness is an essential prerequisite if we are to begin and sustain the loving relationships within our families. Forgiving one another after a relationship conflict may be one of Jesus' most neglected teachings (Matt 18:15), however it is certainly one of his most important teachings if we are to maintain loving relationships with our family and others.

Who first talked to you about forgiveness?

Forgiveness is God's invention for coming to terms with a world in which people are unfair to each other and hurt each other deeply. God began by forgiving us. And he invites us all to forgive each other.

Lewis B. Smedes (1921-2002)

Forgiveness Is Not...

- **Forgiveness is not about making excuses for what another person did to hurt or offend us.**
- **Forgiveness is not about forgetting, although that is what many people think.** If a person keeps repeating the same behavior it is probable not to forget. We need to model after God, who forgives us even though he cannot forget the past.

Forgiveness Is...

- **Giving up the need to get even or punish another person who has hurt us. We give up our sinful fight or flight instincts in order to allow for Jesus' loving forgiveness to flow into our broken relationship.**
- **Receiving Holy Communion is a means to exchange our *fight* or *flight* instincts for the healing power for forgiveness. The forgiveness we receive for our sins of *commission* (the wrong we did), as well as the forgiveness for our sins of *omission* (the good we did not do) occurs when we cling to God's promise that, *If we confess our sins...God will forgive us* (1Jn 1:9).**
- **Allowing God to reveal to us his loving relationship with the one we desire to forgive.**
- **Being able to wish the other person, with whom we are at odds, peace and goodwill.**

- Accepting the Christ-like capacity of forgiveness we have received through our reception of God's gift of Holy Communion, even for some of the most horrible transgressions.
- Welcoming Christ's own capacity to forgive another who has hurt us. *God has reconciled us to himself through his Son, and now invites us to reconcile our broken relationships with each other* (2 Cor 5:18).
- Holding *in prayer* the name of one who has hurt us and for whom we desire to reflect the healing power of Christ's forgiveness.
- Receiving the *real presence* of Christ, his true body and blood, his own supernatural power and ability to accept another in love, even after a divisive argument or disagreement.

Unforgiving

When we don't forgive…

× We obsessively dwell on past hurts with bitterness
× We become more judgmental of others
× Our relationship will die a slow death
× Our anger spreads to other relationships
× Our physical health and wellness is weakened

Write & Share with a Partner…

Recall a time when Christ helped you to forgive?

....

....

....

....

Peter asked, Master how many times do I forgive a friend who has hurt me? Seven times? Jesus replied, Hardly! Try seventy times seven!

Matthew 18:22

My dear Lord Jesus Christ, increase in me your grace to love my neighbor with all my heart as I do myself. You have given us the command to forgive and the promise to help us.

Martin Luther (1483-1546)

How we Forgive

In the closing passages of *The Hiding Place*, evangelist Corrie Ten Boom tells a story that helps us understand how we are able to forgive others, even in extreme situations: After World War II and her release from a Nazi concentration camp, Corrie Ten Boom lectured and preached on the need to forgive our enemies. The struggle to forgive was brought home to her with stunning force after one of her guest preachings when Corrie was greeted by a man whom she recognized as the Nazi guard in the shower room at her concentration camp. *How grateful I am for your message*, he said. *To think that, as you say, the Lord has washed all my sins away!* Corrie then recalls: *Suddenly, his hand thrust out to shake mine. And I, who had preached so often the need to forgive, kept my hand at my side. As all of the angry and vengeful thoughts were boiling through me, I saw my sin. Lord Jesus, I prayed, forgive me and help me to forgive him. I felt nothing, not the slightest spark of charity. And so again I breathed a silent prayer.*

Jesus I cannot forgive him; give me your forgiveness. As I took his hand, a most incredible thing happened. From my shoulder along my arm and through my hand a current seemed to pass from me to him, while into my heart sprang a love that almost overwhelmed me. And so I discovered that it is not on our forgiveness any more than on our goodness that the world's healing hinges, but on his. When Jesus tells us to forgive our enemies, he gives to each of us along with the command, the love we need to forgive!

How has Christ helped you in being forgiving?

> God has reconciled his relationships with us through his Son, and now invites us to reconcile our relationships with each other. God uses us to persuade people to drop their differences and use reconciliation to make things right in their relationships. (2 Cor 5:18-19)

Forgiven to Forgive

Forgiveness is God's means of purification. When God forgives us he is purifying, cleansing, and removing our sinful desire to *fight* with, or to *flight* from, another person with whom we are at odds. Scripture teaches: *If we admit to God our part and are remorseful over a broken relationship, he will heal us. God will forgive our sins and purge us from our need for revenge* (1 John 1:9). Our ability to be forgiving is totally dependent upon the free gift of forgiveness God gives us. The most important way that we

receive God's forgiving love is through our participation in his gift of Holy Communion. The Eucharistic meal gives us Christ's own capacity to love and to forgive others even when it is not natural for us. Through our reception of the *real presence of Christ in, with, and under bread and wine*, we receive Christ's own power to forgive and love another person. When we receive God's forgiveness, he empowers us with his own gifts of *love, peace, and joy*. With God's forgiveness we no longer have a need to *get even* or to pretend a friend no longer exists. Christ's *real presence* transforms our revenge and condemnation into a desire to wish another well. We all need to regularly reflect upon our ability to access God's forgiving love, which we receive through Holy Communion. Our lives are changed as we grow in our dependency upon God's free gift of forgiveness.

What do you think of forgiveness as a means of purification?

On the Lord's Day, when you have been gathered together, break bread and celebrate the Eucharist. But first confess your sins so that your offering may be pure. If anyone has a quarrel with a neighbor, that person should not join you until the quarrel has been reconciled. Your sacrifice must not be defiled. In this regard, the Lord has said: "In every place and time offer me a pure sacrifice. I am a great king, says the Lord, and my name is great among the nations.

Didache (2nd century)

God always gives us the strength to forgive!

The World's Way of Resolving Relationship Conflicts

FIGHT	FLIGHT
Responding to a relationship conflict with an angry attack, until one person backs down and the other one "*wins.*"	Physically or emotionally denying a relationship conflict with the intent that it will "*go away.*"

Do you fight or flight more often?

Christ's Way of Resolving Relationship Conflicts

LOVE
Responding to a relationship conflict with Christ's own capacity to relate to one another with love and forgiveness.

How difficult is it for you to respond to conflict with forgiveness?

Resolving Relationship Conflicts

Jesus' important teaching, in the eighteenth chapter of Matthew's Gospel (Matt 18:15), is a constructive way for us to experience forgiveness in our relationship conflicts with family and friends. Jesus' teaching can dramatically and positively affect our relationships. Although this may be one of Jesus' most neglected teachings, it is certainly one of his most important teachings for our daily lives. Untold pain and misery are experienced when we have unresolved conflicts with family and friends.

What do you think motivates you to heal a broken relationship?

A.B.C.'s of Matthew 18:15

A. When you become upset with another person, go directly to them for a private face to face meeting, to experience forgiveness in a broken relationship.

Do not call them on the phone, email them, or post it on a social media site! Do not tell anyone else about your upset, except the person who has upset you. Contact them to set up a face to face meeting.

Before you meet them, it is helpful to put down on paper your feelings and your irrational thoughts. Before meeting with them, work through any irrational thoughts that might be negatively impacting upon the relationship. Some negative and destructive thoughts might be:

x *They should have known better.*
x *I am not good in relationships.*
x *That's just unforgivable.*
x *Women/men are impossible.*
x *That was too cruel to forgive.*
x *A relationship gone badly is over.*
x *Forgiveness does not really work.*

B. **Before a face to face meeting to resolve a relationship conflict with another person, ask for God's help.**

Through the reconciling power of Holy Communion, ask God to give you Christ's own forgiving love before you meet a person with whom you are at odds.

At a face to face meeting, share with one another how each of you experienced hurt, upset, anger, or frustration, by the disagreement which occurred. Instead of saying, *You made me upset,* we want to say...*I was upset.*

C. **The goal of conflict resolution is for two people to experience reconciliation and peace.**

The goal is not to decide who is *right* and who is *wrong*. The goal is to restore the relationship after a divisive conflict. We need to remember that no matter how difficult a face to face reconciliation might be for us, it is what Christ desires. And we can be comforted knowing Christ will be present to give us his capacity to forgive. Our goal is to restore the relationship to its fullest potential. The success of a face to face meeting most often depends upon two important factors:

1. Each person is able to confess their part in the conflict, without blaming the other person.
2. Each person has brought the other person to God in prayer while receiving Christ's reconciling power of Holy Communion.

True reconciliation is not easy, and is rarely quick. It may take several face to face meetings. We always need to remember that no matter how difficult it may become, reconciliation is what Christ desires for our broken relationships because it is the only way to truly restore a broken relationship.

Do you expect to be able to restore most broken relationships?

It is perhaps not so hard to forgive a single great injury. But to forgive the incessant provocations of daily life — to keep on forgiving the bossy father-in-law, the bullying husband, the nagging wife, the selfish daughter, the deceitful son — how can we do it? Only, I think, by remembering where we stand, by meaning our words when we say in our prayers each night "forgive us our trespasses as we forgive those that trespass against us." We are offered forgiveness on no other terms. To refuse it is to refuse God's mercy for ourselves. There is no hint of exceptions and God means what he says.

C.S. Lewis (1898-1963)

Prayer has always enhanced my ability to love and forgive!

Praying, Listening, and Forgiving

God intends prayer to be a resource that enhances our listening and forgiving. And yet, prayer remains one of the most neglected and most difficult resources to use appropriately. Many Christians are uncertain about how to pray spontaneously. However, God makes it clear: *For where two or three are gathered in my name, I am there with them* (Matt 18:20). God promises to understand our needs and he desires to help us. Prayer should be a natural part of our listening and our forgiving. To initiate a spontaneous prayer we might say something like: *Maybe it would be good if we shared these concerns with God in prayer* or, *We have both decided on some specific goals, would you like to pray about them to ask for God's help?*

Although most of our prayers that are prayed within the context of forgiveness and reconciliation will likely be a spontaneous-style prayer, we might also choose to use a prayer book. Also, the Lord's Prayer is always appropriate for any situation, and can be prayed by itself or with other prayers.

Have you tried asking for God's help when needing to forgive?

If you are distressed by anything external, the pain is not due to the thing itself, but to your estimate of it; and this you have the power to revoke at any moment.

Marcus Antonius (83-30 B.C)

Reconciliation refers to doing away with enmity and bringing together parties who were formerly hostile to each other... Christ has entrusted us with a ministry of reconciliation, (2Corinthians 5:18-21), and thus the church must be ultimately concerned about matters of justice and peace...The church must always remember God's truth, peace and justice as revealed by the cross of Christ are intended not only for the church and believers, but also for the entire world...Like its Lord, the church must do works of love and mercy and seek justice for everyone, whatever the cost... We must be compassionate in order to see and hear the cry of the oppressed and the downtrodden and must identify with just and righteous causes.

Yusufu Turaki (b.1957)

The true Christian is like sandalwood, which imparts its fragrance to the axe which cuts it down, without doing any harm in return.

Sadhu Sundar Singh (1889-1929)

There are often bound to us, in the closest intimacy of social or family ties, natures hard and ungenial, with whom sympathy seems to be impossible, and whose continued daily presence necessitates a constant conflict with an adverse influence. There are, too, enemies, - open or secret, - whose enmity we may feel yet cannot define. Our Lord, going before us in this hard way, showed us how we should walk. It will be appropriate to the solemn self-examination of the period of Lent to ask ourselves, Is there any false friend or covert enemy whom we must learn to tolerate, to forbear with, to pity and forgive? Can we in silent offices of love wash their (our enemies) feet as our master washed the feet of Judas? And, if we have no real enemies, are there any bound to us in the relations of life whose habits and ways are annoying and distasteful to us? Can we bear with them in love? Can we avoid harsh judgments, and harsh speech, and the making known to others our annoyance? The examination will probably teach us to feel the infinite distance between us and our divine Ideal, and change censoriousness of others into prayer for ourselves.

Jean Ingelow (1820-1897)

Write & Share with a Partner...

What are some of the most important insights you discovered in Sphere One: Caring for family?

. . . .

. . . .

. . . .

. . . .

♪♪♪♪♪♪♪♪♪♪♪♪♪♪♪♪♪♪♪♪♪♪♪♪♪♪♪♪♪♪

Jesu, Jesu, Fill us with your Love

Jesu, Jesu, fill us with your
Love, show us how to serve
The neighbors we have from you.

Kneels at the feet of his friends.
Silently washes their feet,
Master who acts as a slave to them.
Jesu, Jesu, fill…

Neighbors are wealthy and poor,
Varied in color and race,
Neighbors are near-by and far away.
Jesu, Jesu, fill…

These are the ones we will serve,
These are the ones we will love,
All these are neighbors to us and you.
Jesu, Jesu, fill…

Kneel at the feet of our friends,
Silently washing their feet,
This is the way we will live with you.
Jesu, Jesu, fill…

Tom Colvin (1925-2000)

 We end our session by joining hands in a circle to pray together the Lord's Prayer.

342 | Seven Habits of Jesus

Insights for developing my Caring HABIT:

*How will adding the habit of caring for my family **help** me live a more Christ-centered life?*

. . . .

. . . .

. . . .

. . . .

. . . .

. . . .

. . . .

. . . .

*How often will I **attempt** to do the habit of caring for family?*

. . . .

. . . .

. . . .

. . . .

. . . .

. . . .

. . . .

. . . .

. . . .

*How will the habit of caring for family **become** part of my life?*

....

....

....

....

....

....

....

*How is caring for family **important** to my maturity as a disciple of Christ?*

....

....

....

....

....

....

....

*What is my **timeframe** to make caring for family a habit?*

....

....

....

....

....

....

Self-Study for Caring
Love (7a)

Do not use your freedom as an opportunity for the flesh, but through love be servants of one another (Gal 5:13).

Christian holiness is love, just as the lack of love is the lack of holiness. The nature of pure love is beyond us, because it is of God only. When Christ fills our hearts we are able to be humble and give our lives to God. Sin is remembering oneself and forgetting others. All sins are, to a greater or lesser degree, a renunciation of love. Instead of giving ourselves to those in need, we can so often be absorbed with ourselves. Love defeats pride, destroys selfishness, and leads us to God. True holiness and true love are one in the same.

Explore Scripture:
John 13:34-35; John 15:12-13; 1 John 3:14-18; Rom 13:9-10

What are examples of selfishness in your life?
What are examples of love in your life?

Listening to my family has always helped me to care for their needs!

I ask for God's help when I need to forgive!

Use your answers from the Insights questions to help

make **CARING** *a*
Sphere One: Family

Help

Attempt

Become

Important

Timeframe

---

*How will adding the habit of caring for my family **help** me live a more Christ-centered life?*

....

....

....

....

---

*How often will I **attempt** to do the habit of caring for family?*

....

....

....

....

How will the habit of caring for family **become** part of my life?

....

....

....

....

How is caring for family **important** to my maturity as a disciple of Christ?

....

....

....

....

What is my **timeframe** to make caring for family a habit?

....

....

....

....

> *Second Sphere of Caring: Society*
> *Means: God-given Talents*

7b. CARING

Caring for Society

car·ing (vb)
>   1. Unselfish concern for others
>   2. Christ-like love for those in need
>   3. Paying attention to another's needs

Opening Prayer

O God---when I have food, help me to remember the hungry; When I have work, help me to remember the jobless; When I have a warm home, help me to remember the homeless; When I am without pain, help me to remember those who suffer; And remembering, help me to destroy my complacency and stir up my compassion. Make me concerned enough to help. Amen.

Anonymous

Caring Goal

The true meaning and purpose of our lives is to recognize that God has put us on earth to *love one another as God has loved us. Because God is love, the most important lesson he wants us to learn is how to love. It is in loving that we are most like God.* Mother Theresa often said, *It's not so much what we do for others, but how much love is in all that we do.* Why is it so important that Christians lovingly care for one another? Because Christ tells us it is not possible to love God without loving one another. Our love of God is revealed in our capacity to love others, especially those in need of our help.

> # *Write & Share with the Group...*
> *Is the workplace a good location for caregiving?*
>
> ....
> ....

Caring through Work

The work place is the second sphere in which we are called to be caregivers. **In the book of Genesis, God describes himself as a diligent and conscientious worker. God continues to labor in our world as the Sustainer of all life.** Therefore, when we work we reflect the very image and character of God. Our daily work is important because God uses the fruit of our labor (vocation) to benefit both our family and society. As a model of the life we are to live as workers, Jesus spent nearly his entire life working as a carpenter. *The true meaning and purpose of our lives can only be discovered through our concern for others* (Rom 12:5). As Martin Luther said, *We are not saved by our service to others, but have been saved for service to others.*

We work to help others, not out of duty, but out of gratitude for Christ saving us. We were not given life on earth only to take from life, but also to give back to life. All who have been given life by God have an important part to play in contributing Christ's mission in our world. To know this truth about our lives is what gives true meaning to the work God has provided for us to do.

How do you perceive yourself as a co-laborer with God?

There came to me, as I awoke, the thought that I could not accept this happiness as a matter of course, but must give up something in return for it. I settled with myself that I would consider myself justified in living until I was thirty for science and art, in order to devote myself from that time onward to the direct service of humanity.

Albert Schweitzer (1875-1965)

Made to Work

At the time of our birth, God gave each of us a unique talent. God gives us this unique talent to perform a certain type of work that supports God's design for the well-being of society. God has designed us, and gifted us, with the ability to make our world a better place. God did not make us to take **from** life, but to give something back **to** life. Jesus told his disciples, *Only when you give your life away to help others will you be able to have life as it was intended to be* (Mark 8:35). *The way of Christ resists selfish ambition and considers the needs of others* (Phil 2:3). As a model of the type of lives we are to live as *workers*, Jesus spent nearly his entire life using his earthly talent by working as a carpenter. God has gifted us all with a special and unique blend of talents, skills, and opportunities so that our lives might make a positive impact upon society.

In Genesis, work is to be a means through which basic needs might be met, as human beings *till and keep* the garden in which God has placed them (Gen 2:15). Work is seen not as an end in itself, but as a means for sustaining humans and the rest of creation. Due to sin, the work God gives to humans also becomes toil and anguish (Gen 3:17).

Injustice often deprives people of the fruits of their work (Prov 13:23), which benefits others instead.

God calls us to use our freedom and responsibility, our capacities, and know-how to participate productively in his world. As stewards of what God has entrusted to us, we should use our available resources to generate jobs for the livelihood of more people. To a limited extent, our wealth should benefit others so that they also might live productive lives.

Unfortunately, what matters for many in jobs today are the wants or desires of one's earning potential, instead of a sense of *vocation* or *calling* to make society a better place. Often, for too many, work becomes a means toward increased consumerism. We are freed from such economic captivity by the new life and dignity that is ours in Christ.

What does it mean to you that God gives everyone a unique talent?

I am not told that I am to like my neighbor; I am ordered to love him or her. Luther's explanation of our relation to the neighbor brings us close to a right understanding. Our neighbors in the biblical sense, are those persons who live in God's creation with us in the solidarity of our life together on this earth. Though I cannot will myself to feel an oceanic affection for all people, I can acknowledge my bond with the whole creation. In that bond I am to recognize the authenticity, the thereness, the concrete life and existence of the other. In the broad context of human solidarity the exercise of love is realized in transaffectional justice.

Joseph Sittler (1904-1987)

Luther on Work

Martin Luther created a revolutionary new attitude about how the work that we do for our daily life is given to us as a vocational calling or assignment by God himself to make society a better place. Dr. Max Weber, a world renowned sociologist, documented how Luther's idea of vocation, and calling to a particular type of work, enabled ordinary Christians for the first time in history to see significance in their daily work. Weber was able to show how Luther's teachings about work, as a calling by God, unleashed one of history's greatest periods of economic activity and energized the economies of the Western nations.

How can you best share your vocational talents with others?

An important part of life is working together for the good of society.

Gifted with a Talent

A talent is an ability, or an aptitude, to do something well. The Bible tells us that our talent has been given to us by God so we will be able to care for others through the work that we do. At the time of our birth, God gave each of us a talent (skill or ability) so we might be able to make society a better place, in a way that fits in with God's grand design for a *new heaven and new earth* (Rev 21). By identifying and understanding our unique God-given talent, we can discover how best to contribute to the well-being of our society.

How does God use your work to care for others?

> *God gives to all people certain talents and abilities to serve society through their daily work. Whether we are Christian or not, all who serve society through their daily work are serving God. God compels even the godless people of this world to serve one another to restrain the powers of evil which would otherwise destroy creation. Only the Christian is aware that their daily work is a vocational calling from God. While the daily work of a Christian can appear to have nothing to do with God, one recognizes that the whole creation is God's workshop.*
>
> Taito Kantonen (1900-1993)

Discovering Our Talent

Every society throughout the ages has had a way to help young adults identify their God-given inborn talents. In recent years society has turned to a variety of psychosocial indicators, or talent inventories, to assist our young adults in identifying their God-given talents. One of the most reliable, accurate, helpful, and popular inventories was developed by Dr. Carl Jung. Just after the Second World War, Jung's talent inventory was further refined into a tool called the **Myers-Briggs Type Indicator (MBTI)** by two American researchers, Myers and Briggs. The MBTI indicator asks a series of questions to reveal how we process information. The MBTI identifies the following four hidden mental procedures we go through when we process information:

1. How we <u>energize</u> ourselves to make decisions
2. How we <u>gather</u> information to decide
3. How we <u>process</u> facts toward a decision
4. How we <u>execute</u> our decision into actions

Preferred Preferences

Our four mental preferences (energize, gather, process, and execute) describe the four ways that we process information. These four mental preferences describe our *preference type* according to the MBTI Type Indicator. Our preference type is determined by the way we process information within each of the four functions. For the function of: 1.)**Energize**, we can be energized as either an Extrovert (**E**) or as an Introvert (**I**). For the function of: 2.)**Gather**, we can gather with either Sensing (**S**), or with iNtuition (**N**). For the function of: 3.)**Process**, we process by either Thinking (**T**) or Feeling (**F**). Finally, for the mental function of 4.)**Executing**, we act by either Judging (**J**), or through Perceiving (**P**).

Four Preferred Functions

(E) Extroversion	1. Energize	Introversion (I)
Energized from the outside world	How we are energized to decide	Energized from the inside world

(S) Sensing	2. Gather	INtuition (N)
Gather info by the facts	Info to make a decision	Gather info by the big picture

(T) Thinking	3. Process	Feeling (F)
Evaluate the logical results	Arriving at a decision	Guided by personal values

(J) Judging	4. Execute	Perceiving (P)
Acting in a planned way	How one acts out a decision	Acting in a flexible way

There are four questions we can answer in order to determine how we use our four preferred preferences.

1. Am I energized as an Extrovert or Introvert?
2. Do I gather information as a Sensor or Intuitive?
3. Do I process information with Thinking or Feeling?
4. Do I act out my decisions with Judging or Perceiving?

I never knew anything about this personality stuff!

Talent Indicator

There are a variety of talent indicators available in use. However, the MBTI is one of the most reliable and trusted of all the indicators in use today. Many mental health professionals are qualified to administer the MBTI. If this general description of the MBTI is helpful, it would be advisable to learn about your MBTI type from a qualified licensed professional. You can learn more from the Center for the Association of Personality Type website.

The purpose of a preference indicator is to determine which of the four preferences, out of the eight preferences, is preferred. Each mental function has two preferences, but one is preferred most of the time. For instance, we are primarily energized by and prefer either (E) extroversion or (I) introversion. To gather information we will prefer (S) sensing or (N) intuition. To process information we will generally prefer (T) thinking or (F) feeling. And, to act on the information we have processed, we will prefer (J) judging or (P) perceiving.

How would knowing your type preferences make a difference?

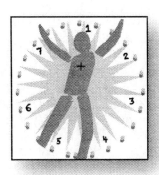

TALENT INDICATOR
Discovering Your Preferred Preferences Code

Directions: On each of the next four pages, the two opposite preferences for each of the four mental operations will be contrasted through the use of General Descriptions and a Checklist.

<u>FIRST</u> – **Read the *general descriptions* for each mental function.** For example, a description for Extraverts (E) and a description for Introverts (I) are presented. **As you read through each description, underline those key words that best describe you.**

<u>SECOND</u> – **Look over the contrasting *lists* for Extraverts (E) and for Introverts (I).** You do not need to give it too much thought, just your first impression is adequate. Use your first impression to check mark either the Extravert (E) box or the Introverts (I) box. **Then, at the bottom, total the check marks for Extraverts (E) and those for Introverts (I).**

<u>THIRD</u> – **Review the words you underlined in the descriptions for Extroverts (E) and for Introverts (I). Determine which words have more *weight*, and best describe your preferred mental operation. Then, review the two check-list totals. Using both the descriptions and the checklist, choose at the bottom of the page either: Extraverts (E) or Introverts (I).**

Note: If you are not able to clearly identify your preferred preference for either (E) or (I), you may find it helpful to repeat this process at another time. You may also find it helpful to share your results with a trusted friend who knows you well. The greatest obstacle in knowing our preferred preference, is wanting to have a preferred preference code that we think we *should* have, instead of accepting the preferred preference code and talent we have been given by God. Remember, all preferred preferences are God-given and therefore good!

HOW WE **ARE ENERGIZED** TO PROCESS INFORMATION EITHER AS AN:
EXTRAVERT (E) OR AN INTROVERT (I).

Underline those words that best describe you in each of the following descriptions:

DESCRIPTION OF EXTRAVERTS (E)

Extraverts (E) enjoy action, interaction, and activity. They are energized by people and the world around them. They like to share their thoughts and feelings with others, receive feedback, and then modify their ideas based on those interactions. Usually, they act first and then reflect on their actions. They are often friendly, talkative, and easy to know. They express their emotions rather easily. Extraverts can seem superficial to Introverts, mostly because they act before they reflect. Extraverts use both Extraversion (E) and Introversion (I) to get energized, but most of the time they prefer Extraversion (E).

DESCRIPTION OF INTROVERTS (I)

Introverts (I) enjoy quiet reflection and are energized by their inner world of thoughts and ideas. They draw energy by being alone and reflecting. Introverts tend to prefer situations where they can work alone or one-on-one. They prefer to process their thoughts and feelings silently, sharing them only when they are well processed. Introverts feel stressed out by too many activities. Introverts can seem overly serious to Extraverts, mostly because they always reflect before they act. They can be reserved, quiet and difficult to know. They need a lot of private time and may seem withdrawn to Extraverts. Introverts (I) use both Introversion (I) and Extraversion (E) to get energized, but most of the time they prefer Introversion (I).

Look over the following lists that contrast Extraverts (E) and Introverts (I).
Check the box ☑ that best describes your preference.

Extraverts (E)			Introverts (I)
Doing a lot	☐	*or* ☐	Reflecting a lot
Drawn to activities	☐	*or* ☐	Drawn to quiet time
Uses many words	☐	*or* ☐	Uses few words
Likes to talk	☐	*or* ☐	Likes to be quiet
More sociable	☐	*or* ☐	More reflective
Say what you think	☐	*or* ☐	Ponder thoughts
Outer energy	☐	*or* ☐	Inner energy
Live it first	☐	*or* ☐	Understand it first
More aggressive	☐	*or* ☐	More passive
Breadth of knowledge	☐	*or* ☐	Depth of knowledge
Extraverts (E)	☐	☐	**Introverts (I)**

Total Number of checks

After reading the descriptions and reviewing the lists, most of the time, my preference for **being energized** is done as an:
(check one)

(E) Extravert ☐   ☐ Introvert (I)

360 | Seven Habits of Jesus

HOW WE **GATHER INFORMATION** TO THINK OCCURS AS EITHER A: **SENSOR (S)** OR **INTUITIVE(N).**

Underline those words that best describe you in each of the following descriptions:

DESCRIPTION OF SENSORS (S)

Sensors (S) pay close attention to the information they gather through their five senses (sight, sound, feel, taste, smell). Facts, sounds, textures, and details make up their world. They are good at identifying the reality of a situation based upon factual data. Sensors like to look at the specific parts and pieces of any situation. They live mostly in the present moment, enjoying what is there. They prefer handling practical matters. Sensors like to work hands-on and usually take one step at a time toward their goals. They like set procedures and established routines. They may seem materialistic and literal-minded to Intuitives. Sensors (S) use both Sensing (S) and Intuition (N) to gather information, but most of the time they prefer Sensing (S).

DESCRIPTION OF INTUITIVES (N)

Intuitives (N) pay close attention, not to the way it is, but to the way it could be. They gather information with their hunches, insights, and their creative ideas. Instead of relying upon their five human senses, they rely on a sixth sense, called intuition. Intuitives like situations that allow for new developments and discovering the possibilities. They look at patterns and connections in life as a way of imagining what the future might be. They are not so systematic and do not care for routines. Change, variety, dreaming, innovation, are words they like. Intuitives (N) use both Sensing (S) and Intuition (N) to gather information, but most of the time they prefer Intuition (N).

Look over the following lists that contrast Sensing (S) and Intuition (N).
Put a check in the box ☑ that best describes your preference.

Sensors (S)			Intuitives (N)
Practical, common sense	☐	*or* ☐	Innovative, insight
Concrete, accuracy	☐	*or* ☐	Abstract, creative
Routine approach	☐	*or* ☐	Novel approach
Current reality	☐	*or* ☐	Future possibilities
Real world	☐	*or* ☐	Future world
Seen	☐	*or* ☐	Unseen
Five Senses	☐	*or* ☐	Sixth sense
Routine directions	☐	*or* ☐	Innovative hunches
Enjoyment	☐	*or* ☐	Anticipation
Conserve	☐	*or* ☐	Change
Sensors (E)	☐	☐	**Intuitives (I)**

Total Number of checks

After reading the descriptions and reviewing the lists, most of the time, my preference for **gathering information** is done as a:
(check one)

(S) Sensor ☐   ☐ Intuitive (N)

HOW WE **PROCESS** THE INFORMATION GAHERED EITHER AS A:
THINKER (T) OR **FEELER (F)**

Underline those words that best describe you in each of the following descriptions:

DESCRIPTION FOR THINKERS (T)

Thinkers (T) like to be in settings that rely on logic, consistency, and fairness, when decisions are made. They do not like to proceed in any situation until they have had plenty of time to analyze it. Thinkers are more interested in the task at hand than they are about relationships. Thinkers take pride in academic degrees and job titles. They decide with their heads instead of their hearts. They can quickly find flaws and be critical. They may seem cold and aloof to Feeling types. Thinkers (T) use both Thinking (T) and Feeling (F) to process information, but most of the time they prefer Thinking (T).

DESCRIPTION FOR FEELERS (F)

Feelers (F) use a set of values to process information. Most of these values are strongly held beliefs that Feelers have about their relationships with others. At work, those with a Feeling preference often consider their relationship with colleagues as important as the work they do. They decide with their hearts instead of their heads. They are very concerned for harmony with others. They can quickly find the good of a situation, overlooking the problems. Feelers (F) are good at empathizing and understanding the problems of their family and friends. Feelers (F) use both Thinking (T) and Feeling (F) to process information, but most of the time they prefer Feeling (F).

Look over the following lists that contrast Thinker (T) and Feelers (F).
Put a check in the box ☑ that best describes your preference.

Thinkers (T)			**Feelers (F)**
Head	☐	*or* ☐	Heart
Usually objective	☐	*or* ☐	Usually subjective
Logical	☐	*or* ☐	Compassionate
Firm principles	☐	*or* ☐	Personal values
Business first	☐	*or* ☐	Friendship first
Find the flaw	☐	*or* ☐	Find the positive
Impartial	☐	*or* ☐	Partial
Works with facts	☐	*or* ☐	Works with people
Explains	☐	*or* ☐	Understands
Aloof	☐	*or* ☐	Personable

Thinkers (T) ☐ ☐ **Feelers (F)**

Total Number of checks

After reading the descriptions and reviewing the lists, most of the time, my preference for **processing information** is done as a:
(check one)

(T) Thinker ☐   ☐ Feeler (F)

> HOW WE **EXECUTE** THE INFORMATION PROCESSED EITHER AS A:
> **JUDGER (J)** OR **PERCEIVER (P)**

Underline those words that best describe you in each of the following descriptions:

DESCRIPTION OF JUDGERS (J)

Judgers (J) like to plan their work and work their plan. They believe that if you fail to plan, you have already planned to fail. Those with a preference for Judging (J) are attracted to places of work and leisure that are well ordered. They tend to believe that work should come first – only then are they free to play. A Judging (J) lifestyle is decisive, planned, and orderly. This preference functions best with clear limits and categories. They handle deadlines and plan well in advance. Judgers (J) use both Judging (J) and Perceiving (P) to execute or act out the information they have processed, but most of the time they prefer Judging (J). (Note: Judging (J) does not mean being judgmental, but wanting to come to closure on things.)

DESCRIPTION OF PERCEIVERS (P)

Perceivers (P) find that planning can get in the way of living life to the fullest. Those with a Perceiving preference tend to be open and spontaneous as they adapt to what comes their way. They like to be a part of situations that call for plenty of flexibility. Perceivers want their play to be a part of their work – they try to make both life and work more fun. They enjoy jobs that allow for plenty of adventure. They do best at jobs that call for them to respond to emergencies. Perceivers (P) use both Judging (J) and Perceiving (P) to execute or act out the information they have processed, but most of the time they prefer Perceiving (P). (Note: Perceiving (P) does not mean being perceptive, but enjoying plenty of options.)

Look over the following lists that contrast Judging (J) and Perceiving (P).
Put a check in the box ☑ that best describes your preference.

Judgers (J)				**Perceivers (P)**
Organized, efficient	☐	*or*	☐	Flexible, unplanned
Decisive, deadlines	☐	*or*	☐	Discoveries, curious
On time	☐	*or*	☐	On a roll
Systematic order	☐	*or*	☐	Spontaneous options
Establishes closure	☐	*or*	☐	Maintains openness
Clear limits	☐	*or*	☐	Freedom to explore
Following the plan	☐	*or*	☐	Going with the flow
Scheduled	☐	*or*	☐	Unplanned
Urgent	☐	*or*	☐	Lots of time
Work then play	☐	*or*	☐	Work with play

Judgers (J) ☐   ☐ **Perceivers (P)**

Total Number of checks

> After reading the descriptions and reviewing the lists, most of the time, my preference in **living out** my life of service is through:
> (check one)
>
> (J) Judger ☐   ☐ Perceiver (P)

Identifying Your Preferred Preference Code

All people have been given all eight preferences (E/I, S/N, T/F, J/P). However, God has uniquely created each of us with four preferred preferences which can be described by a four letter preferred preference code.

Each of the preference letters of each four letter code always appear in the same order –

Extraversion or Introversion	Sensing or iNtuition	Thinking or Feeling	Judging or Perceiving

Based upon the: * Written descriptions of each preference.
               * The score of your four check lists.

Your **Preferred Preference Code** is:

E/I	S/N	T/F	J/P

(Circle one letter in each box.)

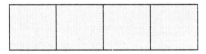

(Write your Code above.)

Write & Share with a Partner...

How well does your four letter code describe you?

....

....

....

....

Knowing each of our types and preferences will really help us to get along and work together!

ON THE FOLLOWING SIXTEEN PAGES, FIND YOUR PREFERRED PREFERENCE CODE. USE THIS INFORMATION TO DISCOVER HOW BEST TO USE YOUR GOD-GIVEN, INBORN TALENT TO BE A CHRIST-LIKE SERVANT AT YOUR DAILY WORK.

ISTJ

"Dependable managers of facts" "Doing what should be done"

GENERAL CHARACTERISTICS... Serious, quiet, earns success by concentration and thoroughness. Practical, orderly, matter-of-fact, logical, realistic, and dependable. Sees to it that everything is well organized. Takes responsibility. Makes up their own minds as to what should be accomplished and works toward it steadily, regardless of protest or distractions. Most responsible of all the types.

ISTJ WORK TITLE - "THE INSPECTOR"... Responsible and trustworthy, will see the job through to the end, a "no-nonsense" person, task oriented.

AT WORK, THE ISTJ NEEDS... Organization and structure in which to work. Projects to complete and tasks to accomplish. Opportunities to organize and preserve data or materials. An understanding of their role.

FRUSTRATED AT WORK BY... Unrealistic and emotional situations. Wasted time and broken rules. Permissiveness and a lack of respect for the system.

"Hold them in the highest regard in love because of their work"
(1Thessalonians 5:13).

SPIRITUAL STRENGTHS: Being the upholders of the faith traditions. Within the Christian community, they are dependable and hard working. They build upon their past spiritual experiences and can make steady growth in their maturity in Christ.

SPIRITUAL WEAKNESSES: Being so focused on work that they can easily forget they are "saved by grace." Becoming too legalistic about the Christian lifestyle. Dwelling on their need for self-improvement. Not very patient or understanding of different types.

SPIRITUAL HELPS: Needs time alone with God each day. Structured Bible study that allows for a "special message" from God. Reading about real life experiences of God' grace in action. Religious objects or symbols that represent God's grace, his underserved love.

ISTP

"Reserved practical analyzers" "Ready to try anything once"

GENERAL CHARACTERISTICS... Cool onlookers – quiet, reserved, observing and analyzing life with detached curiosity and unexpected flashes of original humor. Usually interested in cause and effect, how and why mechanical things work, and in organizing facts using logical principles. Excels at getting to the core of a practical problem and finding the solution. Most pragmatic of all the types.

ISTP WORK TITLE - *"THE OPERATOR"*...Cool observer of life, interested in impersonal principles, the how and why of things, does not waste personal energy.

AT WORK, THE ISTP NEEDS... Variety, skills and techniques to master. Challenge of problems to solve and something to fix. Freedom to work independently. A sense of bringing about something new and important.

FRUSTRATED AT WORK BY... Restrictions, emotional situations. Being told how to work. Anything slow. Social requirements.

"But whoever lives by truth comes into the light so that it may be plainly seen that what he has done has been done through God" (John 3:21).

SPIRITUAL STRENGTHS: Always contributing quietly behind the scenes. Can draw upon a storehouse of facts that interests them in the Bible or Church history. Within Christian community, they find the best ways to get a project completed without complications or conflict.

SPIRITUAL WEAKNESSES: Often neglects prayer time. Often finds worship to be too awkward and illogical. Not so concerned about the needs of others in their daily lives. Reduces life and faith to a logical formula. Can isolate themselves from spiritual community.

SPIRITUAL HELPS: Regular disciplined study of the Bible and spontaneous prayer afterward. Benefits from a spiritual mentor or director. Reading theological or doctrinal material about faith. Experiencing the presence of God in daily life, especially within the natural world.

ESTP

"Promoters of practical change" "Adaptable ultimate realist"

GENERAL CHARACTERISTICS...*Good at on-the-spot problem solving. Likes action, enjoys whatever comes along. Tends to like mechanical things and sports, with friends on the side. Adaptable, tolerant, pragmatic; focused on getting results. Dislikes long explanations. Are best with real things that can be worked, handled, taken apart, or put together. Most spontaneous of all the types.*

ESTP WORK TITLE - *"THE PROMOTER"*...An adaptable realist, makes the most of every situation, highly observant, fun loving.

AT WORK, THE ESTP NEEDS... Challenge and excitement. They love to put out fires and to rally the troops. Lots of action and adventure. Don't tell them, they love to be asked.

FRUSTRATED AT WORK BY... Restrictions. Being told how to do their work. Complex theory. Long explanations. Orders and demands. Too much structure.

"Therefore, everyone who hears my words and puts them into practice is like a wise man who built his house on the rock" (Matthew 7:24).

SPIRITUAL STRENGTHS: Reminds others of the "present moment" and the joys of life. They lovingly pay attention to what needs fixing. Within Christian community, they add a "spark" to whatever they are doing; their enthusiasm is contagious.

SPIRITUAL WEAKNESSES: Difficult to always take things on faith. Skeptical about some things as "spiritual," with an overemphasis on "real" life. Regular experiences of dry periods of faith. Lacks commitment to a faith community. Spends too much time in activities without much reflective time.

SPIRITUAL HELPS: In-depth Bible study with a focus on the practical applications of the faith. Quiet time, especially in nature for rest and meditation. Needs opportunities for spontaneous prayer and a group with which to share the faith. Needs to be open to dramatic answers to personal prayers, sometimes in the form of the paranormal.

ESTJ

"Realistic practical organizers" "Society's natural administrators"

GENERAL CHARACTERISTICS... Practical, realistic, matter-of-fact, with a natural head for business or mechanics. Not interested in abstract theories; wants learning to have direct and immediate application. Likes to organize and run activities. Often make good administrators; are decisive, quickly loves to implement decisions; takes care of routine details. Most spontaneous of all the types. Most hard-charging of all the types.

ESTJ WORK TITLE - *"THE SUPERVISOR"*...Practical and realistic, a natural in business, gets things done, has no time to waste.

AT WORK, THE ESTJ NEEDS... Predictability and order. Standards and measurements for success. Tell them what needs to be done and they'll make it happen.

FRUSTRATED AT WORK BY...A lack of realism. Missed deadlines. Broken rules and wasted time. Emotional responses.

> *"Be diligent in these matters; give yourself wholly to them"*
> *(1 Timothy 4:15).*

SPIRITUAL STRENGTHS: Models consistency in their use of the spiritual disciplines/practices. Uses their own experiences to build upon and grow. Within Christian community, they challenge others with the reality of the situation and can suggest an efficient plan of attack.

SPIRITUAL WEAKNESSES: Many and regular thoughts of doubt. Living the faith in too much of a "religious" and routine manner. Becoming too focused on rules. More concerned with the structure of a congregation than relationships. Strictly traditional with little room for change. Doubting the relevance of an experience of the Holy Spirit.

SPIRITUAL HELPS: Needs a daily routine of traditional devotion and prayers. Needs quiet times alone to practice spontaneous prayer from the heart. Could benefit from a prayer group. Can develop empathy for others through a service project that directly helps people in need. Connect Bible study to personal values.

ISFJ

"Sympathetic manager of details" "A high sense of duty"

GENERAL CHARACTERISTICS... Quiet, friendly, responsible, and conscientious. Works devotedly to meet their obligations. Lends stability to any project or group. Thorough, painstaking, and accurate. Their interests are usually not technical. Can be patient with necessary details. Loyal, considerate, perceptive. Concerned with how other people feel. Most loyal of all the types.

ISFJ WORK TITLE - "THE PROTECTOR"...A loyal and devoted worker, sympathetic listener, dependable person, a real team player.

AT WORK, THE ISFJ NEEDS... An orderly work environment with human interaction. Opportunities to respond to the needs of others. Harmonious relationships. Praise and appreciation.

FRUSTRATED AT WORK BY... Criticism and injustice. Having to stop in the middle of a project. Too much complexity and cold, impersonal logic.

"Pursue righteousness, Godliness, faith, love, endurance, gentleness"
(1Timothy 6:1).

SPIRITUAL STRENGTHS: Provides stability to any group. Models a sensible and practical way to live out the spiritual disciplines/practices. Humble and quiet in their caring for others. Within Christian community, they add a sense of dignity and respect.

SPIRITUAL WEAKNESSES: Being so conscientious that they neglect their own spiritual needs. Too concerned what others think of them. False sense of humility, not taking credit for a job well done. Not open to theological thinking, spontaneous prayer with others, or shared planning for a project.

SPIRITUAL HELPS: Needs a spiritual director to help plan for personal practices of spiritual growth. Structured daily Bible study and contemplative prayer. Being alone in nature to "sense" God's presence. Devote less time to service and more time to mystical experiences of the faith. Read and reflect upon theological subjects of the faith.

ISFP

"Loyal modest helpers" "See much, shares little"

GENERAL CHARACTERISTICS...*Retiring, quietly friendly, sensitive, kind, and modest about their abilities. Shuns disagreements, does not force their opinions or values on others. Usually does not care to lead, but are often loyal followers. Often relaxed about getting things done because they enjoy the present moment and do not want to spoil it by undue haste or exertion. Most artistic of all the types.*

ISFP WORK TITLE - *"THE COMPOSER"*...Modest about abilities, a loyal follower, guided by values, a free spirit.

AT WORK, THE ISFP NEEDS...Challenge and variation. Opportunity to act on their values. Freedom to incorporate and internalize music, rhythm, color, and texture into their life.

FRUSTRATED AT WORK BY...Restrictions. Being told how to do work. Limitations and time constraints. Social functions and being forced to conform.

> *"Truly I tell you, just as you did it to one of the least of these who are members of my family, you did it to me" (Matthew 25:40).*

SPIRITUAL STRENGTHS: Provides loving, gentle and behind-the-scenes help. Can easily experience God in the natural world. Can be very charitable. Within Christian community, they offer immediate one-on-one help to people in need.

SPIRITUAL WEAKNESSES: Too modest to accept recognition that is due. Not assertive with others. Does not have a regular schedule of Scripture study or prayer. Difficulty following through on a project or their own spiritual development. Avoids theological analysis and reason. Avoids working under pressure or meeting deadlines.

SPIRITUAL HELPS: Needs role models for their spiritual journey. Meditating on God in nature. Joining a Bible study/prayer group to schedule spiritual growth. Use a daily prayer journal. Expecting to experience God's presence in daily life, sometimes in a dramatic way. Benefits from singing in the choir.

ESFP

"Realistic relational adapters" "Do it while you can"

GENERAL CHARACTERISTICS...*Outgoing, accepting, friendly, enjoying everything and making things more fun for others by their enjoyment. Likes action and making things happen. Knows what is going on and joins in eagerly. Finds remembering facts easier than mastering theories. Are best in situations that need sound common sense and practical ability with people. Most generous of all the types.*

ESFP WORK TITLE - *"THE PERFORMER"*...A hands-on operator, a natural negotiator, life of the party, lots of fun, exciting company.

AT WORK, THE ESFP NEEDS... Challenge, excitement, and the opportunity to be a hero. Respect for their skills, talents, and approach to problems and needs of the organization. Positive feedback and recognition.

FRUSTRATED AT WORK BY... Restrictions. Being told how to work. Anything slow. Not being allowed to operate and contribute. Injustice and cruelty.

"A cheerful heart is good medicine" (Proverbs 17:22).

SPIRITUAL STRENGTHS: Preservers of the faith from one generation to the next. Focused on warm, caring, service to others. They make others feel welcomed in their home and at church. Within Christian community, they know what are the most important priorities for the whole group.

SPIRITUAL WEAKNESSES: Neglecting to make time for a relationship to God. Not thinking about their future spiritual maturity. Being too generous with others while neglecting their own needs. Not wanting to act alone. Not very organized and difficulty in working on a project through to completion.

SPIRITUAL HELPS: Benefits from group Bible study/prayer. Needs specific experiences of God in daily life. Prefers to pray spontaneously as they go through the day. Needs to pray alone more often. Encouraged by sacred pictures, fasting, incense, lighting candles. Helpful to regularly mediate on the passion of Christ.

ESFJ
"Practical popular harmonizers" "Caring hospitality experts"

GENERAL CHARACTERISTICS...*Warm-hearted, talkative, popular, conscientious, born cooperators, active committee members. Needs harmony and may be good at creating it. Always doing something nice for someone. Works best with encouragement and praise. Main interest is in things that directly and visibly affect people's lives. Most harmonizing of all the types.*

ESFJ WORK TITLE - *"THE PROVIDER"*...Active committee member, sociable, strong value systems, always doing something nice for others.

AT WORK, THE ESFJ NEEDS... Harmony, encouragement, praise, and emotional support. A structured work environment with many opportunities to work with people.

FRUSTRATED AT WORK BY... Criticism and a lack of appreciation for peoples' needs. Complex theory and abstract thought. Impersonal decisions. The challenging and breaking of established rules.

> *"For I am not seeking my own good, but the good of many, so that they may be saved"* (1Corinthians 10:33).

SPIRITUAL STRENGTHS: Provides an emphasis on service and caring for others as the primary witness of the faith. They make people feel welcomed, loved, and valued in a variety of settings. Within Christian community, keeps the genuine needs of people front and center.

SPIRITUAL WEAKNESSES: Denying problems with others until they "explode." Being a "caretaker" and a "doormat" for those they love. Ignoring their own needs for spiritual growth. Can be too pessimistic about the Kingdom. Finds it difficult to be alone with God.

SPIRITUAL HELPS: Individual and group Bible study that identifies a connection to daily life. Participate in regular Christian fellowship events. Prayerfully grow in praying to God as a friend. Use a spiritual journal. Regularly schedule time to meditate. Work at evangelism and outreach.

INFJ

"People-oriented innovators" "An inspiration to others"

GENERAL CHARACTERISTICS... *Succeeds by perseverance, originality, and desire to do whatever is needed or wanted. Puts their best efforts into their work. Quietly forceful, conscientious, concerned for others. Respected for their firm principles. Likely to be honored and followed for their clear visions as to how best serve the common good. Most contemplative of all the types.*

INFJ WORK TITLE - "THE FORESEER"... Concerned for others, serves the common good, puts their best efforts into work, single-minded concentration.

AT WORK, THE INFJ NEEDS... Support for ideas and opportunity to put them into practice. Variety and freedom from dull routine. Recognition and appreciation for their unique contribution. A cause to work for.

FRUSTRATED AT WORK BY... Being told how to do things. Not being listened to. Lack of feedback and impersonal attitudes. Criticism and confrontations.

> *"Therefore, encourage one another and build each other up, just as you are doing"* (1Thessalonians 5:11).

SPIRITUAL STRENGTHS: Understanding the feelings and the motivations of others. Can make helping others enjoyable for all involved. Have a high sense of integrity and follow-through. Within Christian community, they can be visionaries and are good at long-range planning.

SPIRITUAL WEAKNESSES: Finds it difficult to ask for other's help. Reluctant in sharing ideas or talents. Not assertive in relationships. Not so interested in the activities of other people. Can be too judgmental of others. Tends toward perfectionism and idealism. Difficulty enjoying life.

SPIRITUAL HELPS: Journal writing. Find a spiritual mentor who will encourage action. Meditative prayer could be practical twice a day. Use imagination to make the Scriptures come alive. Very open to the voice of God in Bible study. Regularly experience God's love as a new insight.

INFP

"Imaginative quiet helpers" "Noble service to others"

GENERAL CHARACTERISTICS...*Quiet observers, idealistic, loyal. Important that outer life be congruent with inner values. Curious, quick to see possibilities, often serves as catalyst to implement ideas. Adaptable, flexible, and accepting unless a value is threatened. Wants to understand people and ways of fulfilling human potential. Little concern with possessions or surroundings. Most idealistic of all the types*

INFP WORK TITLE - *"THE ADVOCATE"*...A peacekeeper, undertakes a great deal, absorbed in creative projects, deeply caring, idea oriented.

AT WORK, THE INFP NEEDS... To handle significant projects from start to finish. Support for ideas. Encouragement and respect for their unique contribution. Freedom from structure and rules.

FRUSTRATED AT WORK BY... Their own inner standards of perfection. Routine and inconsequential details. Conflict and unpleasantness. A lack of purpose.

> *"Do not conform any longer to the pattern of this world, but be transformed by the renewing of your mind"* (Romans 12:2).

SPIRITUAL STRENGTHS: Brings a caring and personal focus to wherever they are serving. Adds harmony and unity to any group. Reminds others of their ideals. Within Christian community, they provide a positive and optimistic vision of the future together, and the benefit of working toward that vision.

SPIRITUAL WEAKNESSES: Difficulty accepting "constructive criticism." Can't get enough affirmation or support from those they love. Not assertive or skilled in facing conflicts. Comes across to others as too idealistic and impractical. Consumed with their own ideas. Disorganized, avoids a routine for Bible study and prayer.

SPIRITUAL HELPS: Journal writing. Find a spiritual mentor who will encourage actions. Meditative prayer could be practiced twice a day. Use imagination to make the Scriptures come alive. Very open to the voice of God in Bible study. Regularly experiences God's love as a new insight.

ENFP

"Enthusiastic planners of change" "Giving life an extra squeeze"

GENERAL CHARACTERISTICS...*Warmly enthusiastic, high-spirited, ingenious, imaginative. Able to do almost anything that interests them. Quick with a solution for any difficulty and ready to help anybody with a problem. Often rely on their ability to improvise instead of preparing in advance. Can usually find compelling reasons for whatever they want. Most optimistic of all the types.*

ENFP WORK TITLE - *"THE CATALYST"*...Charming and interesting, people oriented, knows everyone and everything going on, able to do almost anything they want.

AT WORK, THE ENFP NEEDS... Acceptance and appreciation for their unique contribution and creativity. Recognition for achievements and a lot of encouragement. They need harmony and care.

FRUSTRATED AT WORK BY... Criticism and cold logic. Impersonal attitudes and doing things by the book. Lack of positive feedback and dull routine.

"Whatever is true, whatever is noble, whatever is right, whatever is pure, whatever is lovely, whatever is admirable – if anything is excellent or praiseworthy – think about such things" (Philippians 4:8).

SPIRITUAL STRENGTHS: Offers warmth and enthusiasm to others. Adds zest to group endeavors. Shares resources and personal belongings with others. Within Christian community, they promote the value of relationships and the need to nurture them.

SPIRITUAL WEAKNESSES: Neglects personal, physical, and emotional needs. Learns just enough about a subject to be "dangerous" or to just get by. Being attracted to the newest and latest fad, but failing to bring closure to where they are at. Lacks self-discipline. Avoids alone time, meditative prayer.

SPIRITUAL HELPS: Needs structure and routine if they are to grow spiritually. Schedule spiritual disciplines/practices. Make time each day to pray alone. A prayer partner can be helpful. Fellowship with a small group of like minds. Get out into the world of nature. Join the choir; be active in worship.

ENFJ

"Enthusiastic visionary" "Passionate and persuasive leader"

GENERAL CHARACTERISTICS..._Responsive and responsible. Feels real concern for what others think or want, and tries to handle things with due regard for other's feelings. Can present a proposal or lead a group discussion with ease and tact. Sociable, popular, sympathetic. Responsive to praise and criticism. Likes to facilitate others and enable people to achieve their potential. Most persuasive of all the types._

ENFJ WORK TITLE - *"THE MENTOR"*...Popular and sociable, charismatic charm, a natural communicator, warmly enthusiastic.

AT WORK, THE ENFJ NEEDS... Opportunities to lead people, especially through face-to-face interaction with others. Harmony and support for ideas. Recognition, appreciation, and a cause or leader to work for.

FRUSTRATED AT WORK BY... Cold, impersonal logic. Overly task-oriented jobs. Being left out. A lack of feedback. Criticism and a lack of appreciation.

"For I know the plans I have for you' says the Lord, 'plans to prosper you and not to harm you, plans to give you hope and a future" (Jer 29:11).

SPIRITUAL STRENGTHS: Supports with warmth and much encouragement. Believes in the positive potential of all people. Others look up to them because of their values and integrity. Within Christian community, they invite others to live up to their ideals and potentials.

SPIRITUAL WEAKNESSES: Becomes too invested in the failure or success of an endeavor. Assumes their way is the most noble. Avoids conflict for harmony. Takes the "weight of the world" on their shoulders. Avoids expressing negative feelings with others, even with God. Ignores the details and facts of a project. Daily, too planned, structured, and organized.

SPIRITUAL HELPS: Needs quiet time with God to discern his will. Benefits from good experiences of Christian community and worship. Prayer groups are helpful. Needs to trust the sudden ideas that pop into their minds as the "voice" of God. Study the lives of leaders in the Bible/Church. Regularly retreat from leadership responsibilities.

INTJ

"Logical innovators" "Always room for improvement."

GENERAL CHARACTERISTICS... *Have original minds and great drive for their own ideas and purposes. Have long-range vision and quickly find meaningful patterns in external events. In fields that appeal to them, they have a fine power to organize a job and carry it through. Skeptical, critical, independent, determined, have high standards of competence and performance. Most independent of all the types.*

INTJ WORK TITLE - *"THE STRATEGIST"*...Interested and innovative, single-minded concentration, unimpressed with authority, a high achiever

AT WORK, THE INTJ NEEDS... Support for ideas and projects. Freedom from routine and mundane details. Problems to work on and solve. To see ideas worked out and applied.

FRUSTRATED AT WORK BY... Routine, redundancy, being sidetracked by others' needs and opinions. Being told what to do or how to do things.

"I devoted myself to study and to explore by wisdom all that is done under heaven" (Ecclesiastes 1:13).

SPIRITUAL STRENGTHS: Provides the systems and organizational framework to create a better world. They change the way other people view things. Designs and adjusts structures for the future. Within Christian community, they break new ground and act independently from outmoded ways.

SPIRITUAL WEAKNESSES: Reluctant to share their "real self" with others. Needing answers to everything. Not feeling as competent as they would like. Expecting others to see the future as they do. Being lost in thoughts, not paying attention to others or the situation. Can be too aloof and arrogant. Too few friends. Unable to enjoy life with others.

SPIRITUAL HELPS: A spiritual guide is needed in helping with relationship issues. Needs long periods of theological Scripture study and meditative prayer. Silent retreats are helpful. Keeping a spiritual journal of thoughts. Contemplation to emotionally experience God's presence in their heart. Needs plenty of service to others and leisure time with loved ones.

INTP

"Inquisitive reserved analyzers" "A love for problem-solving"

GENERAL CHARACTERISTICS...*Quiet and reserved. Especially enjoys theoretical or scientific pursuits. Likes solving problems with logic and analysis. Interested mainly in ideas, with little liking for parties or small talk. Tends to have sharply defined interests. Needs careers where some strong interest can be used and useful. Most conceptual of all the types.*

INTP WORK TITLE - *"THE DEFINER"*...Lives in a world of ideas, skilled with hair-splitting logic, strongly defined interests, enjoys theoretical and scientific subjects.

AT WORK, THE INTP NEEDS...Freedom to work independently. Opportunities to design, problems to solve. Variety and support for ideas. Positive feedback, recognition and a reason for what they are doing.

FRUSTRATED AT WORK BY...Being told what to do and how to do it. Unintelligent demands. Routine and redundancy. Overly emotional responses.

"And this is my prayer: That your life may abound more and more in knowledge and depth of insight" (Philippians 1:9).

SPIRITUAL STRENGTHS: Searches for the logic in all things spiritual. Able to formulate an action plan for a long-term goal. Keeps the faith from becoming too sentimental. Within Christian community, they provide a clear, theological understanding to the faith.

SPIRITUAL WEAKNESSES: Gets too wrapped up in skepticism. Regularly tries to intellectualize the faith, ignoring the heart. Ignores the needs of others until it becomes a serious problem. Minimizing the needs of loved ones. Not realizing how they are negatively affecting others. Difficulty in stopping to "smell the roses." Does not express feelings.

SPIRITUAL HELPS: Needs intellectually demanding Bible study. Regularly scheduled times for verbal prayer from the heart and silent meditation. Benefits from a spiritual director that keeps them accountable to their loved ones and the regular use of certain spiritual disciplines. Needs to express emotions in their relationships and their prayers.

ENTP

"Analytical planners of change" "Always an exciting challenge"

GENERAL CHARACTERISTICS... *Quick, ingenious, good at many things. Stimulating company, alert and outspoken. May argue for fun on either side of a question. Resourceful in solving new and challenging problems, but may neglect routine assignments. Apt to turn to one new interest after another. Skillful in finding logical reasons for what they want. Most inventive of all the types.*

ENTP WORK TITLE - "THE INVENTOR"... Stimulating company, alert and outspoken, argues on both sides of an issue, confident of abilities.

AT WORK, THE ENTP NEEDS...A working environment where they can go from one project to another, solving major problems and leaving details to others. Recognition and support for ideas.

FRUSTRATED AT WORK BY... Dull routine, boring details, emotional responses to rational issues. Redundancy and restrictions. Being told how to do things.

"Not that I have already obtained this or already reached the goal; I press on to make it my own, because Christ Jesus has made me his" (Philippians 3:12).

SPIRITUAL STRENGTHS: Brings enthusiasm and energy to any new direction of their own spiritual maturity. Provides a positive way to deal with problems. Within Christian community, they are resourceful with strategies and structures in the implementation of a new project for mission or ministry.

SPIRITUAL WEAKNESSES: Not very systematic or patient with the details of life. Lacking in self-discipline. Difficulty in following a daily schedule of spiritual practices. Wants to be "one-up" with others socially and at work. Very progressive. Not considerate of others. Avoids the facts (truth) in "selling" their idea.

SPIRITUAL HELPS: Needs to be less competitive by balancing it with regular voluntary service to others – social outreach. Regular, theological studies of the Bible. Establishing routines and a schedule for spiritual growth. Attend worship regularly. Develop a more personal relationship with God through prayer. Plenty of time for quiet contemplation.

ENTJ
"Totally innovative organizers" "Natural born leaders"

GENERAL CHARACTERISTICS...*Frank, decisive, leaders in activities. Develops and implements comprehensive systems to solve organizational problems. Good at anything that requires reasoning and intelligent talk, such as public speaking. Are usually well informed and enjoy adding to their fund of knowledge. Most commanding of all the types.*

ENTJ WORK TITLE - *"THE FIELD MARSHALL"*...A natural leader, thinks on their feet, exudes confidence, always well informed.

AT WORK, THE ENTJ NEEDS... Mental challenges and interesting problems to solve. Recognition. Positive feedback and an absence of routine. Respect for ideas.

FRUSTRATED AT WORK BY... Emotional responses to rational situations. Routine and petty details. The inabilities and weaknesses of their co-workers. Wasted time.

> *"Dear children, let us not love with words or tongue alone,*
> *but with actions and in truth"* (1John 3:18).

SPIRITUAL STRENGTHS: Understands how the many different parts of spiritual growth fit together to create "fullness in Christ." They bring well-reasoned theology to the struggles of faith. Within Christian community, they are helpful leaders in developing long-range plans for the congregation.

SPIRITUAL WEAKNESSES: Overpowers others in relationships. Overly rational, reducing everything to certain formulas for living. Holds high standards for themselves and others. Needs to share appreciation to others. Does not take time to listen to others. Not tolerant of others. Too rigid in scheduling life. Avoids attention to detail. Lacks alone time.

SPIRITUAL HELPS: Needs good experiences of fellowship and worship. They enjoy leading a Bible study or prayer group. Needs to develop the habit of praying/meditating alone at the beginning and end of each day. Needs to be open to Godly insights and inspirations during sleep. Benefits from regular times to reflect on the Bible after a short study.

Do Not Use Your Type to:

- × Think you are better than others
- × Make excuses for your weaknesses
- × Stereotype others negatively

Use Your Type to:

- + Help you understand how God has uniquely blessed you to make society a better place
- + Understand how to grow in your service to others
- + Identify your spiritual weaknesses, strengths, and how God intends you to grow towards maturity in Christ.

Why does everyone always think their type is better?!

Your Talent at Work...

Read the overview of your type (i.e. ESTJ). <u>Underline</u> those descriptions that best describe your talent. Describe how your inborn talent helps you at work:

....

....

....

....

....

....

Write & Share with a Partner...

What are some of the most important insights you discovered in Sphere Two: Caring for Society?

....

....

....

....

♪♪♪♪♪♪♪♪♪♪♪♪♪♪♪♪♪♪♪♪♪♪♪♪♪♪♪♪

Jesu, Jesu, Fill us with your Love

Jesu, Jesu, fill us with your
Love, show us how to serve
The neighbors we have from you.

Kneels at the feet of his friends.
Silently washes their feet,
Master who acts as a slave to them.
Jesu, Jesu, fill...

Neighbors are wealthy and poor,
Varied in color and race,
Neighbors are near-by and far away.
Jesu, Jesu, fill...

These are the ones we will serve,
These are the ones we will love,
All these are neighbors to us and you.
Jesu, Jesu, fill...

Kneel at the feet of our friends,
Silently washing their feet,
This is the way we will live with you.
Jesu, Jesu, fill...

Tom Colvin (1925-2000)

 We end our session by joining hands in a circle to pray together the Lord's Prayer.

Insights for developing my Caring HABIT:

*How will adding the habit of caring for society **help** to me live a more Christ-centered life?*

....

....

....

....

....

....

....

....

*How often will I **attempt** to do the habit of caring for society in a Christ-like way?*

....

....

....

....

....

....

....

....

....

....

....

*How will the habit caring for society **become** part of my life?*

....

....

....

....

....

....

....

*How is caring for society **important** to my maturity as a disciple of Christ?*

....

....

....

....

....

....

....

*What is my **timeframe** to make caring for society in a Christ-like way a habit?*

....

....

....

....

....

....

Self-Study for Caring
Vocation (7b)

I (Paul) beg you to lead a life worthy of the calling to which you have been called (Eph 4:1).

Vocation is our service to God through our service to our neighbor. God is interested in what we do with our time and energy every day of our lives. God is concerned about what we do every day, not just on Sundays. God does not call us out of the world. Instead, he calls us into the world to do our daily work, to do the work of our vocational calling, to serve him through our occupation, our family, community, and church. Our baptism reminds us that it is truly *God's work, our hands*. Whether our work is of service to others is of greater importance than whether it is challenging, interesting, or rewarding.

Explore Scripture:
Luke 10:38-42; Eph 4:11-13; Col 3:20-24; 1 Peter 2:9

What difference does it make to you if you help a friend in need as a vocation instead of an obligation?

....

....

....

....

I believe God has given all of us unique ways to care for society.

I believe we need to work together for the good of all.

Use your answers from the Insights questions to help

make **CARING** *a*

Sphere Two: Society

Help

Attempt

Become

Important

Timeframe

---

*How will adding the habit of caring for society **help** to me live a more Christ-centered life?*

....

....

....

....

---

*How often will I **attempt** to do the habit of caring for society in a Christ-like way?*

....

....

....

....

How will the habit caring for society **become** part of my life?

....

....

....

....

How is caring for society **important** to my maturity as a disciple of Christ?

....

....

....

....

What is my **timeframe** to make caring for society in a Christ-like way a habit?

....

....

....

....

The Third Sphere: Creation
Means of Caring: Christ's Mission

7c. CARING

Caring for God's Creation

car·ing (vb)
1. Unselfish concern for others
2. Christ-like love for those in need
3. Paying attention to another's needs

Opening Prayer

Lord, make me an instrument of your peace, Where there is hatred, let me sow love; where there is injury, pardon; where there is doubt, faith; where there is despair, hope; where there is darkness, light; where there is sadness, joy; O Divine Master, grant that I may not so much seek to be consoled as to console; to be understood as to understand; to be loved as to love. For it is in giving that we receive; it is in pardoning that we are pardoned; and it is in dying that we are born to eternal life. Amen.

St. Francis of Assisi (1181-1226)

Caring Goal

The true meaning and purpose of our lives is to recognize that God has put us on earth to *love one another as God has loved us. Because God is love, the most important lesson he wants us to learn is how to love. It is in loving that we are most like God.* Why is it so important that Christians lovingly care for one another? Because Christ tells us it is not possible to love God without loving one another. Our love of God is revealed in our capacity to love others, especially those in need of our help.

Write & Share with the Group...

What are some ways that you care for God's creation?

....

....

The whole earth is a living icon of God's face.
St. John Damascene (675-749)

Caring for Creation

As we participate in the seven habits of Jesus we are given his own perspective of the world as God's creation. We begin to see the world, and all people, as a place filled with the Creator's loving presence. The love of Christ within us develops our capacity to experience the loving presence of God in life itself. As we grow *in Christ* we realize that God's presence cannot be restricted to the church, the Bible, prayer, or the so-called religious areas of life. As we deepen our relationship with Christ through *the seven habits*, we are given the opportunity to experience the fullness of God's presence in the three spheres of our daily lives: family, work, and the world. In his loving generosity our Creator God has given us everything we need to fully enjoy life. *We receive it from his hands with humble thanksgiving* (1Tim 4:4; 6:17). And, *we work toward becoming his stewards of the creation* (Gen 1:26-28).

Are you familiar with what the Bible teaches about creation?

God Loves the World

God's most profound involvement with the world was through his Son. The third chapter of John's Gospel says, *For God so loved the world that he gave his only Son* (John 3:16a). Through faith we trust that God's Son is now mysteriously and deeply involved in all that happens in our world. We primarily understand Christ's involvement in our world through his mission of reconciliation. Christ's mission is to restore (reconcile) our broken relationship with God, one another, and the world so that God's original intent for his creation might be recovered. Christ's mission is in the process of bringing wholeness into the world. *Christ is the image of the invisible God, he is the firstborn of all creation; for in him all things in heaven and on earth were created, things visible and invisible, whether thrones or dominions or ruler or power—all things have been created through him and for him...through him God was pleased to reconcile to himself all things, whether on earth or heaven, by making peace through the blood of the cross* (Col 1:15-16; 20). **Christ is the Lord of all the creation and is the great reconciler between God and his created world. Christ, the cosmic Lord, is in the process of restoring the world to its original design.** There is no reason to believe that the world will be destroyed as some have falsely imagined. We trust that Christ the Lord will restore the world to its original design, before evil entered it (Romans 8:21). *Paradise Lost* in Genesis will be *Paradise Found* in the future. One day there will be a *new heaven and a new earth* (2 Peter 3:13, Rev 21:1). Meanwhile, the whole of God's Creation is groaning with the birth pangs of a new creation (Romans 8:18-23).

What does it mean that Christ Jesus is the Lord of creation?

Mission of Reconciliation

The Bible is a missionary book about a missionary God. In Old Testament times, God formed the Israelites into the people he had chosen to spread his mission of life and love to all people. In New Testament times, Christ commissioned his disciples to spread his mission of love to all people: a mission to live in a loving relationship with God and with one another. The book of Acts describes the Holy Spirit as a missionary Spirit that empowers believers to share the life and love God has for all people. The God of the Christian faith is a missionary God who is manifesting his mission to give all people access to a new life and a loving relationship with him. Authentic Christianity is not a faith that escapes the world for religion and personal piety. Christianity powerfully draws us into Christ's mission, which has now become the most powerful force in our world. Christ's mission pulls people out of their self-centeredness, fills them with love, and then compels them to further his mission of life and love throughout the world.

Are you a participant in God's mission of life and love?

Apprehend God in all things, for God is in all things. Every single creature is full of God and is a book about God. If I spent enough time with the tiniest creature — even a caterpillar — I would never have to prepare a sermon. So full of God is every creature.

Meister Eckhart (1260-1329)

Christians really get into Christ's Mission in the world!

Write & Share with a Partner...

How have you recognized or participated in Christ's Mission of Reconciliation within the whole world?

....

....

....

....

How We Care for Creation

A Better Understanding of God

God is the God of nature as well as of religion. God made the universe, sustains it, and still pronounces it good (Gen 1:31). We need to be grateful to God for all the good gifts he has given us—the capacity to love, the family, the beauty of nature, for work and leisure, for friendship and the arts, etc... Our God would be better understood if we did not limit his involvement to religion and religious activities. It may not be helpful to refer to a local church as *God's House*. The universe, and beyond, is the true habitation of God. If there is one thing we clearly learned from Jesus, the Son of God, it is that God is very critical of some religion and does not like it when religious people remove him from their daily lives. The living God is the God of creation as well as the God of the covenant. The Bible begins with Adam not Abraham. God's concerns are not only *sacred* but also *secular*. We must not be so heavenly minded that we fail to do any earthly good.

> *The power of God is present at all places, even in the tiniest tree leaf. Do you think God is sleeping on a pillow in heaven?...God is wholly present in all creation, in every corner, behind you and before you.*
>
> Martin Luther (1483-1546)

A Better Understanding of People

The Bible makes it quite clear that all people are made in *God's likeness* and possess unique capabilities, which distinguish us from the animals. And yet, we all have the *genetic flaw* of sin, which has been passed down to us from creation's first parents. Sin limits our abilities as godlike creatures, which have the capacity of God to love and forgive. God has given all people the ability: to reason and evaluate our lives; to make moral choices; to love and to be loved; to admire beauty; to worship, pray, and live in communion with God; and, a capacity to exercise lordship over creation as God's stewards (caretakers). **All people have been made by God to care for the whole of the creation. Our lives are to cooperate with God's work of caring for the world**. The Evangelical Lutheran Church in America (ELCA) has a saying, *God's work, our hands*. Throughout the ages the likeness of God working through people has founded hospitals and schools; abolished the slave trade; improved the conditions of workers; eliminated childhood labor; cared for the orphaned, widows, the sick and dying; and most importantly, acted in solidarity with the poor and hungry, the deprived and disadvantaged. Why have Christians led the way of compassionate caring? Because of the Christian understanding that all of creation is made by God and all people are made in his image.

A Better Understanding of Salvation

There has always been a tendency in the church to limit the full nature of God's salvation. Salvation, as it is explained in Scripture, is more than just a *ticket to heaven*. Our experience of salvation begins now in this life and continues in a new heaven and earth right here within God's creation. Salvation has implications for how we will take seriously the stewardship of our present and future home. Jesus taught his disciples that entering God's Kingdom is an earthly reality (Mark 10:24-26). Jesus taught that salvation through God's kingdom on earth involves confronting and overcoming evil, expecting wholeness for all people, and living a caring alternative to many values of society. When we are *saved* we enter a new age of living in God's future creation. **Scripture provides no reason for us to imagine that eternal salvation will be somewhere outside of the Lord's transformed *new heaven and new earth*. *(For God so loved the world.* John 3:16)**

Many of those churches within a liturgical tradition end their worship services with a variation of the sending phrase: **Go in peace, to serve the Lord!** A similar sending phrase was used by the first Christians and can be translated as: *Now don't stay around here, get out into the world which God made, for that is where we belong if we are to live, love, serve, and die for Christ.*

What is your understanding of a restored heaven and earth?

God writes the Gospel, not in the Bible alone, but also on trees, and in the flowers and clouds and stars.

Martin Luther (1483-1546)

For even creation reveals the One who formed it, and the very work suggests the One who made it, and the world manifests the One who saved it.

St. Iraneus of Lyons (130-200)

Knowing all this makes me love God's creation more than I ever did before!

Responding to Poverty

How should Christians respond to the harsh reality of poverty in today's world? First, we need to approach the problem of poverty in a rational way. We need to know the facts. It's important to know that over half of the world's population lives in poverty. And, less than one-fourth of the world's population lives in affluence yet consumes over half of the world's resources and wealth.

Second, we need to approach the problem of poverty in an emotional way. We need to know how poverty destroys lives. Our indignation must be aroused by the sights and sounds of people living in poverty. If we are to be emotionally moved to act, it can be beneficial to visit a place where people live in extreme poverty. Poverty is demeaning because it reduces people, made in the likeness of God, to struggle just to survive and live life at the level of an animal. Like Jesus did when he saw the hungry crowds, we too need to allow our emotions to move us to compassion in helping the poor.

Third, we need to approach the problem of poverty in a Biblical way. Throughout the Bible, God has revealed his will for the whole creation. We need to study the subjects of wealth and poverty in the Bible. We need to be able to understand what God thinks about wealth and poverty. Is God on the side of the poor? Should we be?

Fourth, we need to be grateful to God our creator for all the good things he has given us to enjoy. Only when we can thank God for all that we have will we be able to give generously to those in poverty. When we are truly able to recognize that all we have is a gift from God, we will be moved to live a simpler lifestyle in order to save the life of a child living in poverty.

What is your experience of witnessing abject poverty?

Without the Word of God no creature has being. God's Word is in all creation, visible and invisible. The Word is living, being, spirit, all verdant greening, all creativity. All creation is awakened, called, by the resounding melody, God's invocation of the Word. All of creation is a symphony of praise to God.

Hildegard of Bingen (1098-1179)

Crises of Creation

With sinful self-centeredness, people have sorely abused God's world, his own creation. As a result, God's created world is now in a state of crisis. Environmental issues disproportionally affect the poor, disadvantaged, and those with limited resources. Misuse of resources, pollution, disease, collapsed fisheries, soil loss and erosion, lack of fresh water, and poor quality of life adversely affect those in poverty because they are least able to address the distress and to resolve issues efficiently. There are four global factors that sorely put the creation in a state of crisis:

1. Population Growth
2. Climate Change
3. Resource Consumption
4. Water availability

Crisis 1: Population Growth

It is estimated that by the year 2050 there will be more than 10 billion people living on planet earth and more than three-fourths of them will be living in poverty. Recent improvements in infant mortality, food production and distribution, and health care have resulted in rapid population growth, especially among the poor. A growing challenge is to find how it will be possible to feed and house a greater proportion of those living in poverty.

By working with Christian agencies at home and around the world, we may help break the cycle of poverty through health clinics, microloans, water wells, animal husbandry, food pantries, and soup kitchens. And, more than temporary help, we need to support efforts to find innovative solutions that get at the root causes of the problems of future overpopulation. Our involvement with relief and development agencies that address world hunger, malaria, and refugee resettlement will continue to make a positive impact on a growing world population. The church has a long history of being present in communities, working to care for and serve where the needs are the greatest. Because we care about what happens to all people, we work together with partners from around the world to participate in God's work of caring throughout our global community.

One constructive response to the increasing numbers of those living in poverty is the gifting of small family farms. The Evangelical Lutheran Church in America (ELCA) has a program called *Good Gifts* which fundraises to provide the establishment of family farms to help families work their way out of abject poverty. (www.elca.org/goodgifts)

There are some simple things I can do each day as a response to population growth.

There are many ways to respond to the population growth crises, here are just a few:

- Support organizations that provide health and sex education throughout the world
- Learn about the environmental crisis and the need for ecological justice
- Support development agencies & organizations that assist local communities in impoverished areas to become self-sustaining
- Buy locally rather than purchasing food that traveled a great distance
- Buy only what you will consume, and then use all you buy
- Put only what you will eat on your plate, and then eat all on your plate
- Eat less, eat fresher
- Eat fewer (or no) animal proteins each week. Have a *hunger* meal each week, which is the type of meal a person living in poverty would eat
- Take the savings from eating less and support hunger issues (www.bread.org)

How is being poor different than poverty?

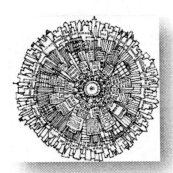

Crisis 2: Climate Change

Of all the global threats that face our planet, climate change is one of the most serious! The destruction of nature, and the many effects of global warming are major concerns for the future of God's creation. Climate change is one of the most pressing issues facing all of God's creation. The evidence is mounting that earth's climate is changing dramatically—sea levels are rising, rainfall patterns are changing, the polar icecaps and glaciers are melting, weather disasters are increasing. And the effects of these changes are already impacting most heavily on people and nations struggling in poverty; those least able to adapt to changing conditions because they have few resources to do so. The great paradox of climate change is that those least responsible for the emission of pollutants harmful to the earth will be most severely affected and least able to adapt to changing conditions. As caring Christians, we strive to seek justice and help for those living in poverty who will be impacted the most by climate change. As climate change escalates, the world's food supply will become increasingly insecure and hunger in many

regions will increase. Despite human actions that result in harm to God's creation, we must remember that God is in, with, and under the redemption of his creation. We are each called to be God's hands in the world. As children of the Creator, we must examine our own role and responsibilities for climate change. How might we act in our families, congregations, and communities to raise awareness about climate change in a reasoned and impassioned way? The United States has only 5% of the world's population, but creates nearly 25% of the entire human global warming problem. If the U.S. became part of the solution, the positive impact on the world would be enormous. Each of us can also bring imagination and creativity to finding solutions:

- Lobby for alternative energy sources from your energy company (solar/geothermal/wind)
- Purchase Energy Star appliances and high efficiency heating/cooling units and windows
- Change thermostat setting when away from the home
- Program your thermostat to run at 80* in summer and 68* in winter
- Clean and replace appliance filters regularly
- Use energy-efficient lighting (LED or CFL)
- Trade lights for natural light when possible
- Run full laundry loads and dishwashers
- Use a microwave or slow cooker (crock pot) rather than an oven/range
- Set refrigerators from 36* to 42* and freezers from -5* to -2*. Set your water heater at 120*F.
- Use cold water when washing and rinsing clothes
- Adequately insulate houses
- Use a fuel-efficient vehicle
- Walk, bike, carpool, or use alternative means of transportation (mass transport) when possible
- Sign up for the ELCA e-Advocacy Network
- Contact your government representative and ask them to support legislation to reduce carbon dioxide emissions from power plants and other energy conservation policies.

Who was the first person to talk to you about climate change?

Crisis 3: Resource Consumption

Depletion is occurring to the non-renewable resources of plankton in oceans, animal species and their habitats, trees and other green surfaces, clean air, and water. The depletion of natural resources is a common concern for all environmentalists. With the incredibly fast-paced acceleration of globalized industrialization, coupled with urbanization and modernization, the scarcity of natural resources has become an increasing crisis. There is now a common consensus that preventing the depletion of natural resources for the greater good of the environment and future generations is a global issue that needs to be addressed with urgency. A simple but very effective solution is to create awareness that once certain resources have been used up they cannot be replaced. As stewards in God's world, we are called to examine our use of these nonrenewable resources. Too often people feel that what they are doing is just a small effort and will not affect much. However, a growing number of combined effects can make a remarkable impact.

Within the developed countries, the average person disposes their body weight in waste every other month. Waste reduction begins by simplifying our lives and reducing our consumption, both in our homes and communities. Waste reduction is important because all the products we buy, and their packaging, will eventually require disposal. The family who reduces consumption and waste in the home helps protect the environment. Waste reduction refers to: Reducing the amount of waste produced, and reducing toxic substances in that waste.

The best way to discover where you can reduce waste is to actually sort through your trash. What does each family member throw away? What materials take up the most space? Is anything reusable or repairable? Can we reduce the amount of disposable products we use? Can we substitute products and packaging made of reusable, recyclable, or nonhazardous materials? If we are throwing away unusable leftover products, can we give them to someone else, or buy these things in smaller sizes?

Those Christians who care about creation and take nonrenewable resources seriously make informed choices. They choose sustainable forms of energy where possible. They monitor their use of utilities. When possible, they buy food goods and services from businesses that have sound environmental policies. Concerned Christians take their environmental responsibilities seriously. They often seek out and join conservation clubs and societies. They avoid over-consumption and unnecessary waste and recycle as much as possible. A *Green Team* at congregations can model how to conserve and recycle. To get a *green team* started at your congregation, contact: www.greenfaith.org

Waste reduction starts at the shopping center. When you go shopping follow these guidelines: **Buy** *durable products* instead of those that are disposable or cheaply made; **Repair/restore** *used items* before replacing them; **Buy** *items you can recycle locally* through curbside collection or recycling centers; **Avoid** *excess packaging* when choosing product brands. **Buy** products in bulk; **Buy** only what is needed. **Make** a shopping list, and then stick to that list.

- Read about easy to do alternatives for simple living (www.greenamericatoday.org/programs/LivingGreen)
- Reuse or repurpose products that still have utility
- Participate in recycling programs in your community
- Avoid extra packaging, recycle cardboard and plastic wrapping
- Compost kitchen, lawn, and garden waste

- Avoid the use of paper and plastic bags for shopping by using reusable canvas bags
- Minimize the use of bottled water, drink filtered tap water
- Use recycled, post-consumer paper products for kitchen, bathroom, and cleaning
- Use cloth towels instead of paper
- Use electronic media instead of printing on paper
- Recycle glass, tin, plastic, newsprint, cardboard, etc
- Recycle batteries and damaged electronics
- Do not put chemicals or grease down the drain
- Buy products with recycled and less packaging
- Save and use leftovers
- Buy locally
- Purchase earth friendly products
- Buy Fair Trade products
- Become aware of legislative efforts to protect the environment
- Write government representatives and officials

How important to you is resource conservation?

Mice are really good at repurposing products that still have utility.

Crisis 4: Water

Worldwide, there are severe shortages of water. The world now drains more from rivers and aquifers than is returned by the annual rain and snow fall. We are drawing down underground aquifers faster than they can be replenished, and many major rivers are so over-tapped they run dry before they get to the sea. Agriculture uses 70% of fresh water: it takes 1,000 tons of water to grow one ton of grain. One ton of beef requires 15,000 tons of water to produce. Water shortages will eventually cause major food shortages and threaten the lives of all the earth's plants and animals.

- Turn off water promptly in the sink and when showering
- Install low-flow shower heads, faucet aerators, and water efficient toilets
- Repair water leaks immediately
- Wash only full loads of dishes and laundry
- Use recycled water for lawn and car washing
- Don't fertilize lawns or allow runoff to water bodies
- Reduce the amount of animal proteins eaten
- Avoid using bottled water and advocate for clean, healthy tap water for all
- Become aware of legislative efforts to protect water supplies and promote conservation efforts
- Support politicians who are aware of resource issues and sponsor protective measures
- Use non-toxic dish detergent and laundry detergent
- Use safe cleaning products that are either purchased or homemade
- Avoid spray or disposal products for cleaning, air-freshening, and cooking

What are three ways you could respond to water conservation?

Crisis Management

An encouraging number of Christian aid organizations are addressing a wide range of environmental concerns. The US, which consumes 25% of the world's resources, with only 4% of the world population, must be a leader in the response to these crises. Some other nations have become proactive in correcting their country's exploitation of the environment. Most encouraging, there are now a growing number of young adult advocates who are championing the needs of the environment.

As people baptized into the Trinity's mission of reconciliation, we need to become involved in some area, on some level, to help resolve one of these four crises that are threatening God's creation. In the past, Christians have been on the cutting edge of managing and resolving human and environmental crises—problems of disease, slavery, widows and orphans, refugees and prisoners, mental illness, the hungry, and abject poverty. May we grow to realize that God intends for our care of creation to reflect our love for the Creator.

Sociological research teaches us that our core values are shaped before the age of thirteen years old. Unless *caring for creation* was made to be one of our pre-teen core values, we will most likely not have it as a value. Possibly, our best effort in caring for creation as an adult would be to instill in our pre-teen children and grandchildren the crucial importance of addressing the crises of creation. For example, in the 1960s, the Environmental Protection Agency launched the anti-litter campaign. In retrospect, it was an extremely effective program because they targeted their campaign efforts to those under the age of thirteen! Scientists and environmentalists tell us it is not too late to resolve the impending crises of creation! However, if we fail to act, we will reach a point of *no return*.

What do you think keeps you from caring more for creation?

For when one considers the universe, can anyone not believe that the Divine is present, pervading, embracing and penetrating in everything? All things depend upon God who is, and nothing can exist which does not have its being in God who is.

St. Gregory of Nyssa (335-395 AD)

Some people, in order to discover God, read books. But there is a great book: Look above you! Look below you! Note it. Read it. God never wrote that book with ink. Instead he set before your eyes the things that he had made. Can you ask for a louder voice than that?

St. Augustine (354-430)

More Simple Lifestyle

It is unarguable that IF...we have received a new life from Christ the Lord of he*aven and earth*, THEN...our lifestyle should also be new. We must foster a culture of creation care, a generational shift from consumption to conservation. We do this by promoting a new ethic in all we do, reflecting this love for God's world.

A. Individuals can make a difference by:
    a. Reducing waste (Reduce, Reuse, Recycle)
    b. Conserving resources and using less.
    c. Giving an environment tithe of 10% above your weekly offering to go directly to causes and development opportunities for people living in poverty.
B. Each congregation needs to be an awareness center to explore the theological foundation for caring for the creation.
C. Congregations can offer *green* programs, such as recycling, gardens, cleanups, sustainable building projects, and energy audits to help the community live a simpler lifestyle. These programs can be based in schools, churches, neighborhoods, and communities. Outdoor ministry programs should be models for sustainable, simple, and connected living.

It is important for us to make lifestyle adjustments to show and be good stewards of creation. For example, find ways to make your yard eco-friendly. There are organic ways to grow a lawn without pesticides or herbicides. Plant low maintenance grass and use manual or electric gardening tools. Plant trees and shrubs in strategic places to lower the heating/cooling costs in your home. Make your property a sanctuary for animals, and consider turning part of your yard into a natural prairie with native grasses and wild flowers.

Other ways to be a good steward:

- Spend more time intentionally in the natural world
- Learn about the planet's ecosystems and the dangers of habitat and species destruction
- Promote nature-based educational programs in schools
- Engage in family activities out in nature
- Take 10 minutes a day to retreat into and enjoy nature
- Use devotional materials that enhance your love of nature and your care for it
- Advocate for environmentally-friendly legislation and policies
- Participate in local restoration or cleanup projects
- Join an environmentally focused club or organization
- Invest in socially-responsible funds that foster care for the creation

How much would it take for you to be a better steward?

Living a new life and caring for creation is fun!

414 | Seven Habits of Jesus

Look a Dog in the Eye

For the greatness of humanity, to which we are called and which gives us dominion over the earth, is not to manifest itself in brutal exploitation of the creation...but in a consideration for it...This consideration consists in humanity's self-knowledge — that we can attain our destiny or that we can lose it, and that we may relate to him who gives life...That is just what the rest of creation neither knows nor can do. Because human beings, however, do know and have the ability, because we may look up to our Creator, the rest of creation becomes like a talent entrusted to us...Paul once used the enigmatic phrase "groaning of the creation" (Rom 8:22) and indicated that it too cried out for redemption. Once when I was a young man, I asked an elderly servant of God how he made sense out of it. He simply said, "Look a dog in the eye, then you will know." Now, I don't believe for a minute that he gave me an adequate explanation of that phrase, but since that time I have never ceased to ponder what he said.

When I look at a dog, and he looks at me, those words come back again and again. And although one must guard against sentimentality and reading too much into the situation, I nevertheless cannot shake the feeling that a real dialogue with the creation takes place. And this is the way it sounds: "My little canine friend, you are just one particular part of creation. The two of us – in contrast to innumerable fellow creatures of yours – have been brought together in a remarkable way and live with one another. If something bad would happen to you, I would be very upset. And I know that if something happened to me, that your canine heart would be affected. You notice at once if something is bothering me. And if I am happy, then you make the most droll attempts to show me that you rejoice with me, because you are such a unique part of creation, because you have bound your canine destiny to me, a human being, our limitations can become, at times, particularly painful. Our lives are more fully linked than I can say or you can bark. Animals remind us of an unfallen world where Adam gave names to his brothers and sisters in creation, and conversed with them. They remind us of a world once again called into being when Francis of Assisi preached to the birds as his beloved fellow creatures.

Helmut Thielicke (1908-1985)

Write & Share with a Partner...

What are some of the most important insights you discovered in Sphere Three: Caring for God's creation?

....

....

....

....

The authors would like to acknowledge Dr. Monica Folk and Rev. Dr. Johan Bergh for their collaborative input and assistance on 7C: Caring for Creation

♫♫♫♫♫♫♫♫♫♫♫♫♫♫♫♫♫♫♫♫♫♫♫♫♫♫♫

Jesu, Jesu, Fill us with your Love

Jesu, Jesu, fill us with your
Love, show us how to serve
The neighbors we have from you.

Kneels at the feet of his friends.
Silently washes their feet,
Master who acts as a slave to them.
Jesu, Jesu, fill...

Neighbors are wealthy and poor,
Varied in color and race,
Neighbors are near-by and far away.
Jesu, Jesu, fill...

These are the ones we will serve,
These are the ones we will love,
All these are neighbors to us and you.
Jesu, Jesu, fill...

Kneel at the feet of our friends,
Silently washing their feet,
This is the way we will live with you.
Jesu, Jesu, fill...

Tom Colvin (1925-2000)

We end our session by joining hands in a
circle to pray together the Lord's Prayer.

Insights for developing my Caring HABIT:

*How will adding the habit of caring for creation **help** me live a more Christ-centered life?*

....
....
....
....
....
....
....
....

*How often will I **attempt** to do the habit of caring for creation in a Christ-like way?*

....
....
....
....
....
....
....
....
....
....

*How will the habit caring for creation **become** part of my life?*

. . . .
. . . .
. . . .
. . . .
. . . .
. . . .
. . . .

*How is caring for creation **important** to my maturity as a disciple of Christ?*

. . . .
. . . .
. . . .
. . . .
. . . .
. . . .
. . . .

*What is my **timeframe** to make caring for creation in a Christ-like way a habit?*

. . . .
. . . .
. . . .
. . . .
. . . .
. . . .

Self-Study for Caring
God Created Me (7c)

In the beginning, God created...And it was very good (Gen 1:1,31).

God makes all things good. He takes great care to place our first parents in the garden to care for the things that he created. When we read about the creation in the first book of the Bible (Genesis), we recognize that the Bible reveals God as the Creator. We also identify that creation is not a one-time event. God continues to provide for us and all of creation—not because we deserve it, but because of God's undeserved love for us. God created each of us to be in relationship—with God, one another, and all creation.

Explore Scripture:
Psalm 23:1; Isa 64:8; Isa 66:13; Jer 17:13

What does it mean to you that God created the world and all people to be very good?

....

....

....

....

God provided everything for the first mice that were in the garden!

God still provides everything we need because he loves us!

Use your answers from the Insights questions to help

make **CARING** *a*

Sphere Three: Creation

Help

Attempt

Become

Important

Timeframe

---

*How will adding the habit of caring for creation **help** me live a more Christ-centered life?*

....

....

....

....

---

*How often will I **attempt** to do the habit of caring for creation in a Christ-like way?*

....

....

....

....

How will the habit caring for creation **become** part of my life?

....

....

....

....

How is caring for creation **important** to my maturity as a disciple of Christ?

....

....

....

....

What is my **timeframe** to make caring for creation in a Christ-like way a habit?

....

....

....

....

Disciples Die Twice

The New Testament makes it quite clear that the disciples of Christ will die twice. The first time we die is when we are baptized; our sinful self is drowned in the waters of baptism. And, the second time we die occurs when we physically die at the end of our earthly journey.

Our First Dying in Baptism

The only way to enter eternal life is by dying, says Scripture. This is the meaning of Paul's teaching—*The price we pay for being sinners is death* (Rom 6:23). Sin is an offense to God and death is its penalty. And yet, if we were to die for our sins, it would be the end of us! For this reason, God sent his Son into the world. God's Son took on the sin of all people of all time, by taking our place and dying the death we deserved. When Christ calls us to be his disciples, he calls us to die to ourselves so that we might be given a new life in his kingdom. Within the creation, God only acts in ways that are consistent with his nature. Therefore, he would not just instantly pardon sinners, because he is a God of justice and in this way evil would be allowed to go uncontrolled. Neither could God punish sinners because of his infinite love for all people. This is why a God of justice and love resolved the plight of human sinfulness through the ancient sacrificial system he himself had established in antiquity to forgive sins. The ancient sacrificial system was a system of *exchange*. The Biblical word *exchange* also means *on behalf of*. When Jesus died, he died *on our behalf*. This is the primary effect of Jesus' death on our behalf. God allowed Jesus' death to ritually *exchange* our sins to the Lamb of God, just as a sacrificial lamb in the Old Testament died symbolically in exchange for the people's sin. Christ exchanged our sins for his own righteous relationship to the Father. This *great exchange*, says Martin Luther, is the most important event that will ever occur in history.

The cross was God's supreme act of love for the world and revealed his truest character: love. Through the cross, God defines true love: *recognizing another's need and freely reaching out to help.* The cross reveals that God does not bring troubles or suffering, but like a loving parent, comes to our rescue and helps us. Just as God was lovingly united with his Son on the cross, God is now lovingly united with us in all the troubles of our lives.

The cross rendered satan *limited,* like a disease-ridden fruit tree, a mortally wounded animal, or a disarmed warrior. And yet, even though satan has been defeated, he has not yet conceded defeat. For this reason, the Cross gives Christians power over satan. Through Christ's victory over satan, Christians are given POWER OVER...our sinful nature, our spiritual dying, satan and his demons, and the Law's condemnations.

The Old Testament sacrificial system foreshadows and symbolizes how Jesus died for our sins as an *exchange.* When Jesus died on the cross, the sinful nature of all people and of all times was transferred or *exchanged* to Jesus as the *pure and undefiled sacrificial Lamb of God.* Jesus became the *scapegoat* for the sins of the world. Only Jesus' death, as the Son of God, was a sacrifice large enough to carry the sins of the whole world. When Christ died on the Cross, he sacrificially died *on behalf* of our sinful nature. Jesus took upon himself our sinful infected nature and bore the punishment of death for it. Jesus died *on our behalf...* Jesus died *in our place...* Jesus paid the price *for our punishment...* Jesus *returned us to God...* Jesus *exchanged his life for ours.*

Our Second Dying in Death

For most people, including Christians, the process of dying and physical death inspires terror and anxiety, not to mention that death is often messy and undignified. Scripture refers to our physical death as *our last enemy* (1 Cor 15:26). Christ has conquered death by his resurrection. God has promised that those who die with Christ will live eternally with him. God made death a way to life. If we want to live, we must die. *For all who live and believe in me will never die* (John 11:25), says Jesus. The resurrection of Jesus is significant to the baptized for at least three reasons:

1. God validated the effectiveness of Jesus' death on the cross for the salvation of the world.
2. God revealed to us that to be his child is to be *acted upon* by him. Salvation, is not, and cannot be, a do it yourself (diy) project.
3. God revealed his plan to redeem his creation back to its original design, from before evil had entered it, giving us a sure hope of living in a *new heaven and a new earth*. All the baptized are promised to receive a resurrected body like Jesus' resurrected body. The creation, that even now is *groaning*, will be reborn into a renewed, redeemed, and restored creation.

When we reflect upon the future of God's creation and our life within in it, we can always say, *The best is yet to come.* Death is the way to life. If we want to live we must die... we must die twice—once as a disciple and once at the end of our earthly pilgrimage.

Lord, when the signs of age begin to work our bodies and minds; when the illness that will diminish us from within and without makes itself known to us; and at the very last moment when we feel we are losing hold of reality and placed back into the great forces of life that first formed us; in all these times, may we understand and have the faith needed to accept that all these events are signs that you, our Creator and Redeemer, are painfully parting the very fibers of our being in order to penetrate us to the core of our being to purify us and bear us away to be with you for eternity.

Teilhard de Chardin (1881-1955)

God's gracious love surrounds us each day; we know this because of Jesus Christ. God protects us even though we do not always know it. He gives us inner peace and a deep sense of joy, which comforts us even when there is pain. Trusting in God's gracious love and abiding presence, we bless one another and are confident he is with them.

The Lord bless you and keep you; the Lord make his face to shine upon you, and be gracious to you; the Lord look upon you with favor and give you peace.

Numbers 6:24-26

The grace of our Lord Jesus Christ, the love of God, and the Communion of the Holy Spirit be with you all!

2 Corinthians 13:13

We close this book with the very last words of the Bible (Revelation 22:21). These last words offer us strong affirmation that Christ's daily desire for all his disciples is to remain open to his gracious love so that we might always have new life!

The grace of the Lord Jesus be with all of you. Amen.

Revelation 22:21

I think I already recommended the book, *All God's Creatures Go to Heaven?*

Almighty Father, we praise you for raising up our Lord Jesus from death and for giving us the power of his resurrection. Grant that we may believe this with all our heart, mind, and soul. Keep us steadfast in the faith. May we know Christ always as the Lord and King of all Creation, who now sits at your right hand of power. Give us faith to trust in Christ as our King of kings and Lord of lords. Amen.

-Martin Luther

APPENDIX

Utilizing the Companion Website
www.7HabitsofJesus.com

You can now access a companion website that has been designed to be used by discipleship training students in conjunction with this book! Type: **www.7HabitsofJesus.com** into your browser or device to explore the site now: **The Seven Habits of Jesus webpage has some tabs that are visible to the public and others that require a student password. The public tabs include:** a general *Welcome* page that contains updates and information about The Seven Habits of Jesus. The *About the Book* page includes general information about this workbook along with ordering, sales, copyright, and permissions information. Located on the *Discipleship Training* page, the reader will be able to find out more about Discipleship Training seminars and events. The *Contact* page is the final publicly visible part of the website.

There is also a section of the website that is not visible to the public without first entering a password. There are icons of a smart phone device in the margins throughout this workbook. These icons indicate that supplemental material is available on that topic via the *Student Login* **tab of the Seven Habits of Jesus webpage. Specific instructions for utilizing the** *Student Login* **pages of the website can be found by clicking on or going to the** *Student Login* **tab.** The website is also mobile friendly, so you can access all of the supplemental material, chat forum, and other Seven Habits of Jesus information while in your fellowship group meetings, partnership meetings, or self-study!

When prompted, your Student Login password is: NewLife

Christian Glossary

Atonement
Being at one with God through the sacrificial death of Jesus.

Baptism
Cleansing us of our sinful connection to satan through the indwelling of Christ's own Spirit.

Baptismal Renewal
Usually a daily event through which Christ's death brings death to our self-centeredness. And, Christ's resurrection gives us Christ's own capacity to love and forgive.

Caregiving
The loving concern Christians share with people and creation, which comes from Christ living in our hearts.

Church
All who have been invited into God's family by the Holy Spirit to become the Body of Christ to the world.

Confession
Acknowledging our sins of thought, word, and deed before God.

Creed
A statement of belief. The three Christian creeds are the: Apostles', Nicene, and Athanasian.

Disciple
One chosen by God to join in Christ's mission to the world.

Evangelism
Verbally sharing with another who is not baptized the benefits of receiving Christ's indwelling Spirit of death and resurrection.

Faith Formation
Participation in the faith-nurturing practices, or the habits of Jesus, to more fully participate in Christ's mission of reconciliation in the world.

Forgiveness
To let go or dismiss our sins.

God's Voice
The voice (message) of God, which God speaks to us through the reading of the Bible.

Gospel
The good news of eternal salvation given to us by God, through Christ's sacrificial death on the cross.

Grace
God's love and forgiveness of sins freely given to undeserving sinners. (The *means of grace* which offer us forgiveness are the renewal of our baptism and Holy Communion.)

Justification
God's declaration that our relationship with him has been made right through Christ's sacrificial death.

Law & Gospel
God's law in the Bible tells us what we ought, should, could, and must do to please God. God's gospel in the Bible tells us what Christ promises without any help from us.

Lord's Prayer
The prayer given by Jesus to his disciples to teach them how to spontaneously pray to God at all times.

Luther
Martin Luther (1483-1546), a priest in the Roman Catholic Church, who challenged the church of his day and ignited the Reformation. Translated the Bible for everyday people and taught them how to read the Bible.

Lutherans
A Christian denomination who's roots go back to Martin Luther. They emphasize the cross, the Bible, baptism, Holy Communion, and the Gospel.

Praying
The conversation, or spontaneous dialogue, we have with God in which we ask for his help and guidance. Meditative prayer offers us the opportunity to experience our Lord Jesus within our inner sanctuary (heart, soul).

Reconciliation
God's action to restore our relationship to himself, one another, and the creation. Most often described as Christ's mission of reconciliation.

Repentance
Turning away (usually 180°) from our sinful self-centeredness toward a renewed relationship with the Triune God.

Sacraments
An act that imparts God's grace with visible means, connected with a promise from God and commanded by Christ.

Salvation
God's effort (work), through his Son, to rescue us from our sinful alienation and rebellion, so that we might live in an eternal relationship with God.

Sanctification
The work of the Holy Spirit that daily invites us to be renewed in our relationship with Christ, who lives in our hearts.

Tithing
An offering, given at weekly worship, the amount of which is ten percent of one's weekly income.

Trinity
The biblical teaching that God has revealed himself in three persons—*Father, Son, and Holy Spirit*—who are fully and eternally God.

Two Kingdoms
One kingdom, or realm, is about salvation and eternal life. The other kingdom or realm is about the world and daily life.

Vocation
The type of work God has gifted us to do in order to make society a better place

The Science of Forming Habits

All of our life, so far as it has definite form, is but a mass of habits.

William James (1892)

Habits

Everyday our lives are filled with an endless sequence of habits. And yet, nearly all of these habits are so automatic that we hardly recognize them as habits. Few people are aware of the multitude of habits that fill their daily lives. And, even fewer understand how habits are formed and change us. Even when we are convinced that daily Bible reading is something we would like to do, unless we know something about creating and sustaining a habit, we will most likely not realize our goal of daily Bible reading.

Brain Science

It has been more than two decades since research at Massachusetts Institute of Technology (MIT) discovered how habits are formed. Inside the brain, close to the brain stem where the brain meets the spinal column, is where the *habit maker*, the basal ganglia, does its work. This is in the area of the brain that controls our automatic behaviors such as respiration. The most important function of the basal ganglia is to store routine habits, and when needed, to activate them. By creating and controlling habits the basal ganglia can free-up the brain from a multitude of less important activities and routines.

Creating Habits

It is often said, *we are creatures of habit*. However, for most of us, starting and maintaining a habit such as reading the Bible can be a very discouraging experience. The most difficult aspect about creating a habit is to learn how habits are created. **Habit formation requires the combined cooperation of both the conscious and the unconscious areas of the brain.**

Conscious Brain

The conscious area of the brain is involved with the logical reasons *for* and *against* creating a new habit, or maintaining an already established habit. The rational reasons *for* or *against* a habit can be determined by developing two parallel lists. In general, the longer list of reasons *for* or *against* will determine the conscious brain's willingness to either sustain a habit or create a new one.

Another way to enlist the help of the conscious brain is to develop a logical plan of *what, when, where, why,* and *how.*

Example: How to read the Bible five times each week

A. **WHAT: I plan to accomplish**
   Read the Bible for fifteen minutes, five days each week
B. **WHEN: I will practice this habit**
   After eating breakfast and before going to work
C. **WHERE: I will practice this habit**
   At the kitchen table after eating my breakfast
D. **WHY: I want to practice this habit**
   I would like to listen to God's voice through Bible reading
E. **HOW: I will benefit from this habit**
   It will strengthen my relationship with God

Unconscious Brain

The unconscious brain is involved in creating hundreds of thousands of routine habits, all of which are a mystery to us. Most of these habits are formed within the area of the brain refered to as the basal ganglia. Unfortunately, brain science has not progressed enough to describe in any detail how the unconscious brain creates or sustains habits. **However, brain science has isolated the components the brain uses in forming and sustaining habits within the basal ganglia. These components are: Triggers, Routines, Rewards.** It is not a simple three step process. Instead, the life of a habit is the complicated result of a dynamic interplay between the factors of a trigger, routine, and reward. We can learn something about the way in which the basal ganglia forms habits with the use of an example. Let's analyze a jeweler's afternoon habit of walking to a local coffee shop.

Routine

We begin to understand the jeweler's habit by paying attention to the habit's routine. The habit's routine can often reveal what *triggers* and what *rewards* are forming the habit. The jeweler's afternoon routine involves leaving his store and walking to a nearby coffee shop, where he purchases a large coffee and takes a twenty minute break. Most days the jeweler meets a few friends at the coffee shop. Even though his extra-large coffee and a pastry seem to describe the motivation behind his habit, it is not that obvious. Behind every habit (routine) is a *trigger* and a *reward*.

Trigger

Most of our needs, that lead to the formation of a routine, are not physical or mental, but an emotional trigger. Once we can identify some of the emotional needs that are triggering routine, we are able to identify if a habit needs to be altered. In the case of our jeweler, that which triggered his daily coffee shop routine was being isolated in the back room of his jewelry store with little or no social interaction. His real need was not for the sweet pastry, coffee, or even the caffeine, but for more social interaction, which he experienced at the coffee shop. The jeweler's emotional need for social interaction might be experienced with a better routine, which would be less expensive and healthier. If he would have been aware of the *trigger* behind his routine he could have spent a half hour or so each afternoon talking to customers at his jewelry store. This would be a more constructive routine for him to practice.

Reward

A reward is a type of benefit that strongly increases or enhances the chance that we will repeat a specific routine. Sometimes we are able to identify a reward, and the routine it is reinforcing. Sometimes we are not. The jeweler's reward, at first, might be identified as a caffeine fix or a sugar high, however once the jeweler was able to identify his daily routine, he was able to isolate the actual trigger and the reward. The reward of the coffee shop was actually the social interaction he was not experiencing at his store, since he spent most of his time in the back room.

Our Habits

It is a helpful exercise to regularly evaluate those habits of which we are aware. It is beneficial to analyze our regular habits. We might want to ask:

> *Am I satisfied with my regular routines?*
> *Is there a routine or habit I would like to add?*
> *Are the triggers and rewards healthy?*

As we think about the seven habits of Jesus (Remembering, Listening, Praying, Preparing, Returning, Inviting, and Caring) we want to ask:

> *How might these habits of Jesus become my habits?*

We will each answer that question in our own unique way. **The *Make it my Habit Worksheets* located at the end of every chapter have been designed to assist in using both the conscious and the unconscious areas of the brain to take on the habits of Jesus in our daily lives.**

Discipleship/ Faith Formation
- Bibliography -

Augustine. "The Confessions of St. Augustine.
Orleans, MA: Paraclete, 1986.

Bonhoeffer, Dietrich. "The Cost of Discipleship."
New York: Simon & Schuster, Touchstone, 1995.

Brother Lawrence. "The Practice of the Presence of God."
New York: Doubleday, 1977.

Braatan/Jenson. "Christian Dogmatics." (vol. 1 & 2)
Philadelphia: Fortress, 1984.

Chesterton, G.K. "Orthodoxy."
New York: Doubleday, 1990.

Foster, Richard J. "Celebration of Discipline."
San Francisco: Harper, 1988.

------. "Devotional Classics" Rev. Ed.
San Francisco: Harper, 2005.

------. "Sanctuary of the Soul."
Downers Grove, IL: InterVarsity Press, 2011.

GIA Publications, Inc. 7404 S. Mason Ave. Chicago, IL
60638. www.giamusic.com.

"Go Make Disciples." Edit. By Dennis Bushkofsky.
Minneapolis: Augsburg, 2012.

Hope Publishing Company. 380 S. Main Pl. Carol Stream,
IL 60188. www.hopepublishing.com.

Lewis, C.S. "Mere Christianity."
San Francisco: Harper, 2001.

McNeal, Reggie. "Missional Renaisance."
San Franscisco: Jossey-Bass, 2009.

Nee, Watchman. "The Normal Christian Life."
Carol Stream, IL: Tyndale, 1977.

Rouse, Richard W. "A Field Guide for the Missional
Congregation." Minneapolis: Augsburg, 2008.

Schaeffer, Francis. "True Spirituality."
Carol Stream, IL: Tyndale, 1979.

Schmalzle, Robert. "New Life."
Nairobi, Kenya: Kolbe Press, 2008.

Singh, Sadhu Sundar. "With and Without Christ."
New York: Harper & Brother, 1929.

"Spiritual Classics." Edit. By Richard J. Foster.
San Francisco: Harper, 1999.

Stott, John. "Authentic Christianity."
England: Inter-varsity Press, 1996.

Stott, John. "Basic Christianity."
England: Inter-varsity Press, 2002.

Van Gelder, Crain. "The Ministry of the Missional Church."
Grand Rapids: Baker Books, 2007.

Willard, Dallas. "The Divine Conspiracy."
San Francisco: Harper, 1998.

-------. "Renovation of the Heart."
Colorado Springs, CO: NavPress, 2000.

-------. "The Great Omission."
New York: HarperOne, 2006.

Notable Saints Triumphant
- A Short List -

Ambrose, Bishop of Milan (333-397)
The first great Latin doctor of the church.
Anselem (1033-1109)
Doctor and archbishop of Canterbury.
Athanasius (296-373)
Bishop of Alexandria and called the "Father of Orthodoxy."
Augustine, Bishop of Hippo (354-430)
The most eminent theologian of the Latin Church Fathers.
Bede, the Venerable (673-735)
English Historian, theologian, and doctor of the church.
Bonhoeffer, Dietrich (1906-1945)
German Lutheran pastor executed by Hitler's Nazis.
Boniface (672-754)
Anglo-Saxon missionary who organized Frankish Church.
Calvin, John (1509-1564)
One of the foremost reformation reformers.
Catherine of Sienna (1347-1380)
Patron Saint of Italy, author of "Divine Doctrine."
Chesterton, G.K. (1874-1936)
Roman Catholic English humorist, prolific author.
Chrysostom, John (344-407)
Bishop of Constantinople, revered as a great preacher.
Clement of Rome (36-96)
Third bishop of Rome and first of the Apostolic Fathers.
Erasmus, Desiderius (1466-1536)
European author and first to publish the Greek New Testament.
Francis of Assisi (1182-1226)
Founder of the Franciscan Order of Friars.
Gertrude the Great (1256-1302)
German Benedictine nun and mystic who influenced Luther.
Gregory of Nazianzus (330-389)
Father of Eastern Church and bishop of Nyssa.
Gregory the Great (540-604)
First Medieval bishop of Rome.
Ignatius of Loyola (1491-1556)
Spanish churchman and founder of the Jesuits.
Jerome (340-420)
Church father, translated the Bible into the Latin Vulgate.
Julian of Norwich (1332-1420)
Anchorite mystic who authored "Divine Love."

A' Kempis, Thomas (1380-1471)
German priest who authored "The Imitation of Christ."

Kierkegaard, Soren (1813-1855)
Danish Lutheran theologian and philosopher.

Lewis, C.S. (1898-1963)
English scholar, author and Christian apologist.

Luther, Martin (1483-1546)
Augustinian Friar and priest whose reforms led to Lutheranism.

Martin of Tours (316-397)
Luther's namesake converted Gaul to Christianity.

Melanchthon, Philip (1497-1560)
Colleague of Luther, authored "Augsburg Confession."

Origen of Alexandria (185-254)
Father of the Eastern Church, teacher and author.

Romero, Oscar (1917-1980)
Roman Catholic archbishop of El Salvador, assassinated by military.

Savonarola, Girolamo (1452-1498)
Italian friar, executed as a reformer.

Underhill Evelyn (1875-1941)
English novelist and poet of the church of England.

Walther, C.F.W. (1811-1887)
Lutheran pastor and theologian, helped create the Lutheran Church
Missouri Synod.

Watts, Isaac (1674-1748)
English Puritan theologian and great hymn writer.

Wycliffe, John (1320-1384)
English priest and scholar critic of the Pope and the Church.

Zinzendorf (1700-1760)
Bishop of the Brethren and founder of Moravian Church.

Revised Common Lectionary
Three year cycle
A. Matthew   B. Mark   C. Luke

First Sunday of Advent

A	Isaiah 2:1-5	B	Isaiah 64:1-9	C	Jeremiah 33:14-16
	Psalm 122		Psalm 80:1-7, 17-19		Psalm 25:1-10
	Romans 13:11-14		1 Corinthians 1:3-9		1 Thes 3:9-13
	Matthew 24:36-44		Mark 13:24-37		Luke 21:25-36

Second Sunday of Advent

A	Isaiah 11:1-10	B	Isaiah 40:1-11	C	Malachi 3:1-4
	Psalm 72:1-7, 18-19		Psalm 85:1-2, 8-13		Luke 1:68-79
	Romans 15:4-13		2 Peter 3:8-15a		Philippians 1:3-11
	Matthew 3:1-12		Mark 1:1-8		Luke 3:1-6

Third Sunday of Advent

A	Isaiah 35:1-10	B	Isaiah 61:1-4, 8-11	C	Zephaniah 3:14-20
	Psalm 146:5-10		Psalm 126		Isaiah 12:2-6
	James 5:7-10		1 Thessalonians 5:16-24		Philippians 4:4-7
	Matthew 11:2-11		John 1:6-8, 19-28		Luke 3:7-18

Fourth Sunday of Advent

A	Isaiah 7:10-16	B	2 Samuel 7:1-11, 16	C	Micah 5:2-5a
	Psalm 80:1-7, 17-19		Psalm 89:1-4, 19-26		Psalm 80:1-7
	Romans 1:1-7		Romans 16:25-27		Hebrews 10:5-10
	Matthew 1:18-25		Luke 1:26-38		Luke 1:39-45

Nativity of our Lord - Christmas Eve

A	Isaiah 9:2-7	B	Isaiah 9:2-7	C	Isaiah 9:2-7
	Psalm 96		Psalm 96		Psalm 96
	Titus 2:11-14		Titus 2:11-14		Titus 2:11-14
	Luke 2:1-14		Luke 2:1-14		Luke 2:1-14

Nativity of the Lord - Christmas Day

A	Isaiah 52:7-10	B	Isaiah 52:7-10	C	Isaiah 52:7-10
	Psalm 98		Psalm 98		Psalm 98
	Hebrews 1:1-4		Hebrews 1:1-4		Hebrews 1:1-4
	John 1:1-14		John 1:1-14		John 1:1-14

First Sunday After Christmas

A	Isaiah 63:7-9	B	Isaiah 61:10-62:3	C	1 Sam 2:18-20, 26
	Psalm 148		Psalm 148		Psalm 148
	Hebrews 2:10-18		Galatians 4:4-7		Colossians 3:12-17
	Matthew 2:13-23		Luke 2:22-40		Luke 2:41-52

Second Sunday After Christmas

A	**B**	**C**
Jeremiah 31:7-14	Jeremiah 31:7-14	Jeremiah 31:7-14
Ps 147:12-15, 19, 20	Psalm 147:12-15, 19, 20	Ps 147:12-15, 19-20
Ephesians 1:3-14	Ephesians 1:3-14	Ephesians 1:3-14
John 1:10-18	John 1:10-18	John 1:10-18

Epiphany of the Lord

A	**B**	**C**
Isaiah 60:1-6	Isaiah 60:1-6	Isaiah 60:1-6
Psalm 72:1-7, 10-14	Psalm 72:1-7, 10-14	Psalm 72:1-7, 10-14
Ephesians 3:1-12	Ephesians 3:1-12	Ephesians 3:1-12
Matthew 2:1-12	Matthew 2:1-12	Matthew 2:1-12

Baptism of the Lord - First Sunday After Epiphany

A	**B**	**C**
Isaiah 42:1-9	Genesis 1:1-5	Isaiah 43:1-7
Psalm 29	Psalm 29	Psalm 29
Acts 10:34-43	Acts 19:1-7	Acts 8:14-17
Matthew 3:13-17	Mark 1:4-11	Luke 3:15-17, 21-22

Second Sunday After Epiphany

A	**B**	**C**
Isaiah 49:1-7	1 Samuel 3:1-10	Isaiah 62:1-5
Psalm 40:1-11	Psalm 139:1-6, 13-18	Psalm 36:5-10
1 Corinthians 1:1-9	1 Corinthians 6:12-20	1 Cor 12:1-11
John 1:29-42	John 1:43-51	John 2:1-11

Third Sunday After Epiphany

A	**B**	**C**
Isaiah 9:1-4	Jonah 3:1-5, 10	Neh 8:1-3, 5-10
Psalm 27:1, 4-9	Psalm 62:5-12	Psalm 19
1 Corinthians 1:10-18	1 Corinthians 7:29-31	1 Cor 12:12-31a
Matthew 4:12-23	Mark 1:14-20	Luke 4:14-21

Fourth Sunday After Epiphany

A	**B**	**C**
Micah 6:1-8	Deuteronomy 18:15-20	Jeremiah 1:4-10
Psalm 15	Psalm 111	Psalm 71:1-6
1 Corinthians 1:18-31	1 Corinthians 8:1-13	1 Cor 13:1-13
Matthew 5:1-12	Mark 1:21-28	Luke 4:21-30

Fifth Sunday After Epiphany

A	**B**	**C**
Isaiah 58:1-9a	Isaiah 40:21-31	Isaiah 6:1-8
Psalm 112:1-9	Psalm 147:1-11, 20c	Psalm 138
1 Corinthians 2:1-12	1 Corinthians 9:16-23	1 Corinthians 15:1-11
Matthew 5:13-20	Mark 1:29-39	Luke 5:1-11

Sixth Sunday After Epiphany

A Deuteronomy 30:15-20
Psalm 119:1-8
1 Corinthians 3:1-9
Matthew 5:21-37

B 2 Kings 5:1-14
Psalm 30
1 Corinthians 9:24-27
Mark 1:40-45

C Jeremiah 17:5-10
Psalm 1
1 Cor 15:12-20
Luke 6:17-26

Seventh Sunday After Epiphany

A Leviticus 19:1, 2, 9-18
Psalm 119:33-40
1 Corinthians 3:16-23
Matthew 5:38-48

B Isaiah 43:18-25
Psalm 41
2 Corinthians 1:18-22
Mark 2:1-12

C Gen 45:3-11, 15
Ps 37:1-11, 39,40
1 Cor 15:33-50
Luke 6:27-38

Eighth Sunday After Epiphany

A Isaiah 49:8-16a
Psalm 131
1 Corinthians 4:1-5
Matthew 6:24-34

B Hosea 2:14-20
Psalm 103:1-13, 22
2 Corinthians 3:1-6
Mark 2:13-22

C Exodus 34:29-35
Psalm 99
2 Cor 3:12-4:2
Luke 9:28-36

Transfiguration Sunday - Last Sunday after the Epiphany

A Exodus 24:12-18
Psalm 2 or Psalm 99
2 Peter 1:16-21
Matthew 17:1-9

B 2 Kings 2:1-12
Psalm 50:1-6
2 Corinthians 4:3-6
Mark 9:2-9

C Exodus 34:29-35
Psalm 99
2 Cor 3:12 - 4:2
Luke 9:28-43

Ash Wednesday

A Joel 2:1-2, 12-17
Psalm 51:1-17
2 Cor 5:20-6:10
Matthew 6:1-6, 16-21

B Joel 2:1-2, 12-17
Psalm 51:1-17
2 Corinthians 5:20b-6:10
Matthew 6:1-6, 16-21

C Joel 2:1-2, 12-17
Psalm 51:1-17
2 Cor 5:20-6:10
Matt 6:1-6, 16-21

First Sunday in Lent

A Genesis 2:15-17; 3:1-7
Psalm 32
Romans 5:12-19
Matthew 4:1-11

B Genesis 9:8-17
Psalm 25:1-10
1 Peter 3:18-22
Mark 1:9-15

C Deut 26:1-11
Psalm 91:1-2, 9-16
Romans 10:8b-13
Luke 4:1-13

Second Sunday in Lent

A Genesis 12:1-4a
Psalm 121
Romans 4:1-5, 13-17
John 3:1-17

B Genesis 17:1-7, 15-16
Psalm 22:23-31
Romans 4:13-25
Mark 8:31-38

C Genesis 15:1-12,17-18
Psalm 27
Philippians 3:17-4:1
Luke 13:31-35

Third Sunday in Lent

A Exodus 17:1-7
Psalm 95
Romans 5:1-11
John 4:5-42

B Exodus 20:1-17
Psalm 19
1 Corinthians 1:18-25
John 2:13-22

C Isaiah 55:1-9
Psalm 63:1-8
1 Cor 10:1-13
Luke 13:1-9

Fourth Sunday in Lent

A 1 Samuel 16:1-13
Psalm 23
Ephesians 5:8-14
John 9:1-41

B Numbers 21:4-9
Psalm 107:1-3, 17-22
Ephesians 2:1-10
John 3:14-21

C Joshua 5:9-12
Psalm 32
2 Cor 5:16-21
Lk 15:1-3, 11b-32

Fifth Sunday in Lent

A Ezekiel 37:1-14
Psalm 130
Romans 8:6-11
John 11:1-45

B Jeremiah 31:31-34
Psalm 51:1-12
Hebrews 5:5-10
John 12:20-33

C Isaiah 43:16-21
Psalm 126
Philippians 3:4b-14
John 12:1-8

Passion Sunday - Sixth Sunday in Lent

A Isaiah 50:4-9a
Psalm 31:9-16
Philippians 2:5-11
Matthew 26:14-27:66

B Isaiah 50:4-9a
Psalm 31:9-16
Philippians 2:5-11
Mark 14:1-15:47

C Isaiah 50:4-9a
Psalm 31:9-16
Philippians 2:5-11
Luke 22:14-23:56

Maundy Thursday (Holy Thursday)

A Exodus 12:1-4,11-14
Psalm 116:1-2, 12-19
1 Corinthians 11:23-26
John 13:1-17, 31b-35

B Exodus 12:1-4, 11-14
Psalm 116:1-2, 12-19
1 Corinthians 11:23-26
John 13:1-17, 31b-35

C Ex 12:1-4, 11-14
Ps 116:1-2, 12-19
1 Cor 11:23-26
Jn 13:1-17, 31b-35

Good Friday

A Isaiah 52:13-53:12
Psalm 22
Hebrews 10:16-25
John 18:1-19:42

B Isaiah 52:13-53:12
Psalm 22
Hebrews 10:16-25
John 18:1-19:42

C Isaiah 52:13-53:12
Psalm 22
Hebrews 10:16-25
John 18:1-19:42

Holy Saturday

A Jeremiah 31:1-6
Psalm 118:1-2, 14-24
Colossians 3:1-4
Matthew 28:1-10

B Jeremiah 31:1-6
Psalm 118:1-2, 14-24
Colossians 3:1-4
Matthew 28:1-10

C Jeremiah 31:1-6
Psalm 118:1-2, 14-24
Colossians 3:1-4
Matthew 28:1-10

Easter Day

A Acts 10:34-43
Psalm 118:1-2, 14-24
Colossians 3:1-4
John 20:1-18

B Acts 10:34-43
Psalm 118:1-2, 14-24
1 Corinthians 15:1-11
John 20:1-18

C Acts 10:34-43
Ps 118:1-2, 14-24
1 Cor 15:19-26
John 20:1-18

Second Sunday of Easter

A Acts 2:14a, 22-32
Psalm 16
1 Peter 1:3-9
John 20:19-31

B Acts 4:32-35
Psalm 133
1 John 1:1-2:2
John 20:19-31

C Acts 5:27-32
Psalm 118: 14-29
Revelation 1: 4-8
John 20: 19-31

Third Sunday of Easter

A Acts 2:14a, 36-41
Psalm 116:1-3, 10-17
1 Peter 1:17-23
Luke 24:13-35

B Acts 3:12-19
Psalm 4
1 John 3:1-7
Luke 24:36b-48

C Acts 9:1-6
Psalm 30
Revelation 5:11-14
Luke 24:36b-48

Fourth Sunday of Easter

A Acts 2:42-47
Psalm 23
1 Peter 2:19-25
John 10:1-10

B Acts 4:5-12
Psalm 23
1 John 3:16-24
John 10:11-18

C Acts 9:36-43
Psalm 23
Revelation 7:9-17
John 10:22-30

Fifth Sunday of Easter

A Acts 7:55-60
Psalm 31:1-5, 15-16
1 Peter 2:2-10
John 14:1-14

B Acts 8:26-40
Psalm 22:25-31
1 John 4:7-21
John 15:1-8

C Acts 11:1-18
Psalm 148
Revelation 21:1-6
John 13:31-35

Sixth Sunday of Easter

A Acts 17:22-31
Psalm 66:8-20
1 Peter 3:13-22
John 14:15-21

B Acts 10:44-48
Psalm 98
1 John 5:1-6
John 15:9-17

C Acts 16:9-15
Psalm 67
Rev 21:10,22:1-5
John 14:23-29

Ascension of our Lord

A Acts 1:1-11
Psalm 47
Ephesians 1:15-23
Luke 24:44-53

B Acts 1:1-11
Psalm 47
Ephesians 1:15-23
Luke 24:44-53

C Acts 1:1-11
Psalm 47
Ephesians 1:15-23
Luke 24:44-53

Seventh Sunday of Easter

A Acts 1:6-14
Psalm 68:1-10, 32-35
1 Peter 4:12-14; 5:6-11
John 17:1-11

B Acts 1:15-17, 21-26
Psalm 1
1 John 5:9-13
John 17:6-19

C Acts 16:16-34
Psalm 97
Revelation 22:12-21
John 17:20-26

Day of Pentecost

A Acts 2:1-21
Psalm 104:24-34, 35b
1 Corinthians 12:3b-13
John 20:19-23

B Acts 2:1-21
Psalm 104:24-34, 35b
Romans 8:22-27
John 15:26-27; 16:4b-15

C Acts 2:1-21
Ps 104:24-34, 35b
Romans 8:14-17
John 14:8-17

Trinity Sunday

A Genesis 1:1-2:4a
Psalm 8
2 Corinthians 13:11-13
Matthew 28:16-20

B Isaiah 6:1-8
Psalm 29
Romans 8:12-17
John 3:1-17

C Prov 8:1-4, 22-31
Psalm 8
Romans 5:1-5
John 16:12-15

Second Sunday After Pentecost

A Deuteronomy 11:18-28
Psalm 31:1-5, 19-24
Romans 3:22b-28
Matthew 7:21-29

B Deuteronomy 5:12-15
Psalm 81:1-10
2 Corinthians 4:5-12
Mark 2:23 - 3:6

C 1 Kings 8:22-23, 41-43
Psalm 96:1-9
Galatians 1:1-12
Luke 7:1-10

Third Sunday After Pentecost

A Hosea 5:15-6:6
Psalm 50:7-15
Romans 4:13-25
Matthew 9:9-13, 18-26

B Genesis 3:8-15
Psalm 130
2 Corinthians 4:13 - 5:1
Mark 3:20-35

C 1 Kings 17:17-24
Psalm 30
Galatians 1:11-24
Luke 7:11-17

Fourth Sunday After Pentecost

A Exodus 19:2-8a
Psalm 100
Romans 5:1-8
Matthew 9:35-10:8

B Ezekiel 17:22-24
Psalm 92:1-4, 11-14
2 Corinthians 5:6-17
Mark 4:26-34

C 2 Sam 11:26 - 12:10
Psalm 32
Galatians 2:15-21
Luke 7:36 - 8:3

Fifth Sunday After Pentecost

A Jeremiah 20:7-13
Psalm 69:7-10, 16-18
Romans 6:1b-11
Matthew 10:24-39

B Job 38:1-11
Psalm 107:1-3, 23-32
2 Corinthians 6:1-13
Mark 4:35-41

C Isaiah 65:1-9
Psalm 22:19-28
Galatians 3:23-39
Luke 8:26-39

Sixth Sunday After Pentecost

A Jeremiah 28:5-9
   Psalm 89:1-4, 15-18
   Romans 6:12-23
   Matthew 10:40-42

B Lamentations 3:23-33
   Psalm 30
   2 Corinthians 8:7-15
   Mark 5:21-43

C 1 Kings 19:15-21
   Psalm 16
   Galatians 5:1, 13-25
   Luke 9:51-62

Seventh Sunday After Pentecost

A Zechariah 9:9-12
   Psalm 145:8-14
   Romans 7:15-25a
   Matt 11:16-19, 25-30

B Ezekiel 2:1-5
   Psalm 123
   2 Corinthians 12:2-10
   Mark 6:1-13

C Isaiah 66:10-14
   Psalm 66:1-9
   Galatians 6: 7-16
   Lk 10:1-11, 16-20

Eighth Sunday After Pentecost

A Isaiah 55:10-13
   Psalm 65: 9-13
   Romans 8:1-11
   Matthew 13:1-9, 18-23

B Amos 7:7-15
   Psalm 85:8-13
   Ephesians 1:3-14
   Mark 6:14-29

C Deut 30:9-14
   Psalm 25:1-10
   Colossians 1:1-14
   Luke 10:25-37

Ninth Sunday After Pentecost

A Isaiah 44:6-8
   Psalm 86:11-17
   Romans 8:12-25
   Matt 13:24-30, 36-43

B Jeremiah 23:1-6
   Psalm 23
   Ephesians 2:11-22
   Mark 6:30-34, 53-56

C Genesis 18:1-10a
   Psalm 15
   Colossians 1:15-28
   Luke 10:38-42

Tenth Sunday After Pentecost

A Isaiah 44:6-8
   Psalm 86:11-17
   Romans 8:12-25
   Matthew 13:24-43

B Jeremiah 23:1-6
   Psalm 23
   Ephesians 2:11-22
   Mark 6:30-34, 53-56

C Genesis 18:1-10a
   Psalm 15
   Colossians 1:15-28
   Luke 10:38-42

Eleventh Sunday After Pentecost

A 1 Kings 3:5-12
   Psalm 119:129-136
   Romans 8:26-39
   Matt 13:31-33, 44-52

B 2 Kings 4:42-44
   Psalm 145:10-18
   Ephesians 3:14-21
   John 6:1-21

C Genesis 18:20-32
   Psalm 138
   Colossians 2:6-15
   Luke 11:1-13

Twelfth Sunday After Pentecost

A Isaiah 55:1-5
   Psalm 145:8-9, 14-21
   Romans 9:1-5
   Matthew 14:13-21

B Exodus 16:2-4, 9-15
   Psalm 78:23-29
   Ephesians 4:1-16
   John 6:24-35

C Ecclesiastes 2:18-23
   Psalm 49:1-12
   Colossians 3:1-11
   Luke 12:13-21

Thirteenth Sunday After Pentecost

A		B		C	
A	1 Kings 19:9-18 Psalm 85:8-13 Romans 10:5-15 Matthew 14:22-33	**B**	1 Kings 19:4-8 Psalm 34:1-8 Ephesians 4:25-5:2 John 6:35, 41-51	**C**	Genesis 15:1-6 Psalm 33:12-22 Heb 11:1-3, 8-16 Luke 12:32-40

Fourteenth Sunday After Pentecost

A	Isaiah 56:1, 6-8 Psalm 67 Rom 11:1-2a, 29-32 Matthew 15:21-28	**B**	Proverbs 9:1-6 Psalm 34:9-14 Ephesians 5:15-20 John 6:51-58	**C**	Jeremiah 23:23-29 Psalm 82 Heb 11:29-12:2 Luke 12:49-56

Fifteenth Sunday After Pentecost

A	Isaiah 51:1-6 Psalm 138 Romans 12:1-8 Matthew 16:13-20	**B**	Joshua 24:1-2a, 14-18 Psalm 34:15-22 Ephesians 6:10-20 John 6:56-69	**C**	Isaiah 58:9b-14 Psalm 103:1-8 Hebrews 12:18-29 Luke 13:10-17

Sixteenth Sunday After Pentecost

A	Jeremiah 15:15-21 Psalm 26:1-8 Romans 12:9-21 Matthew 16:21-28	**B**	Deuteronomy 4:1-2, 6-9 Psalm 15 James 1:17-27 Mark 7:1-8, 14-15, 21-23	**C**	Proverbs 25:6-7 Psalm 112 Heb 13:1-8, 15-16 Luke 14:1, 7-14

Seventeenth Sunday After Pentecost

A	Ezekiel 33:7-11 Psalm 119:33-40 Romans 13:8-14 Matthew 18:15-20	**B**	Isaiah 35:4-7a Psalm 146 James 2:1-10, 14-17 Mark 7:24-37	**C**	Deut 30:15-20 Psalm 1 Philemon 1-21 Luke 14:25-33

Eighteenth Sunday After Pentecost

A	Genesis 50:15-21 Psalm 103:8-13 Romans 14:1-12 Matthew 18:21-35	**B**	Isaiah 50:4-9a Psalm 116:1-9 James 3:1-12 Mark 8:27-38	**C**	Exodus 32:7-14 Psalm 51:1-10 1 Timothy 1:12-17 Luke 15:1-10

Nineteenth Sunday After Pentecost

A	Jonah 3:10-4:11 Psalm 145:1-8 Philippians 1:21-30 Matthew 20:1-16	**B**	Jeremiah 11:18-20 Psalm 54 James 3:13-4:3, 7-8a Mark 9:30-37	**C**	Amos 8:4-7 Psalm 113 1 Timothy 2:1-7 Luke 16:1-13

Twentieth Sunday After Pentecost

A Ezekiel 18:1-4, 25-32   B Numbers 11:4-16, 24-29   C Amos 6:1a, 4-7
  Psalm 25:1-9   Psalm 19:7-14   Psalm 146
  Philippians 2:1-13   James 5:13-20   1 Timothy 6:6-19
  Matthew 21:23-32   Mark 9:38-50   Luke 16:19-31

Twenty-First Sunday After Pentecost

A Isaiah 5:1-7   B Genesis 2:18-24   C Hab 1:1-4, 2:1-4
  Psalm 80:7-15   Psalm 8   Psalm 37:1-9
  Philippians 3:4b-14   Hebrews 1:1-4; 2:5-12   2 Timothy 1:1-14
  Matthew 21:33-46   Mark 10:2-16   Luke 17:5-10

Twenty-Second Sunday After Pentecost

A Isaiah 25:1-9   B Amos 5:6-7, 10-15   C 2 Kings 5:1-3, 7-15
  Psalm 23   Psalm 90:12-17   Psalm 111
  Philippians 4:1-9   Hebrews 4:12-16   2 Timothy 2:8-15
  Matthew 22:1-14   Mark 10:17-31   Luke 17:11-19

Twenty-Third Sunday After Pentecost

A Isaiah 45:1-7   B Isaiah 53:4-12   C Genesis 32:22-31
  Psalm 96:1-9   Psalm 91:9-16   Psalm 121
  1 Thes 1:1-10   Hebrews 5:1-10   2 Timothy 3:14-4:5
  Matthew 22:15-22   Mark 10:35-45   Luke 18:1-8

Twenty-Fourth Sunday After Pentecost

A Leviticus 19:1-2, 15-18 B Jeremiah 31:7-9   C Jer 14:7-10, 19-22
  Psalm 1   Psalm 126   Psalm 84:1-7
  1 Thessalonians 2:1-8   Hebrews 7:23-28   2 Tim 4:6-8, 16-18
  Matthew 22:34-46   Mark 10:46-52   Luke 18:9-14

Twenty-Fifth Sunday After Pentecost

A Micah 3:5-12   B Deuteronomy 6:1-9   C Isaiah 1:10-18
  Psalm 43   Psalm 119:1-8   Psalm 32:1-7
  1 Thes 2:9-13   Hebrews 9:11-14   2 Thes 1:1-12
  Matthew 23:1-12   Mark 12:28-34   Luke 19:1-10

Twenty-Sixth Sunday After Pentecost

A Amos 5:18-24   B 1 Kings 17:8-16   C Job 19:23-27a
  Psalm 70   Psalm 146   Psalm 17:1-9
  1 Thes 4:13-18   Hebrews 9:24-28   2 Thes 2:13-17
  Matthew 25:1-13   Mark 12:38-44   Luke 20:27-38

Twenty-Seventh Sunday After Pentecost

A Zephaniah 1:7, 12-18
Psalm 90:1-8, 12
1 Thes 5:1-11
Matthew 25:14-30

B Daniel 12:1-3
Psalm 16
Hebrews 10:11-25
Mark 13:1-8

C Malachi 4:1-2a
Psalm 98
2 Thes 3:6-13
Luke 21:5-19

Christ The King Sunday

A Ezek 34:11-16, 20-24
Psalm 95:1-7a
Ephesians 1:15-23
Matthew 25:31-46

B Daniel 7:9-14
Psalm 93
Revelation 1:4b-8
John 18:33-37

C Jeremiah 23:1-6
Psalm 46
Colossians 1:11-20
Luke 23:33-43